Theory and History of Literature
Edited by Wlad Godzich and Jochen Schulte-Sasse

The Newly Born Woman

Hélène Cixous and Catherine Clément

Translation by Betsy Wing

Introduction by Sandra M. Gilbert

I.B.Tauris Publishers

LONDON

Published in 1996 by
I.B.Tauris & Co Ltd
45 Bloomsbury Square
London WC1A 2HY

*The preparation of this volume was made possible by a grant
from the Translations program of the National Endowment for the
Humanities, a United States federal agency which supports study
in such fields as history, philosophy, literature, and languages.
The translation was also supported by a grant from the Maison
des Sciences de l'Homme in Paris.*

This book was originally published in France as *La Jeune Née*,
copyright © 1975 by Union Générale d'Editions, Paris.

English translation and introduction copyright © 1986 by the
University of Minnesota.

A full CIP record for this book is available from the British
Library

ISBN 1-86064-137-7

Manufactured in the United States of America

Translator's Note

The notes and bibliographical references are faithful to the style of the French text. Clément and Cixous consistently take what they need from a body of knowledge which they refuse to recognize as anyone else's "property" and make it serve their own purposes.

The prose of Cixous flows in and out of passages by Kleist, Plutarch, and Shakespeare. To maintain her rhythm I have translated these from the French in every instance but one (p. 124). Some of the quotes from Freud are from the Standard Edition (Hogarth Press, 1957) and others are my own translation from the French with reference to this edition. There are a few discrepancies between the French and English interpretations of the German. Quotations from Kafka are from the Schocken edition cited in the notes. All other quotes are my own translation unless the text was originally written in English.

Contents

Introduction
A Tarantella of Theory
Sandra M. Gilbert

> Somewhere every culture has an imaginary zone for what it excludes, and it is that zone we must try to remember today.
>
> Catherine Clément

> Everyone knows that a place exists which is not economically or politically indebted to all the vileness and compromise. That is not obliged to reproduce the system. That is writing. If there is a somewhere else that can escape the infernal repetition, it lies in that direction, where *it* writes itself, where *it* dreams, where *it* invents new worlds.
>
> Hélène Cixous

> When "*The* Repressed" of their culture and their society come back, it is an explosive return, which is *absolutely* shattering, staggering, overturning, with a force never let loose before.
>
> Hélène Cixous

There is a voice crying in the wilderness, Catherine Clément and Hélène Cixous say — the voice of a body dancing, laughing, shrieking, crying. Whose is it? It is, they say, the voice of a woman, newborn and yet archaic, a voice of milk and blood, a voice silenced but savage.

For almost a decade now, Americans, especially American feminist readers, have heard from and of this voice. The first issue of *Signs: Journal of Women in Culture and Society* presented Cixous's by now classic (wo)manifesto, "The Laugh of the Medusa," and later, in *Signs* and in *New French Feminisms* (edited by Elaine Marks and Isabelle de Courtivron) as well as in other publications, we had the chance to become better acquainted with the ferocious soprano that issues from Paris's "psych et po" and other feminist/theoretical groups. But those of us who are, as the current vocabulary would have it, monolingual "anglophones" have had few opportunities to confront the global structures produced by such influential thinkers as Clément and Cixous. We take our pleasures where we can: in American or English journals and anthologies,or in hard-to-translate volumes smuggled home from Parisian discount bookstores like FNAC, or from hungry, intermittent visits to *des femmes*, with its ironic location on the rue des Saints Pères.

Now, though, we can meet the "newly born woman"—the ancient/innocent/fluent/powerful/impossible woman—as she is, or as Clément and Cixous have envisioned her. What will we, products of a culture perhaps stodgier than France's, think of her thieving and flying, her utopian body, her desirous fantasizing and guilty shuddering? Everything about her—as most anglophone readers will no doubt feel—is intense, indeed hyperbolic. She is born of Flaubert and Baudelaire, of Rimbaud and Apollinaire, as well as (Clément and Cixous tell us) of the *Malleus Maleficarum*, Freud, Gênet, Kleist, Hoffmann, Shakespeare, and Aeschylus. Yet is she not in some sense the final figure of our own daydreams and nightmares (or even, in fact, our nightmères)? Is she not the one who erupts at, and disrupts, the edge of female consciousness, the liminal zone between sleeping and waking?

For an American feminist—at least for this American feminist—reading *The Newly Born Woman* is like going to sleep in one world and waking in another—going to sleep in a realm of facts, which one must labor to theorize, and waking in a domain of theory, which one must strive to (f)actualize. By turns dolorous and ecstatic, this extended, collaborative meditation forces us to confront what an old movie once called "monsters from the id," even as it asks us to surrender ourselves to visions of the mysteries controlled by the mistresses of our imaginations. On the surface, though, its structure is comparatively simple. In Part 1, "The Guilty One," Catherine Clément provides an analysis—a superbly sophisticated one—of "images of women," specifically images of the sorceress and the hysteric, as exemplary female figures. In Part 2, "Sorties: Out and Out: Attacks/Ways Out/Forays," Hélène Cixous elaborates brilliant imaginings of liberation, as well as some by now well-known theories of the phallocratic, patriarchal "hierarchization" that has led to the need for liberation. Finally, in Part 3, "Exchange," Clément and Cixous engage in an evidently unpremeditated dialogue that clearly illuminates the differences and similarities in their thinking. Throughout, however, their mutual focus is on the sometimes oppressive, sometimes privileged madness fostered by marginalization, on the wilderness out of which silenced women must finally find ways to cry, shriek, scream, and dance in impassioned dances of desire.

To dance: at the heart of *The Newly Born Woman* is the story of a southern Italian ritual, the tarantella. Early in the book, as she discusses the rebellious "celebrations" with which repressed (female) subjects have responded to their subjugation by patriarchal hierarchies, Clément tells a tale of women in the Mezzogiorno who can be cured of imaginary spider bites only by doing a ceremonial dance, which sometimes lasts for twenty-four hours. A village orchestra plays; a woman/patient dances—dances in a ferocious "festival of metamorphosis" (p. 21)—which subversively, sardonically, with a "tragic happiness" (p. 20), expresses her passionate rage, her raging passion. At the end of the episode, she transcends "the divine bite" and "leave[s] risk behind . . . to settle down again under a roof, in a house, in the family circle of kinship and marriage . . . the men's world" (p. 22). But she has had her interlude of orgasmic freedom.

In some sense, this structure of the hellish/heavenly tarantella governs the shape of *The Newly Born Woman*. In the "Exchange," Clément explains to Cixous that there is a "difference between our discourses. Yours is a writing halfway between theory and fiction. Whereas my discourse is, or I would like it to be, more demonstrative and discursive, following the most traditional method of rhetorical demonstration" (p. 136). But in being "demonstrative and discursive," in revealing how Freud and Breuer (like Kramer and Sprenger, the authors of the *Malleus Maleficarum* [*The Witches' Hammer*]) reiterated and reinscribed conventional sociocultural judgments, Clément herself inflicts, yet again, the ghostly bite of the tarantula—the invisible yet powerful insect of patriarchal lore, lure, and law. In fact, she defines the theory of tarantellas, the cultural causality that would not only justify but explain the need for mad dances. And Cixous, then, whose writing is "halfway between theory and fiction," does the dance, the tarantella of theory necessitated by the hideously potent yet phantasmic incision. Combining autobiography and philosophy, literary analysis and utopian speculation, she transforms herself into the woman whose shrieks and steps mark her as "pure desire, frenzied desire, immediately outside all law" (p. 117).

"Much Madness is divinest Sense," wrote Emily Dickinson in 1862, and in the same year she praised the "Divine Insanity" inspired in her by Elizabeth Barrett Browning's "Tomes of solid Witchcraft." Although she later conceded that "Witchcraft was hung, in History," this poet who defined her own life as a "Loaded Gun" was intuiting the argument about the sorceress and the hysteric, the witch and the madwoman, that Catherine Clément would make more than a

century later. For even if witchcraft *was* "hung, in History," Dickinson trium-
phantly declared, it persists in the "ordinary" life—indeed, in the flesh—of the
woman artist, the perceiving woman: "History and I/Find all the Witchcraft that
we need/Around us, every Day—". Simultaneously drawing on and critiquing
Michelet and Freud, Clément might almost be glossing these lines from
nineteenth-century America. "The sorceress," she writes, "who in the end is able
to dream Nature and therefore conceive it, incarnates the reinscription of the
traces of paganism that triumphant Christianity repressed. The hysteric, who
lives with her body in the past, who transforms it into a theater for forgotten
scenes, bears witness to a lost childhood that survives in suffering" (p. 5). Yet
the roles of both these figures are, she rightly observes, "ambiguous, antiestablishment, and conservative at the same time." Like the fervor that impels the
tarantella, the misrule that governs witchcraft and the rebellious body/language
that manifests hysteria are culturally stylized channels into which *excess* demoni-
cally flows—excess desire, excess rage, excess creative energy—only to be anni-
hilated by the society that drove it in such directions. The tarantella dancer
lapses into fatigued acquiescence; the sorceress is hanged—or burned, quar-
tered, exorcized—leaving only "mythical traces," and the hysteric "ends up inuring others to her symptoms, and the family closes around her again, whether she
is curable or incurable" (p. 5).

It makes sense, then, that Freud confided to Fliess in 1897 that he saw connections between his "hysterical" patients and the possessed, diabolical women
described in the fifteenth-century *Malleus Maleficarum*, which became a standard handbook for witchhunters and inquisitors. The illness or "anomaly" of
womanhood in a culture governed by the invisible but many-legged tarantula of
patriarchal law takes multiple forms, but its one energy derives from the singular
return of the repressed. Dora, with her complicated resentment against her
father and Mr. K., her complex attachment to Mrs. K., and her odd indifference
toward her mother, is simply a little witch. Speaking in tongues, hallucinating,
gagging, accusing Breuer of illicit paternity, Anna O. is another witchy woman.
And Dickinson, too—becoming a gun or a volcano, "hysterically" possessed by
a nameless "master" and uttering (for him) a deadly vocabulary—isn't she a bit
like a witch? Even as she transforms herself into an "it" ("Why make it doubt,
it hurts it so"), "it" cries in her: seeking refuge in writing, she finds a place
where, as Cixous says "*it* writes itself . . . *it* dreams . . . *it* invents new
worlds" (p. 72).

Of course, to represent the historical range and variety of female experience
chiefly in terms of such extreme figures as the sorceress and the hysteric may
seem, on the one hand, hyperbolic and, on the other hand, reductive. Dora's
situation was a special one, after all: how many young girls have become goods
to be traded by their fathers to the husbands of their fathers' mistresses? As for
Anna O., the illness that led to her intense encounter with Breuer was followed

by a long and productive career as a social worker, and Emily Dickinson (my own addition to this cast of characters) carried on sometimes enigmatic yet always brilliant correspondences with such men as Samuel Bowles and Thomas Wentworth Higginson, despite her theatrical self-representations as a gun or a volcano. Reasonable as these *caveats* may seem, however, the paradigms of sorceress and hysteric become increasingly convincing when one contextualizes them with contemporary anthropological theory about—to use the scholar Gayle Rubin's phrase—"sex-gender systems."

Clément herself invokes Lévi-Strauss's hypothesis that "the elementary structures of kinship" are based on an exchange of women as well as his complementary notion that "women's periods, their uncontrolled flow, too close to nature and therefore threatening" paradoxically function as "the *stabilizing* element through which runs the split between nature and culture: simultaneously the rule and the unruly" (pp. 28–29). But American readers will also find the postulates in *The Newly Born Woman* illuminated by Sherry Ortner's well-known article "Is Female to Male as Nature Is to Culture?" Drawing on Simone de Beauvoir and Mary Douglas as well as Lévi-Strauss, Ortner argues that although women's production of signs aligns them with (human) society, their reproductive functions identify them with the (animal) body, so they are universally perceived "as being *closer* to nature than [are] men." Thus, the female role represents "something intermediate between culture and nature, lower on the scale of transcendence than man." Such a position "on the continuous periphery of culture's clearing," she explains, would "account easily for both the subversive feminine symbols (witches, evil eye, menstrual pollution, castrating mothers) and the feminine symbols of transcendence (mother goddesses, merciful dispensers of salvation . . .)".

If Ortner is right—and though her thesis has lately been critiqued by some feminist anthropologists it has not really been refuted—the roles of the sorceress and the hysteric would indeed become exemplary tropes for the female condition. Since the etymological root of the word "hysteria" is the Greek *hyster*, or womb, the hysteric is, after all, the creature whose wandering, even wondering, womb manifests the distinctively female bonding, or bondage, of mind and body, the inescapable female connection between creation and procreation, the destiny that is inexorably determined by anatomy. And the sorceress—the witch, the wisewoman, destroyer and preserver of culture—is she not the *mid*wife, the intermediary between life and death, the go-between whose occult yet necessary labors deliver souls and bodies across frightening boundaries? As Clément tellingly notes, the hysteric weeps but the sorceress does not. In fact, like Kundry, the demonic seductress of Wagner's *Parsifal* who is condemned to a despairing immortality for having mocked Christ on his way to Calvary, the witch laughs at the solemnities of sacrifice that constitute culture. For the hysteric, pathos is the price of carnality; for the sorceress, irony is the privilege of marginality.

Yet, ruled by the womb, the *hyster*, isn't the sorceress/midwife also, like the womb itself, the vessel of a medicinal magic that can kill or cure, a magic whose power must therefore be contained by confinement to what the anthropologists Shirley Ardener and Edwin Ardener have described as a "wild zone" on the edge of culture? Given these points, it is no wonder that Clément, following Freud, succinctly affirms that "the hysteric is the remembrance of the sorceress" (p. 35).

It is not surprising, either, that Clément should meditate on the family romance that the father of psychoanalysis derived from his own meditations on the father-daughter incest reported by his hysterical patients. Tracing Freud's progress toward a theory of infantile sexuality, she shows how the daughter, who charges seduction, herself becomes defined as a seductress and how the plot of seduction and betrayal is further displaced as the history of the nuclear family, enmeshed in cultural codes, turns into a romance of accusation and counteraccusation in which guilt finally settles on the silenced figure who unites sorceress and hysteric in one body—the witchy, bitchy mother. And again American readers can contextualize her narrative with the poems of Emily Dickinson, whose sardonic prayers to "Papa above!" simultaneously seduce and betray the father even while her ecstatic invocations of "strong madonnas" attempt to resurrect and rehabilitate the lost mother.

Concluding her section of *The Newly Born Woman*, Clément tries, as Cixous will, to find ways out—*sorties*. Like her collaborator's, and like many other women's, her imaginative journeys across the frontier of prohibition are utopian, voyages out into a no place that must be a no man's and no woman's land. Specifically, she envisions this acultural no where in terms of a radical bisexuality through which sorceress and hysteric may be enabled to transcend the limits of a destiny that has historically liminalized their desire. For bisexuality, with its fluid pluralization of the erotic, its refusal to be imprisoned in fixity, "is coming out of the show, it is the end of a circus where too many women are crushed to death." The emblem of a *"jeune naissance*, [a] new young birth," it promises us that "they are no more, neither sorceress nor hysteric; and if someone dresses up as one it is an impersonation." In fact, confesses Clément, though "I have dearly loved them," these two monitory and mythic women "no longer exist" (p. 56), and the newborn woman, transcending the heresies of history and the history of hysteria, must fly/flee into a new heaven and a new earth of her own invention.

A new heaven and a new earth: this is the apocalyptic vision that energizes Hélène Cixous's brilliant and mystical tarantella of theory. Reviewing the "hierarchical oppositions" ("Culture/Nature, Day/Night, Father/Mother, Head/Heart, Form/Matter, Man/Woman") (p. 63), through which Western philosophical thought has always organized the world, she excavates the assumptions that have oppressed and repressed female consciousness, alienating woman from the "dark continent" (p. 68) of her own bodily self and channeling female desire into the flights of the sorceress and the fugues of the hysteric. The "way out" of such a system, she declares, is through an escape that is also an attack: woman must challenge "phallo-logocentric" authority through an exploration of the continent of female pleasure, which is neither dark nor lacking, despite the admonitions and anxieties of patriarchal tradition. Out of such a repossession and reaffirmation of her own deepest being, woman may "come" to writing, constructing an erotic aesthetic rooted in a bisexuality that is not a "fantasy of a complete being which replaces the fear of castration . . . a fantasy of unity" (p. 84) but rather—as Clément suggested—a delight in difference, in multiplicity, in continuous awareness of "the other" within the self.

Some American as well as some French feminists have objected with varying degrees of intensity to the biological essentialism that sometimes seems to be implicit in Cixous's concepts of *feminité* or *écriture feminine*, yet as readers of *The Newly Born Woman* will discover, she herself repudiates the notion of persistent and consistent sexual essences. Noting that "there is 'destiny' no more than there is 'nature' or 'essence' as such," she remarks that "it is impossible to predict what will become of sexual difference—in another time" because "men and women are caught up in a web of age-old cultural determinations that are almost unanalyzable in their complexity. One can no more speak of 'woman' than of 'man' without being trapped within an ideological theater where the proliferation of representations, images, reflections . . . invalidate in advance any conceptualization" (p. 83). Her notion of *écriture feminine* is thus a fundamentally political strategy, designed to redress the wrongs of culture through a revalidation of the rights of nature.

American readers are bound to find that such a strategy, along with many of the dreams and dreads that Cixous articulates in the autobiographical opening of "*Sorties*," has English equivalents in the writings of such contemporary theorists as Susan Griffin in *Woman and Nature: The Roaring Inside Her* and Mary Daly in *Gyn/Ecology*—writers who also have attempted to reverse the hierarchies of mind/body that have repressed the female by identifying *mater* and matter, woman and (passive or dangerous) nature. Indeed, even the witty and rational Virginia Woolf may be seen as a crucial feminist precursor of Cixous (and Clément): what is *Orlando* if not an elegantly elaborated fantasy of bi- (or pluri-) sexual liberation—creative "hysteria" unleashed from the *hyster* and dedicated at last to "the other history" which Cixous has called for?

To be sure, recent Anglo-American feminists, heiresses of Wollstonecraft and Woolf, Barrett Browning and Gilman, often seem to begin projects of liberation from more moderately empirical positions than the one Cixous here articulates. Documentation is important to us, and we don't as a rule define our history as primarily "hystery"—or mystery. Yet, if we turn again to Dickinson, we can see that the fevers and fervors of enforced marginalization and compensatory witchcraft, of what she called "races nurtured in the dark," have been crucial to us too. Cixous's sardonically shuddering view of woman as having been "night to his day. . . . Black to his white. Shut out of his system's space. . . . The repressed that ensures the system's functioning" (p. 67) is by no means alien to our consciousness. And of course her story of a girlhood as a dispossessed female Algerian French Jew is one with which almost any immigrant—Jewish-, black-, Chicana-, Italian-, Polish-American—woman can identify. In fact, even if we were, like Dickinson, WASPs, Yankee princesses, couldn't we at least sympathize? That the so-called Myth of Amherst, pacing her father's tur- reted homestead in her white dress, didn't need either the Algerian revolution or the Vietnam war, either the Paris barricades or the New York ghettos, to say "Good Morning—Midnight/I'm coming home," only makes Cixous's point more clear. As culture has constructed her, "woman" *is* "the dark continent" to which *woman* must return.

But returning, a sorceress and a hysteric—that is, a displaced person— everywoman must inevitably find that she has no home, no *where*. Central to Cixous's thinking, and to Clément's, this sense of metaphysical alienation, sym- bolized by geographical dispossession, has also been important in the Anglo- American feminist tradition. Indeed, Cixous's reiteration of points made earlier in England and America seems almost uncanny. "I can never say the word 'patrie', 'fatherland'," she confesses at one point, "even if it is provided with an 'anti'," adding later that "I, revolt, rages, where am I to stand? What is my place if I am a woman? I look for myself throughout the centuries and don't see myself anywhere" (p. 75). Her words echo those of Virginia Woolf in the twentieth century ("As a woman, I have no country. As a woman I want no country" [*Three Guineas*]) and those of Elizabeth Barrett Browning in the nineteenth cen- tury ("I look everywhere for grandmothers and find none" [*Letters*]). We too have been seeking the other country as well as "the other history" for hundreds of years now. "Hysterics," intermittently mad (Woolf) or addicted to opium (Barrett Browning), our ancestresses were also sorceresses who transmitted to us what Dickinson, speaking of Barrett Browning, called "Tomes of solid Witch- craft" in which they too, though not so explicitly, fantasized about a new heaven and a new earth.

If there is any aspect of Cixous's thought that has been and may continue to be problematic for Americans—as it has been for some French women—it is probably the metaphorical system through which her fantasies are transmitted, specifically the complex conceit represented by the now widely used phrase "writing the body." In France, the *Quéstions Feministes* group has argued that "there is no such thing as a direct relation to the body" because everyone's experience of sexuality is constructed by the conventions of her or his culture. Thus they go on to ask whether "this language of the body, this cry-language, is . . . enough to fight oppression?" Or, as Christine Fauré puts it, "How could this changeless body be the source of a new destiny?" Similarly, the American critic Ann Rosalind Jones has conceded that "women's physiology has important meanings for women in various cultures, and it is essential for us to express those meanings rather than submit to male definitions—that is, appropriations—of our sexuality. But," she adds, "the female body hardly seems the best site to launch an attack on the forces that have alienated us from what our sexuality might become. For if we argue for an innate, precultural femininity, where does that position (though in *content* it obviously diverges from masculinist dogma) leave us in relation to earlier theories about women's 'nature'?"

Empirical and skeptical, victims as well as beneficiaries of a *Playboy* society in which the erotic is a commodity and "coming" is *de rigueur* for everybody, some women on both sides of the Atlantic will inevitably wonder whether the *jouissance* implicit in what Cixous calls "coming to writing" is really liberating, even if—as Betsy Wing's valuable glossary reminds us—the currently popular French concept of *jouissance* implies a virtually metaphysical fulfillment of desire that goes far beyond any satisfaction that could be imagined by Hugh Hefner and his minions. Didn't D. H. Lawrence—in *Lady Chatterley's Lover* and elsewhere—begin to outline something oddly comparable to Cixous's creed of woman before she did? Describing the cosmic mystery of Connie's *jouissance*, this often misogynistic English novelist defines an "orgasm" whose implications, paradoxically enough, appear to anticipate the fusion of the erotic, the mystical, and the political that sometimes seems to characterize Cixous's thought on this subject, for Connie's coming to sexuality is also a coming to selfhood and coming away from the historically hegemonic Western "nerve-brain" consciousness that would subordinate body to mind, blood to brain, passion to reason. "She was like the sea," Lawrence enthuses about Connie's metamorphosis, "dark waves rising and heaving . . . the billows of her rolled away to some shore, uncovering her," and later he exults that "her whole self quivered unconscious and alive, like plasm." Similarly, defining the pleasure of the woman writer, Cixous proclaims that "Her libido is cosmic. . . . [She is] spacious singing Flesh. . . . Her rising, is not erection. But diffusion. Not the shaft. The vessel" (pp. 88). The questions raised by such curious parallels—like the issues raised by *Quéstions Feministes*, by Fauré, and by Jones—must be confronted as Cixous's dazzling tarantella of theory explodes on the page before us.

Yet maybe the page itself is the answer to the questions, the page that the woman writer wishes to fill with her desire and that Lawrence, split between Romantic rebellion and patriarchal patronizing, fills *for* Connie Chatterley. In the past, surely—despite the struggles of "sorceresses" and "hysterics" like Barrett Browning, Dickinson, and Woolf—the pen/penis has been the privileged marker that was thought to leave the most significant traces on the apparent vacancy of nature, the blank spaces that had to be filled to "make" history. Thus women's words, traditionally relegated to margins, *are* inevitably the signs of the repressed, enigmatic hieroglyphs of an absence violently striving to become a presence. We in America may not want—as Cixous sometimes seems to tell us we should—to write in milk or blood; we may not always feel it necessary to overturn "mind" by valorizing "body" (because we may think our minds as distinctive, desirous and desirable as our bodies), but we must agree with her passionate assertion that "a feminine text cannot not be more than subversive: if it writes itself it is in volcanic heaving of the old 'real' property crust" (p. 97).

Nor can we fail to join in Cixous and Clément's dream of a transformed language/literature. We have been instructed by the prayers and prophecies not only of Dickinson and Woolf but also of H. D., Gertrude Stein, and Adrienne Rich, among others, so that we too have long yearned for what H. D. called "the unwritten volume of the new," for what Stein defined as a writing in the midst of which "there is merriment," for what Rich has more recently described (by negation) as "a book of myths in which our names do not appear." For us, too, the country of writing ought to be a no where into which we can fly in a tarantella of rage and desire, a place beyond "vileness and compromise" where the part of ourselves that longs to be free, to be an "it" uncontaminated by angel or witch (or by sorceress or hysteric) can write itself, can dream, can invent new worlds.

We too imagine drawing on the strength of nature (whatever that is—and we have to find out). We too fantasize transcending the censorings and censurings of culture (whatever they are—and we need to know). In a poem written more than a decade before *La Jeune Née* was published, Sylvia Plath spoke of this desire in a similar vision of liberation: "I step to you from the black car of Lethe/Pure as a baby." And a century earlier, Emily Dickinson dreamed of dancing "like a bomb abroad," a female/male/indefinable soul. We must be displaced to be re-placed, said Plath and Dickinson with Clément and Cixous. We must fly away to be regenerated. To be innocent as the healthiest processes of nature. To be immune to the hierarchical "principles" of culture. To be newborn.

S. M. G.

The Guilty One

Sorceress and Hysteric

A woman in tears is leaning on an old man's shoulder. She is dressed in crimson and bears signs of violence and of love: "She has bite marks on her face, bruises along her arms; her disheveled hair catches in the rips in her ragged clothes; her eyes seem insensitive to light." She stays silent and listless like this for a long time, "then she awakens, and utters marvelous things." She speaks deliriously of an emerald-colored region, with only one tree standing; she speaks of a Greek or Trojan vessel carrying her off by sea. She became a prostitute for the Greek sailors, and here she is now, found by the old man, just as the tempted Saint Anthony dreams her. "She was the Trojans' Helen whose memory the poet Stesichorus damned. She was Lucretia, the patrician raped by kings. She was Delilah who cut Samson's hair. . . . Innocent as Christ, who died for men, she has consecrated herself to women." These are the words of Simon Magus, performing as Ennoia's showman. Ennoia, Sigheh, Barbelô, Prounikos: woman. "For Jehovah's impotence," he adds, "is shown by Adam's transgression, and the old law, which is opposed to the order of things, must be shaken."

A woman marches on the city, dresses herself in green, and though she has been a wretched peasant, becomes almost sovereign on the strength of accumulated gold. "Never had she been more beautiful. In the black pupil and the yellow white flickered a light no one dared to face, a volcano's sulfurous jet." Then suddenly they are hounding her, cutting her green dress off at the small of her back, the dogs are biting her, and she finds herself again at bay, before the door of her house. "She was spread out there, like the poor screech owl they nail to

3

farmhouse doors, and their blows rained down all over her." Now she finds herself in the heart of the forest. It has become her kingdom; she has become like the animals, "like a wild boar with his acorns"—now her nourishment as well. She lives in the entrance to a caveman's hole. The crows keep her company. People come from all over to consult her, in secret. She is forbidden, menaced by the stake or by the *in-pace*. But she ensures the survival of the pagan forces of desire. "She has a woman's *craving*. Craving for what? For Everything of course, for the Great Universal Everything. . . . To this immense, deep desire, vast as a sea, she succumbs, she sleeps. . . . She slept, she dreamed. . . . The beautiful dream! And how can it be told? That the marvelous monster of universal life was swallowed up inside her; that from now on life, death, everything was held within her entrails, and at the price of such painful labor, she had conceived Nature."

A woman is stretched out on a leather couch; she is suffering. Her eyes blink, she looks down, she wrinkles her brows, her nose; she wrinkles everything. She speaks badly, stutters, hiccups. From time to time, she makes a strange clucking with her tongue like the final sound of a mating grouse. "Fingers crooked and clenched, she makes a motion with her arm as if to push me away, crying out in an anguished voice. 'Don't move! Don't say anything! Don't touch me!' 'Ah,' another time she shudders in terror, 'Suppose I found such an animal in my bed. Just imagine opening the box, there is a dead rat in it, a rat pinned down!' "
She has horrible dreams in which everything turns into serpents; a monster with a vulture's head bites her all over. Men whom she doesn't know attack her; they stand at the foot of her bed. She is afraid—of everything; she hurts everywhere—numb, paralyzed, cramped, twisted, warped. When Freud comes to take care of her, to try to force out these wild beasts that terrify her, she screams, "I am dying of fear. Ah! I can hardly tell you, I hate myself." And she goes on screaming, "I am a woman of the past century."

These three figures of women have three men as their authors. Ennoia, whom Flaubert presents in *The Temptation of St. Anthony*, is a woman suffering in subjection to an old showman who exhibits wild bears and Ennoia herself. The sorceress, as Michelet describes her, is woman finding her autonomy in the satanic dependency of a "counter-culture," a cultural backlash. Emmy von N . . . , 40 years old, from Livonia, is painfully exposed to Freud's eyes. Under hypnosis she spits out the toads and earthworms that she feels have tunneled their way in to inhabit her. Three women suffering for women. One who Hellenistic myth says sacrificed herself for women, as Christ did for men. One who consecrated herself to the Devil for want of something better, to succor other women menaced by the Church's oppression. Finally, one who was able to repeat in the register of symptoms all the history written in feminine mythologies and who suffered from the reminiscenses of the other two—the hysteric. It is true, it is certain, that these three *men* have traits of their own that pertain to femininity. Flaubert, a hysteric himself, the prey of crises that threatened his sanity, identifies himself with Mme. Bovary, but not in the way literary tradition would have it: he identifies in "sexual identity" by wearing a woman's skin. Michelet, who declares himself "Son of Woman," surrounds femininity with a reverse idolatry. Freud, who applies psychoanalysis to and against hysteria (hence against femininity), traverses it with ears open but eyes shut. Nevertheless, these men are filters that are less impervious than others to the myths that women, with no cultural function in the transmission of knowledge, could not themselves elaborate until recently. One must go through the audience of writers, psychiatrists, and judges to reconstitute the mythical stage on which women played their ambiguous role. The last figure, the hysteric, resumes and assumes the memories of the others: that was Michelet's hypothesis in *The Sorceress*; it was Freud's in *Studies on Hysteria*. Both thought that the repressed past survives in woman; woman, more than anyone else, is dedicated to reminiscence. The sorceress, who in the end is able to dream Nature and therefore conceive it, incarnates the reinscription of the traces of paganism that triumphant Christianity repressed. The hysteric, whose body is transformed into a theater for forgotten scenes, relives the past, bearing witness to a lost childhood that survives in suffering.

This feminine role, the role of sorceress, of hysteric, is ambiguous, antiestablishment, and conservative at the same time. Antiestablishment because the symptoms – the attacks – revolt and shake up the public, the group, the men, the others to whom they are exhibited. The sorceress heals, against the Church's canon; she performs abortions, favors nonconjugal love, converts the unlivable space of a stifling Christianity. The hysteric unties familiar bonds, introduces disorder into the well-regulated unfolding of everyday life, gives rise to magic in ostensible reason. These roles are *conservative* because every sorceress ends up being destroyed, and nothing is registered of her but mythical traces. Every hysteric ends up inuring others to her symptoms, and the family closes around her again, whether she is curable or incurable. This ambiguity is expressed in an escape that marks the histories of sorceress and hysteric with the suspense of ellipses. The end of the sorceress, as Michelet tells it, is not the stake, it is being carried off on a black horse "which from his eyes, from his nostrils spurted fire. She mounted him in a leap. . . . As she left she laughed, the most awful burst of laughter, and disappeared like an arrow. . . . One would like to know, but one will not know, what has become of the wretched woman." Emmy von N . . . , like Dora, like other hysterics, disappears little by little from the Freudian horizon. News becomes scarce. Does she find another doctor? We don't know what has become of the wretched woman. One might say that because they touched the roots of a certain symbolic structure, these women are so threatened that they have to disappear. We almost forget that there were thousands of sorceresses burned throughout Europe – real disappearance, sanctioned by real death – for which the ecclesiastical power was legally responsible.

She is innocent, mad, full of badly remembered memories, guilty of unknown wrongs; she is the seductress, the heiress of all generic Eves. Both sorceress and hysteric, in their way, mark the end of a type—how far a split can go. It is the demoniac figure that comes to its end with the sorceress—the end sanctioned by the group in death by fire. The "matrix" alienation, that which fixes the guilt of reproduction on the ill female organs, comes to term with the hysteric. What comes undone in both cases is woman's causality; she/it shifts, changes names at the same time the history of mentalities makes cultural norms evolve. But even if the split shifts, it does not disappear. Somewhere every culture has an imaginary zone for what it excludes, and it is that zone we must try to remember *today*.

This is history that is not over. How could it be? The myth transmits itself making changes in accordance with historical and cultural evolution. It varies, it changes feathers, but it only dies with the people who express it and whose contradictions it serves to resolve. If women begin to want their turn at telling this history, if they take the relay from men by putting myths into words (since that is how historical and cultural evolution will take place), even if it means rereading the most "feminine" of them (Flaubert, Michelet), it will necessarily be from other points of view. It will be a history read differently, at once the same in the Real and an other in the Imaginary. These narratives, these myths, these fantasies, these fragments of evidence, these tail ends of history do not compose a *true* history. To be that, it would have to pass through all the registers of the social structure, through its economic evolution, through analysis of the contradictions that have made and are making its history. This is not my object. Instead, it is a history, taken from what is lost within us of oral tradition, of legends and myths—a history arranged the way tale-telling women tell it. And from the standpoint of conveying the mythic models that powerfully structure the Imaginary (masculine and feminine, complex and varied), this history will be true. On the level of fantasy, it will be fantastically true: It is still acting on us. In telling it, in developing it, even in plotting it, I seek to undo it, to overturn it, to reveal it, to *expose* it.

Culture and Repressive Structures

These "women's stories" are not inscribed in a void or in an ahistorical time when their repetitions would be identical. Each time there is a repetition of memories, a return of the repressed, it will be in a specific cultural and historical context. Moreover, one must be precise about culture's specific dimension. My reference is Lévi-Strauss's statement: "Every culture can be considered as a complex of symbolic systems, in which language, the rules of matrimony, economic relations, art, science, and religion rank foremost. All these systems aim at expressing certain aspects of both physical reality and social reality, as well as, and more importantly, the relations which these two types of reality maintain between them and that the symbolic systems themselves maintain with one another" ("Introduction to the work of Marcel Mauss," *Sociologie et Anthropologie*, p. xix). There are two essential points: the existence of structured symbolic systems and the notion that they express each other. Sartre makes the same point:

> In an alienated society, all the alienations, no matter what their structural level, symbolize one another. It is of little importance whether or not one can reduce them all by regressive analysis to the dominant alienation which is conditioned by the means of production: It is sufficient that they be produced, under the influence of different and irreducible factors, in the midst of this basic alienation, for them to structure themselves in function of it and for them to end up—in their very independence by becoming the expression of it, even if and especially if they deny it. (*L'Idiot de la Famille*, vol. 3)

In their attempt to define the cultural function of the *anomaly*, both Lévi-Strauss and Sartre, who elsewhere contradict each other, seek to situate it in the fault lines of a general system where some correlative structures do not successfully harmonize all their correlations. Societies do not succeed in offering everyone the same way of fitting into the symbolic order; those who are, if one may say so, between symbolic systems, in the interstices, offside, are the ones who are afflicted with a dangerous symbolic mobility. Dangerous for them, because those are the people afflicted with what we call madness, anomaly, perversion, or whom we even label, says Mauss, "neurotics, ecstatics, outsiders, carnies, drifters, jugglers and acrobats." They are "kinds of social classes," Mauss goes on to say, rightly hesitating between defining madmen as a class (since they are situated in a social class *from the point of view of social formation* and at the same time not situated in the symbolic order *from the cultural point of view*) and defining them as an imaginary group. But this mobility is also dangerous—or productive—for the cultural order itself, since it affects the very structure whose lacunae it reflects. "The group asks and even compels these people to represent certain forms of compromise, unrealizable on the collective level, to simulate imaginary transitions, to embody incompatible syntheses" (Lévi-Strauss, *Sociologie et Anthropologie*. *Unrealizable compromises, imaginary transitions, incompatible syntheses*. Madmen embody the impossible configurations of a return to childhood. Shamans claim to have made fictitious voyages, transitions between the here and the beyond. Tumblers perform inaccessible, marvelous but inhuman figures with their bodies. The shamans turn themselves into birds; the tumblers into serpents; the madmen into stones. And more than any others, women bizarrely embody this group of anomalies showing the cracks in an overall system. Or rather, women, who are elsewhere bearers of the greatest norm, that of reproduction, embody *also* the anomaly. Women, whom Marcel Mauss associates with neurotics, ecstatics, drifters, hawkers, jugglers, tumblers, are double. They are allied with what is regular, according to the rules, since they are wives and mothers, and allied as well with those natural disturbances, their regular periods, which are the epitome of paradox, order and disorder. It is precisely in this natural periodicity that fear, terror, that which is offside in the symbolic system will lodge itself. Michelet was right: the sorceress conceives Nature, and woman, the periodic being, takes part in something that is not contained within culture. "The critical periods of their (the women's) life provoke surprises and apprehensions that give them a special position. In fact, it is exactly at puberty, during menstruation, pregnancy and childbirth, and after menopause, that the magical virtues of women reach their greatest intensity" (Marcel Mauss, *A General Theory of Magic*).

Thus women are all decked-out in unrealizable compromises, imaginary transitions, incompatible syntheses. Certainly, the sorceress and hysteric are. One of them, the *sorceress*, serves to connect all the ends of a culture that is hard to endure and to cure all the afflictions that resist the domination of the Church. She makes all the compromises and, above all, is the one who performs the abortions. She executes her transit imaginarily, perched on the black goat that carries her off, impaled by the broom that flies her away; she goes in the direction of animality, plants, the inhuman. The other, the *hysteric*, embodies somewhere an incompatible synthesis – bisexuality. And like all the subgroups that are unsituated in the complex of symbolic systems, women are threatened by the reverse of mobility, by symbolic repressions that are ready to limit the effects of symbolic disorder. In *Tristes Tropiques*, Lévi-Strauss distinguishes two forms of repression (or two forms of integration, one could say). The anthropoemic mode, ours, consists in vomiting the abnormal ones into protected spaces – hospitals, asylums, prisons. The other, the anthropophagic mode, examples of which are found especially in ahistorical societies, consists in finding a place for anomaly, delinquency, and deviancy – a place in the sun at the heart of cultural activity. The history of the sorceress oscillates between the two poles and often ends in confinement or in death. The history of the hysteric, several centuries later, takes place in half-confinement; the hysteric, dolefully reclining, tended and surrounded by doctors and worried family, is a prisoner inside the family; or else, in crisis, she bears the brunt of producing a medical spectacle. This repressive dimension doubles the mobility of those on the margins, but, at the same time, it is the sign of their integration into the system of the whole.

The imaginary groups thus defined have only a fictive independence; only for themselves do they realize, "on the individual level, the illusion of an autonomous symbolism," says Lévi-Strauss. And he adds: "Their peripheral position in relation to a local system does not prevent their being an integral part of the total system in the same way that this local system is." They provide, somehow, the guarantee that locks the symbolic systems in, taking up the slack that can exist between them, carrying out, in the Imaginary, roles of extras, figures that are *impossible at the present time*. That is exactly what makes their real appraisal difficult. Do the abnormal ones—madmen, deviants, neurotics, women, drifters, jugglers, tumblers—anticipate the culture to come, repeat the past culture, or express a constantly present utopia? Michelet himself does not hesitate: it is because the sorceress is the bearer of the past that she is invested with a challenging power. Freud sees the power of the repressed working in the same way: anachronism has a specific power, one of shifting, disturbance, and change, limited to imaginary displacements. Everything occurs as if past resistances persisted through signs and symptoms: "In a certain province," Freud writes, apropos the repressed and its effects through anachronism, "some *fueros* still exist, some traces of the past have survived" (*Origins of Psychoanalysis*). At stake—the whole evaluation of psychoanalysis as a therapeutic function. Is a disturbed, disturbing order reestablished by making the symptom disappear, or does it definitively annul the innovating force that is contained in the past but has become strange, foreign, other in the present? That is how the hysteric, reputed to be incurable, sometimes—and more and more often—took the role of a resistant heroine: the one whom psychoanalytic treatment would never be able to *reduce*. The one who roused Freud's passion through the spectacle of femininity in crisis, and the one, the only one, who knew how to escape him. (This version of hysterical history is, indeed, what keeps the very history of psychoanalysis going.) The whole evaluation of a cultural revolution is still in play—a revolution that simultaneously anticipates a future utopia and results from an effective transformation in the Real of the relations of production. To sum up, it is *the relations between the Imaginary, the Real, and the Symbolic* that are at stake here. If Michelet was right, the Imaginary would be able to act on the Symbolic and on the Real. But it is precisely in inscribing the Imaginary in the Symbolic that the anomaly fails. It is quasi production, but it is not production. Since it is a matter only of individual symbolism and not communicable, the culture cannot take it into account and make it the object of a transmission. This is even more true of hysteria; for though paranoiac writings can be situated at the limit of transmissibility, though one can recognize in them a "margin of human communicability," as Jacques Lacan does (*Premiers écrits sur la Paranoia*), hysterical symptoms, which are metaphorically inscribed on the body, are ephemeral and enigmatic. They constitute a language only by analogy. The heart of the story linking the figures of sorceress and hysteric lies in the subversive weight attributed to the return of the repressed, in the evaluation of the power of the archaic, and in the Imaginary's power or lack of it over the Symbolic and the Real. Still, it must be understood that this question is pertinent only to the extent that these two women now serve as reference, models, and allegory. To pass over into the act, making the transition to actions, moving to the inscription of the Symbolic in the Real, and hence producing real structural transformations, is the only possible gesture of departure from sorcery and hysteria. We are not yet there.

We can follow the thread connecting them, or rather, we can read them in the same scene, caught in the same networks of language. These women, to escape the misfortune of their economic and familial exploitation, chose to suffer spectacularly before an audience of men: it is an attack of spectacle, a crisis of suffering. And the attack is also a festival, a celebration of their guilt used as a weapon, a story of seduction. All that, within the family.

Signs and Marks: The Theater of the Body

"Certainly, before now I had a fantastic desire to see with my own eyes the sorceresses' rapture and their consorting with demons." Jean Bodin, the inquisitor, speaks. With a perverse naïveté, he shows his desire to see, which becomes the necessary condition of sorcery, from the moment when the bewitched, the witches and the wizards, have to give proof of possession in a set ordeal. Better yet: the desire to see—but ultimately all desire—is the sign, the first sign, of the devil; having a "fantastic desire," is already submitting to the dangerous seduction. It is a public spectacle in the light of day. The reverse spectacle, the celebration, in which everyone participates, in which no one is voyeur, is the sabbat. But an audience, ready to satisfy its fantastic desire, is necessary for the spectacular side of sorcery and hysteria. It is, above all, an audience of men: inquisitors, magistrates, doctors—the circle of doctors with their fascinated eyes, who surround the hysteric, their bodies tensed to see the tensed body of the possessed woman. Speaking of a more radical situation, and one more responsibly assumed—the shamanistic cure—Lévi-Strauss describes an equilibrium between offer and demand: the psychopath, the sorceress, the hysteric offer; the group demands.

> But on two conditions: it is necessary, through a collaboration between collective tradition and individual invention, for a structure to elaborate and continually modify itself; that is to say, a system of oppositions and correlations integrating all the elements of a complete situation where sorcerer, patient and spectators, the representations and the procedures each find their place. And it is necessary for the spectators, like the patient and sorcerer, to participate, at least to a certain extent in the abreaction, this lived experience of a universe of symbolic effusions. (Lévi-Strauss, *Structural Anthropology I, The Sorcerer and His Magic*)

This complete situation is manifested in the expressive stagings that surround the sorceress and the hysteric: rituals of beginning, of setting in motion, of waiting expectantly for the attack. From documents that trace the possession at Loudun, Michel de Certeau chooses passages that set the stage for exorcism: "The girls, arriving to be exorcised, are placed on a bench, heads resting on a pillow, hands in handcuffs which are broken easily with the least effort, and they are bound to the bench with two straps across the legs and stomach. Altogether, it gives the impression that lions are being enchained. But as soon as the demon appears, they untie the girls and let them completely free, *so that they are bound as girls and released as demons*" (*The Possession of Loudun*, p. 132, letter from the English writer Killigrew). Women's bodies must be bound so that the constraints will make the demons come out; then, when the spectators have gathered in a circle, when the lions have come into the ring, they are let go—the pleasure of danger, the raging beauty of wild beasts in constrained freedom, of the violent demoniacal forces gripping the women; but no, they are no longer women, no longer girls. The female body served only as intermediary, prop, passage. Passage accomplished, that which is no longer woman but beast, devil, symptom is set free. The girls are not released, the demons are: the girls are *bound*.

Also bound are Emmy von N . . . , Elisabeth von R . . . , Katharina, Lucy bound from all sides. With their contorted faces, sore, tense muscles, and paralyzed limbs, there is no need for handcuffs at all.

The neurasthenic who describes her illness gives the impression of accomplishing a mental task well beyond her strength. Her face is drawn, and grimacing as if she were dominated by some severe emotion, her voice becomes strident, she seeks to express herself, rejects any label that the doctor proposes for her sufferings. . . . The expression on her face is contorted, suffering, her eyes blink, she looks at the ground, eyebrows knit in a frown, the naso-labial creases are deep. She speaks with difficulty, in a low voice, interrupted from time to time by a spasmodic speech disorder to the point of stuttering. (Freud, *Studies on Hysteria*)

There it is: they are bound by the symptom just as the sorceress and the possessed are bound by material cords; and like them, they are ready to break loose, release lions. They come—phantasmic and monstrous—a toad under a rock, an enormous lizard on the stage of a theater, a mouse under a ball of wool, a bat in the bathroom—Emmy's bestiary. Another woman, Cecilie M., has eye pains; dreadful witches come out of them after analysis. Each pain, each symptom hides the figure of a beast: being cold is a link that will release a demon; a prickling sensation somewhere awakens some monstrous parallel. Sorceresses too (still according to Michelet) have their internal beasts. When the demon comes into the woman's body, before possession, "he takes, in revenge, a hundred hideous forms, he snakes a sticky track on her breast, dances on her belly as a toad, or, bat with a pointed beak, he gathers horrible kisses from her frightened lips."

So little by little, the beasts who were set free betray their real face: they are "sinister individuals" who jump from behind a bush at her, a beggar who appears threateningly before her . . . but no, it is her mother's face, dead and disfigured by a stroke, that she finds coming home one night. The lions are us.

At the same time that he was passionately tending hysterics, Freud was interested in sorcery and spoke at length to his friend Fliess about it. The year 1897 is distinctive because of the parallel that Freud makes between what he finds in *Malleus Maleficarum* (*The Witches' Hammer*, a manual for inquisitors) and what he sees in the women he is treating. "You remember having always heard me say that the medieval theory of possession, upheld by the ecclesiastical tribunals, was identical to our theory of the foreign body and the splitting of consciousness." It is unquestionable that there is something foreign in the house. Freud is creating a psychical house, with its odd vat—the psychical apparatus that is forming during this period. But why, he continues, "after having taken possession of these unfortunate women who are his victims, has the devil always fornicated with them, and done so hideously? Why do the confessions extorted by torture have so much similarity to my patients' narratives during psychological treatment?" (*Origins of Psychoanalysis*). So at the same time that sorceresses reemerge in hysterical confessions, the same origin is going to throw light on their story. Freud begins by making a connection between the witches' sabbats and children's games; their gestures are the same, their procedures identical. "The secret gatherings with dances and other amusements are observed everyday in the streets where children play." In the streets! What a peculiar passage from the most clandestine to the most public! In fact, neither the clandestine sabbat nor the children's games are public. They are not seen. Children play in public but secretively; their games are not made to be seen. The spectacle is for later; it is the scene of punishment, of purification, of exorcism. When the institutional spectators of the Church are in place, when the parents are ready to enforce the punishment—that is the spectacle. For the moment, there is play: what sorceresses and hysterics achieve is the updating and actualization of old childhood scenes. The scene will soon take shape. It is a scene of seduction. A terrifying, immense, and paternal character is the principal actor in it, as indefinite as the huge shadow of a he-goat haunting the sabbat nights. Freud goes further.

> In the schema of hysterical attacks that Charcot traces, the explanation of the "clownic" stage is found in the perversion of seducers who, in the grip of an automatic repetition which dates from childhood, indulge themselves by seeking gratification in crazy capers and make pratfalls and impossible faces. Whence the clowning which is specific to hysteria in boys, the imitation of animals and circus scenes which are explained by a fusion of games with sexual scenes.

An entire sequence is set up: acrobatic shamans, witches' flights, clowns, convulsions, and scenes of the hysterics' arched bodies; *magic, spectacle*, and *illness*. Close by is animality, men changing into beasts; and beyond that is the supreme transgression—bestiality—fornication with an animal. If one pursues the image in revery, there is also the circus spectacle and its mystical mythology—the crucified clown, the tragic mime. Going even further, there is the spectacle of cinema, born partly, of course, through the scientific discoveries of the Lumière brothers and many scientists but also in part through the play of buffoons, of Méliès, of carnival stalls. Then, as an accompanying echo, there are the expressive, expressionistic women of the silent films, their mouths open wide in unformulated cries, which florid subtitles repeat. Frightened women, attacked by sleepwalkers in *Caligari*, raped in *Metropolis*, carried off by the monkey-king in *King Kong*. Women, on the other hand, who are amazons, androgynous heroines, beyond bisexuality, and acrobats—Pearl White, Musidora. With the circus and the cinema, we have moved into the institutionalization of hysteria: spectacle cashing in on the exchange of money. A vanished illness is barely evoked by the stale smells of myth floating around, and space is made for cathartic identification, without possible contagion. The history of the sorceress and the hysteric rejoins the history of spectacles: the *fusion of public child's play with private sexual scenes*.

Now Freud, introducing the other half of the couple, the element that looks—the voyeur, doctor, judge, the audience—speaks of the pervert's repetition. The pervert, like the hysteric, repeats a scene they have in common: their seduction of the masculine and of the feminine, one by the other. This seduction passes through suffering. "Moreover," Freud goes on,

> the tortures that they practiced permit understanding of certain obscure symptoms of hysteria. Pins that appear in the most surprising ways, needles scratching these poor creatures' breasts and which x-rays do not reveal, all that can be met again in the story of their seduction. And here we have the inquisitors using their pins again to expose the diabolical stigmata, and the victims begin to invent again the same cruel stories (aided perhaps by the seducer's disguise). Victims and torturers alike recall their earliest youth in the same way. (*Origins of Psychoanalysis*)

To emerge from this coupling of remembrance and reciprocal persecutions, to arrive in the present and no longer return to pantomimes of the past, it will be necessary to get out of the look, to leave the exchange of words, and to break up the circus of transference. Freud will go to the other side of the couch, henceforth a figure from behind and an invisible presence. And he will formulate the fundamental rule—say what comes into your head, don't hide anything anymore—which makes extraordinary things come out during the too ordinary exchange of repetitive words. Transference, now possible, will be carried out in a mirror; and we move on to psychoanalysis.

Attack, Abreaction, Expulsion

When Freud and Breuer give an account of the therapeutic techniques that they use to treat hysteria, they describe a struggle, like the massive one organized by the European inquisitors to fight demons.

> Hence it was a psychical force, repugnance on the part of the ego which had originally provoked the rejection of the pathogenic idea beyond the reach of associations and which was opposed to its return to memory. The hysteric's ignorance was thus a more or less conscious refusal and the therapist's task consisted in conquering (through psychical work) this resistance to associations. This is what the practician achieves, first through "insistence," using a psychical constraint with the aim of drawing the patient's attention to traces of the representations that are sought. But his job is not yet done. We must, as I shall demonstrate, adopt further measures and call on other psychical forces. (*Studies on Hysteria*)

The hysteric is in ignorance, perhaps in innocence; but it is a matter of a *refusal*, an escape, a *rejection*, and this innocence will soon be denounced as guilt, except that it is unconscious. Conquering, forcing, adopting other measures, insisting: the work of those two cathartics Breuer and Freud has still not left the magic circle. Freud calls these practices "a little technical device": "I inform my patient that in a moment, I am going to put pressure on her forehead, and I assure her that, while I am pressing, a memory will arise as an image or else an idea will come to mind." Then it is, after all, dimly conscious: "I rather believe that the advantage of the procedure lies in the fact that, thanks to it, I successfully distract the pateint's attention from his search and conscious reflections, in short from everything that might translate his will; all of this recalls what happens when one stares at a crystal ball, etc." A foreign body, real or metaphorical, must leave the body. Similarly, a shaman, Quesalid, whose memories are described by Lévi-Strauss, expels illness in the form of a sticky, red worm, which he spit out before the eyes of his patient. The worm came from his gums, where he was hiding a bit of fluff which he bloodied just by pressing down with his gums; and Quesalid, the shaman, knows both that it is trickery and that the bloody fluff works because the illness disappears. Conscious? Unconscious? It is not a pertinent question, since native theory works through the metaphorization of the relationship between the world and the body. A foreign body comes out of the body of the shaman, and the patient's body is cured because of it: this is symbolic effectiveness. Bachelard, in *Formation de l'esprit scientifique*, speaking of "the unconscious of a scientific mind," discusses hysteria as if it were an important model, if not the very root of science. He recounts how Strindberg, in *Axel Borg*, gives an account of contemporary therapy:

> This woman felt physically sick but without exactly being so. He (the hero) made up a course of medication, the first of which would cause a real physical discomfort, which would force the patient to abandon her sickly spiritual state and would simply locate the pain in the body. With this end in mind, he took down some *assa foetida*, the most repugnant of all the drugs in his medicine cabinet, and deciding it was more likely than any other to make her completely ill, he took out a large enough dose of it to produce real convulsions. Meaning that the entire physical being had to heave and revolt against this foreign substance, and that all the soul's funcitons would concentrate their forces to get rid of it; consequently, the imaginary sufferings would be forgotten.

Making ill in order to cure; substituting a limited and "real" discomfort for the generalized psychological distress; reducing it to something known, even if (who knows?) what is known is not curable. Similarly, Freud, at the end of *Studies on Hysteria*, admits that the therapy of catharsis consisted in transforming *"hysterical misery into common unhappiness."* And the definitive cure of the witch was to turn her over to the secular arm, which alone could reduce the disorder: reduce it . . . to ashes.

One makes the demon come out by *pressing* on it, as Freud presses on the forehead, as the malodorous remedy will press the stomach to make it vomit. After he has subdued the possessed woman's body, Father Lactance, the exorcist of Loudun, makes her take various acrobatic positions, "ravishing" the spectators; but suddenly the demon kicks up and lets out a curse against God, which the possessed woman expresses "in a hideous voice." "On seeing this, Father Lactance threw the possessed woman's body harshly to the ground, trampled on her with great violence, then, one foot on her throat, repeated several times: 'Super aspidem et basiliscum ambulabis et conculcabis leonem et draconem.' " ("You will walk on the asp and the basilisk, and you will trample on the lion and the dragon.") Desire is truly putting itself in its place, as a reverse figure; it is Mary, the virgin, who "normally" must walk on the serpent—one woman redeeming the other. There is no question of man in this reversal. And yet here is the exorcist putting himself in the Virgin Mary's position, showing her virile side, her repressive function. Virgin and inquisitor trample on the woman-beast, the woman-desire.

At the center of this theater of catharsis unreels the process that Freud and Breuer called "abreaction": "Emotional discharge through which the subject liberates himself from the affect connected to the memory of a traumatic event, thus permitting it to not become or remain pathogenic." Wrested by a physical threat, the confession that one is possessed is a process of abreaction, in the same way that emotional discharge is in the cure: *it comes out*. At the same time that it is, according to Freud, the reactivation of a repressed event—diabolical pact or family seduction—abreaction is also the discharge between language and act: "It is in language that man finds a substitute for the act, thanks to which substitute, the affect can be abreacted almost in the same manner" (LaPlanche and Pontalis, *Vocabulaire de la psychanalyse*, article on abreaction). However, he apparently dispenses with the act: Father Lactance jumps on the body of Mother Jeanne des Anges; Freud presses the hysteric's forehead. But it is not that act that this is all about: it concerns an *original*, guilty act which has inscribed its pathogenic trace on the woman's body. It will come out, this act, in words or in tears, in devil's voice, in excrement, in laughter; but it will come out. Now, curiously, right in the midst of suffering, of contortions and contractions, a phenomenon appears that is apparently unbearable to the spectators, a phenomenon that signals more than any other the presence of the diabolical: joy, pleasure on the witch's luminous face. This time it is Father Recollet, and it is still Mother Jeanne:

> The aforesaid father having taken the aforesaid Sister of the Angels and having commanded Leviathan to appear, her face became laughing and extraordinarily charming. . . . And, on being pressed to obey, the aforesaid sister's charming face was furiously transformed and swept by very violent convulsions. The exorcist, still carrying on, pressed Leviathan to revoke his pact.
>
> Spoken through the mouth of the aforesaid sister: "Who do you think you are talking to?"
>
> Asked: "Who are you?"
>
> Said "Behemoth."
>
> Upon which the exorcist commanded Behemoth to withdraw and Leviathan to rise to the sister's head and fully occupy her mouth and tongue in order to speak in her. And after several violent convulsions accompanied by great contortions all over the aforesaid sister's body, her face once more became all smiles, so charming that it was recognized that Leviathan occupied it. (Michel de Certeau, *La Possession de Loudun*)

Hence when the face is twisted, Behemoth is there; when it is charming, it is Leviathan. When the woman stays silent, it is a grave sign—"taciturnity": not only silence but the absence of tears. "First," one finds in *The Witchs' Hammer*, "to know if a sorceress is caught in the evil spell of taciturnity, the judge will observe if she can cry both when she stands before him and when she is being tortured. . . . One presses and exhorts a witch in vain to cry, if she is really a witch, *she will be incapable of shedding tears*." The priest must look out for false tears—saliva smearing the cheeks—and, putting his hand on the woman's head, he will say the following formula: "I beseech you by the very bitter tears, shed by our Lord and Savior Jesus Christ upon the cross for the salvation of the world, by the burning tears shed upon the wounds of her son by the most glorious Virgin Mary his mother, on the evening of his death, and by all the tears shed in this world by the saints and God's elect whose eyes he wiped: if you are innocent, weep, and if you are guilty, weep not." It is a perfect trap: laughing, not laughing, being gay, being sad, being convulsed—or no longer so, being indifferent: everything is the mark, everything is the sign of the devil. Everything expresses itself, comes out of the body: cathartic expulsion cannot possibly fail.

Attack, Celebration, Issue

The attack, however, is not just a calamity—Mother Jeanne's ecstatic and charming expression when possessed by Leviathan gives the intolerable proof, recognized by Freud in the reference to children's games: going the way of violence, self-punishment, crime against others or against oneself, the attack achieves satisfaction, it resolves a tension within the spectacle like an echo of clandestine celebrations whose memory, one supposes, it remains. Sartre, in *L'Idiot de la Famille*, described the path that leads Flaubert, whom his mother expected first to be a daughter, then a dead boy, to resolve in two ways an insoluble family relationship by means of the hysterical attack: "the 'fall' seen as the negative and tactical response to an emergency," and afterward, "the attack seen as a positive strategy in the light of the facts which followed it, or 'the loser wins' as a conversion to optimism." Flaubert, one fine day or, rather, one moonless night, while driving the family cabriolet accompanied by his brother, Achille, falls as if thunderstruck. For years after he will be stricken by attacks (epilepsy, hysteria—it doesn't much matter under the circumstances) that repeat this first attack, this definitive crossing: crossing—for the attack struck him at the moment the driver of a cart *crossed* in front of his carriage. A witness recounts:

> He became very pale. . . . Then he walked, he ran toward his bed, where he mournfully stretched himself out as sadly as he would have lain himself down alive in a coffin . . . he cried out: "Let's throw away the reins; here is the cart driver, I hear the harness bells! Ah! I see the lantern at the inn!" Then he uttered a groan . . . and the con-

vulsion lifted him up . . . a paroxysm in which his whole being went into a shudder followed invariably by a deep sleep and stiffness which lasted several days.

Sartre demonstrates, in a genesis followed by a case history, an anamnesis of the family, how Flaubert could not help but turn himself into a cadaver to return to a state in which his doctor-father, dissector of corpses, would be forced to take charge of him as simultaneously living and dead. The fall during the attack, the "Fall" in its Christian connotation from the moment quotation marks identify it as myth, remains a tactical solution: a way out. Having arrived at this outcome, it can only *reproduce itself*: "Convulsive attacks are ceremonies that are suffered yet also played, which aim at commemorating what is irreversible, in order to confirm the patient in his neurotic perspective . . . afïd in a certain way, the original attack sets out to reproduce itself symbolically."

If the attack is not repetitive, in a structure entirely different from hysteria, it becomes a single massacre, definitive, a feast day without an anniversary, an isolated festival. That is the case with the Papin sisters. The two of them are a mirroring couple, a double-woman who one evening is no longer able to tolerate the other couple, the master couple, proprietresses. It is an attack, in the sense one might speak of an hysterical "attack." But the murderous woman's body does not mutilate itself. Instead it turns its aggressions against the body of another woman.

> Each of them seizes an opponent, tears her eyeballs out
> alive . . . and knocks her out. Then, with the help of whatever
> comes to hand, hammer, tin pitcher, kitchen knife, they light into their
> victim's bodies, crushing their faces, and uncovering their sexual parts;
> they slash deeply into the thighs and buttocks of one to soil the thighs
> and buttocks of the other with her blood. Afterward, they wash the
> instruments of these atrocious rites, cleanse themselves, and go to bed
> in the same bed. "What a fine mess." That is the formula which they
> exchange and which seems to give a sobering tone, emptied of all
> emotion, which follows, for them, the bloody orgy. (Recounted by
> Jacques Lacan in *Motives of Paranoiac Crime, the Crime of the Papin
> Sisters*)

It's a real festival: an exceptional act against the masters, a bloody saturnalia. But it is an attack that empties all its possibilities of transference at once because it attacks the body of the other. The hysteric and the sorceress are more cunning: the attack is mimed on their own body, implicating the other in the celebration, obliging him to see, since he has the "fantastic desire" to do so, but also obliging him to endure the attack's indefinite repetition. Fair's fair: spectacle in exchange for repetition of spectacle. For Christine Papin and her sister to go on to the act that split things up in reality and cut up real living bodies, transference had to be broken somewhere. It was, by discharging the other couple: two who were alike was bad enough already! but two times two who were alike, in the position of boss and employee, just one more night, a night of short circuit and electrical failure.

No: the sabbat and the hysterical attack provide a return to regular rhythm. The device – setting in complement, face to face, the ones who look and the ones who suffer, the women who suffer – requires it. The device requires that "victims and torturers alike recall their earliest youth" (*Origins of Psychoanalysis*). Perhaps it is a question of a particular phase which, later, one could call "transitivism," some sort of phase of excessive identification. "The child who beats says he was beaten, the one watching someone fall cries. In the same way, it is in an identification with the other that he lives out the whole gamut of reactions of posturing and display, his conduct of which makes their structural ambivalence obvious, the slave identified with the despot, the actor with the spectator, the seduced with the seducer" (Jacques Lacan, *Aggressivity in Psychoanalysis*.) Transitivism of the seduced to the seducer: captation of the *imago* in a relationship with the other that is not yet stable but metastable – uneasy, such that one can pass without fixed identity from body to body: from woman into beast, from woman into woman. But it is also the moment when obvious, wild aggressivity is circulating. The women attack, the ones called "Amazons" by the exorcists of Loudun who, themselves leaping on the possessed women's bodies, move into the Virgin's position. A transition ritual in which civil and symbolic identity has disappeared: "I am a woman of the past century," says Emmy von N . . . .

There is a historically and geographically complex phenomenon that allows us to make what is spectacular and what is pathological, celebration and reminiscence, all add up. In a region of the Mezzogiorno in southern Italy, where the colonies of Magna Graecia were once established, there are women said to have been bitten by tarantulas. These spider bites – these tarantula bites – that cause depression, convulsions, dizziness, and migraines have made them ill. But because tarantulas do not exist in this region, we have to conclude that these are psychical phenomena. Moreover, since the seventeenth century when Father Kircher stuck his curious nose into this story, they have been identified as such. There was one cure: the ancestral therapy of "doing the spider" or "dancing the spider." A sad ritual of celebration, it is a costly ceremony for the woman who engages in it. It requires an orchestra – which is paid, an audience – which accompanies the patient, time – sometimes several days, and the mercy of St. Paul, patron saint of those bitten by the tarantula because, on the road to Damascus, he too was struck down. Ernesto de Martino recounts:

> And before our eyes things really were unfolding as if it were a matter
> of transforming the tarantula-body of the one bitten into an instrument

body and then into a rhythmic and melodic body in order to thus reestablish the relationship with some undisclosed psychological suffering. The musicians were the mediators, stimulators and guides of this evolution. . . . Around ten o'clock, at the musician's first notes, the woman bitten by the tarantula lay motionless on her bed but as soon as they lit into the tarentella, she shrieked sharply and her body arched, thus marking the opening of the ritual day. It was the classic hysterical arc, as it is described in manuals: the arched body supported by the heels and back of the hypertensive neck, arms half flexing. (*La Terre du Remords*)

Spectacle, music, acrobatics, abreaction: this woman, Maria de Nardo, thus repeated her first spider bite — as Flaubert repeated his encounter with the driver of the cart — the spider bite that had been experienced one Sunday at midday during an emotional moment in which she had been disappointed by a first love. Each attack permitted a return to the lost love. In this case, additional elements are introduced: to start with, there is the cathartic role of music and color. Before beginning the ritual, the woman bitten by the tarantula is subjected to a double exploration in music and color and, by showing that she is affected by one color and one chord and unaffected by the others, she "chooses" the color and chord designating "her" spider.

A medieval text explains:

Why do people bitten by the tarantula find such prodigious relief in songs and different melodies? . . . When they hear musical harmonies or songs that please them, their soul delights, and since happiness is an excellent remedy for their affliction, they pull themselves together and come back to life, even though the cause of the pleasure that they feel is something else. Actually, because of the melodies and songs, their humors are drawn from the interior of their bodies to the exterior. (Cited by de Martino in *Sertum de papale de venenis*)

Once again it is a question of expelling the foreign body, the venom, through a violent and irksome action. A forced dance, a tragic happiness: but even more — the repetition of a distant past. Ernesto de Martino shows, in fact, that this historic aftermath to Magna Graecia coincides with the Bacchanalia. In complete confirmation of Michelet's romantic reveries, this local religion is the trace of ancient paganism. And there are myths that add the finishing touches to this image of grubbing peasants who unwittingly reincarnate the pursued heroines of Greek stories: Io, the woman-cow, pursued by the divine bite of Hera's horsefly; Phaedra stung by love; Arachne driven to suicide by Athena, her rival in weaving; Erigone, Icarus's daughter, who hanged herself from a tree, setting off an epidemic of hangings among young girls.

A crisis concerns the realm of women, especially before marriage, a crisis set loose by eros in several forbidden ways, a crisis manifesting itself in flight toward shady and watery solitudes goaded on by a hallucinating, secret enticement which is keenly felt and as irresistible as the anger of an outraged god can be; an animal-like possession corresponding to the rejection of social life and the refusal of civilized human behavior; a drive toward suicide which might well put an end to the pitiful flight; the hypnotic melody which accompanies the frantic run; the revelation of a goal and an end to wandering which at first seemed aimless and endless; the resolution of the crisis in a shady paradise where eternally purifying waters flow, where symbolically and with the help of those divine forces who are at the origin of the drama, reintegration of the woman's disrupted personality is achieved and plenitude of form and human reason is recovered. (de Martino, *La Terre du Remords*)

During the crisis, they become spider, cow, lizard, goat, hanged doll: before the resolution, the festival of metamorphosis takes place. I am not sure that the anthropologist was able to feel the pleasure of frantic flight. He is, however, more sensitive to the rite of the swings: sometimes the bitten woman, on the ritual sheet where she is dancing, goes and grabs onto a string and hangs from it. Kircher remarks that she likes to suspend herself by ropes in the trees. This is "aioresis": the ritual swing. After Erigone's suicide, a festival was instituted to neutralize the madness of the young women who were going to hang themselves, celebrating the Aiora, the virgin's swing, with dolls hung from the branches of trees. (There are other versions of the stories of the hanged that connect swinging with the gathering of mandrakes.) A rhythmic motion, which reproduces the rocking of infancy, pacifies. A motion reproducing the way Arachne was suspended by Athena in the threads of her web. Spider, hanged doll, the pleasure of a swing. The women swing, swing from it, don't give a hang for it, make fun of it: the Greek ritual of sacred swings is the same childish game as that of little girls' swinging.

The pleasure comes about during the crisis, as a substitute for orgasm, mimed in all the forms of displacement, located in the hands' twisting, in acrobatics, in limbs tied in knots, in backs tensed into arcs; and the resolution of the crisis is fatigue, languor, silent immobility. After the spider's dance, when grace is finally manifested, the woman bitten by the tarantula rests:

Grace occurred at exactly 2:55 P.M., five minutes earlier than expected; the kin and witnesses were deeply moved, while the barber-violinist showed us from a distance the hands of his clock to invite our verification of the absolute accuracy of his predictions. Then the orchestra lit into a tarantella of thanksgiving to the saint, with the secondary intention of ascertaining that the bitten woman was really insensitive to the stimulus of music and of dance. But the bitten woman remained immobile on the bed, continuing to look perfectly peacefully at what was going on around her. (*La Terre du Remords*)

She is cured: and, of course, Io's wandering will end at the same time as the *oistros*, the divine bite; but the celebration is over. Returning to social life, leaving the "natural" mode, the marvelous freedom that is animal and desiring, leaving music and dance and their specific tempo is, surely, to leave the deadly proximity of suicide, which is always there and always possible; it is certainly to leave risk behind—the danger of the body that is finally unleashed; it is to settle down again under a roof, in a house, in the family circle of kinship and marriage; and it is to return to the men's world: the celebration is indeed over.

Celebration and Madness

The mythology of the celebration contains the inversion of daily life in its development: feast, binge, drunkenness, dissolute ingestion of food, and regurgitation all demonstrate that it is not simply a matter of getting unusual pleasures but of pushing them to their very limit. Exchanges, undersides: partners cross-breeding, borrowing the forbidden other's clothes—transvestites, masks, and music at a different tempo signifying the break with the tempo of work. It is possible, as exemplified by Mircea Eliade and Roger Caillois, to use the conjunction between origin and reversal as an argument and to see in this inversion a return to the lost origin which, following the course of its history, would therefore conclude with its reverse side. Or, one may, like Lévi-Strauss did, situate "the past" in its mythic dimension: "The celebrations play out the reverse side of social life, not because it was ever once like that, but because it never was and will never be able to be otherwise. The characters of the past have no value as explanation except insofar as they coincide with the characters of the future and the present" (*Structures élémentaires de la parenté*).

Social life is "right side up" (not real social life but whatever the era's mythical image of it is). The festival is "upside down." Everything happens backward, and even bodies find a way to turn upside down. The "Paradises" of Hieronymous Bosch are like that: lovers join, their heads in the air and feet on the wall; proportions reverse, fruits and animals are gigantic and the minuscule elect can straddle them, penetrate them, become absorbed in them. One of the elect caresses himself next to a flower; his head is invisible, entirely underwater; his elongated hands envelop his penis, which is falling back toward the water—yet erecting—toward his head. His legs, which are spread apart for the caress, form a wide V; and in the space between his thighs, a fleshy fruit, red and pierced by a black thorn is swelling. Another figure, his bent legs in the air, has his hands on the ground. Neither his head nor his torso is visible; they are stuck in several wrappings of feathers and shells making the shape of an egg or upside-down flower. The first shell is fruity and pink, the second is made of tawny feathers, and the third is dark and spotted with pale pink. The plover's tail slides between the legs of the upside-down lover. A flowery fruit is drifting; it is a large, round, orange berry with hard and thorny palm leaves bursting from it. A delicate red tuft, vibrant as the trembling fruit of a strawberry tree, comes out of the petals, emerging from a clump of palm leaves. It is completely wrapped in a transparent bluish membrane that is poisonous, a tough yet fragile meninx. A couple of the elect caress each other, protected by a bubble of veins that run throughout the meningeal membrane; wrapped in this flower's pistil, they are emerging from a fruit. Nature and culture abolished, all bodies mingled: animals, fruits, and humans in the same intertwining. Flowers penetrate, fruits caress, animals open, humans are like instruments of this universal *jouissance*. These whimsical illuminations often inscribed in the margins of religious manuscripts, these acrobats contorting their bodies, these grotesques turning order head over heels are like a concerted depravity of the Imaginary. Jurgis Baltrusaitis calls it "the magical antiworld," the passage from the end of the Gothic to the age of discoveries. In the festival, as in the paradise gardens of Hieronymous Bosch, what is at play is the systematic illustration of something that runs opposite to the Real. An Imaginary calculated according to orderly displacements of the proportions of the real world—this is indeed the strategy of fantasy. The sorceress and the hysteric manifest the festival in their bodies, do impossible flips, making it possible to see what cannot be represented, figures of inversion. The exorcist who tamed Mother Jeanne des Anges "with a word caused this body to be placed belly to the ground, head lifted high, arms and feet joined, interlaced and turned backward, and he caused them to come undone and go back into place the same way." The hysteric replays the scene in the Imaginary "I also have discovered," Freud writes to Fliess, "that hysterical headaches were due to a parallel, related to fantasies, which tends to equate the body's two extremities (head and bottom, hair in both places, cheek and cheeks, lips and labia, mouth and vagina), with migraines serving to represent a forced defloration and sickness taking the place, once again, of the realization of desire" (From a letter of 9 June 1899). Hence gymnastic contortions and symptoms are equivalent, and in them woman reveals the unique power to invert her own body. That makes us women want to laugh, a loud and philosophic laughter: Demeter's laughter when faced with Baubô, skirts in the air, showing her bottom. Because Baubô is showing her other head, the head of desire, which

Demeter recognizes in the mockery of culture. Having a headache, swinging like little girls or spiders at the end of their silk, having one's feet on the wall is outmaneuvering the Symbolic order, overturning it: it is festival.

The three central figures, madman, wildman, and child, who always simultaneously signify origin, exclusion, and the future norm are mixed up in this inversion, in the obvious conjunction between a regression to origin and the underside of social life. Woman partakes of all three and she beats all: madwoman, wildwoman, childwoman. The madmens' festival, the savages' wild celebrations, the children's parties: woman is the figure at the center to which the others refer, for she is, at the same time, both loss and cause, the ruin and the reason. She, once again, is the guilty one.

Michelet finds the origin of medieval festivals in the memories of paganism repressed by Christianity: "wonderful feast days, the Middle Age's most beautiful, the Feasts of the Innocents, the Madmen, the Ass." The gilded legend, the one about false saints, marvelous and comforting beasts, ranks animals near man in the hierarchy of God's creatures. "Even outside of the life of legend, in ordinary existence, the humble, homely friends, the brave help-mates in work, rise in man's esteem. They have their rights. They have their feast days." The slippage is complete; there is no longer any difference between the magical beast and the most humble of men—the serf, whose humanity is just barely conceded. The festival is meaningful because it is a festival of beasts, who are in a close relationship to men though are not themselves men. By reducing the serf in the social order to the beast in the counterorder, things are turned upside down. Michelet, who is always sensitive to the collective voice, reads the figure of an oppressed people in the figure of the ass: "It is the people itself, which, as the ass, clings to its image and presents itself, ugly, laughable and humiliated, before the altar! . . . The world of Grace seems to open wide for the least of them, for the simple ones. The people innocently believe it. Hence, the sublime song in which they said to the donkey, as they would have said to themselves: Kneel and say Amen! You've eaten hay and grass enough! Leave the old things, go!"

The inversion is pushed as far as possible:

They proceed to elect a pope, a bishop or an abbott to occupy the throne in masquerade until the evening of Epiphany. These priests wear women's clothes; they strike up obscene and grotesque choruses to liturgical melodies, transform the altar into a tavern table where they feast, burn pieces of worn-out shoes in the censer, in a word, they give themselves over to every conceivable impropriety. Finally, with great pomp a donkey dressed in a rich chasuble is brought into the church; the service is celebrated in his honor. (Roger Caillois, *L'Homme et le Sacré*)

Sometimes they proceed to elect a mad-mother: an even more radical transgression of clerical interdicts.

What is historically repressed, according to Michelet, holds its own future. Madmen, harlequins, tumblers, jugglers, carnies, mad-mothers, those excluded from society, are thus promoted to function as prophets, all the better prefiguring their group's future because they are banished from it for being from the past. A strange dialectic is set up in which going beyond is brought about by the actual gap between a lost past and a future that rediscovers it. Victor Hugo, in *Notre-Dame de Paris*, reconstitutes this configuration, breathing into it, as does Michelet, a spirit of revolt, a liberating capacity. Quasimodo, the misshapen monster, when he first appears, seems to be making a face, but it is his real face. This first foundling unites the virtues of madman and devil: deaf, half-blind, part-dumb, barely escaping the "beautiful flaming brand," nailed to the pillory, he is, nonetheless, soul and savior of Notre Dame. He is, moreover, bearer of the justice that surpasses the unjust justice of human institutions. What is more, he is recognized by the people who cry "Noel" at his miraculous appearances as the pope, as the condemned man given aid, as the one who disrupts asylum by saving Esmeralda. And she, clearly, is Egyptian, dancer, woman accompanied by her goat, bee-woman, wasp-woman, stinging with her dagger anyone who would attempt to rape her. She is "a fairy or an angel," or, as Gringoire puts it, "she is a salamander, a nymph, a goddess, a bacchante of Mount Melaneen!" But the goddess drops a copper piece, and then he recognizes the gypsy. Completely pagan, mythical, there is nothing Christian about her; only the coin will bring her into Christian reality — which is, however, unable to bear her. For the group, she is a marvelous prey; she will die like Erigone — hanged — hanged on a gallows where the hangman stands, pressing on her shoulders. Here Victor Hugo uses as a metaphor a creature that circulates among women: "the spider and the fly." The hangman is the spider; to act like a spider — to act like a man? In Hugo's system, the one who is hanged becomes the pendulum that regulates the huge physical machinery of sexuality. Esmeralda hanged is the sexual organ itself swinging at the end of a rope. The spider is the hangman but also the girl, for in the inversions, set up by Hugo, as in hysterical reversal, executioners and victims are mixed up, are given the same treatment. One day, on a seance table, Hugo drew a hairy-legged spider, who wrote on its own monster body with a quill held by a leg bent back. Across the drawing was written: "Fantastic. . . . Omnia sunt in hoc monstro." The spider produces the symbolic act of writing by turning back on itself in a monstrous coupling. The spider and the fly: the selfsame creature, not yet in existence but possible in Victor Hugo's androgynous fantasy world. Esmeralda has a mad mother: "la sachette," the sacked nun, the recluse, Paquette — raving, holy and damned. She is the same woman grown old; she is the sorceress at the end of her life; she is the one who will hand her daughter over to the executioner.

Claude Frollo, the perverse abbot, is culture perverted; the instrument of order athwart his own disorder; the man vested with hell, who projects it onto the woman to escape it himself. And beyond that, Hugo, like Michelet, playing hermaphrodite games with himself. Hugo, "the bearded woman," as Jean Maurel says:

> This bearded old man is a monumental bearded woman, able to pick up paving stones at a fair; this old Lady, this worn out version of Our Lady, the strange weakness of a white-haired youth. . . . Hugo— antithesis? Who works more frenetically at jamming, subverting and perverting the faith, at contradicting values? Frollo-Quasimodo is led by Esmeralda into dancing the round, the whirling saraband and the circling farandole at the carnival, where everything is scrambled in the game of masks. Our Lady rejoins the court of miracles where roles are exchanged, blind men see, lame men run. Esmeralda: the people's Virgin, Our Lady of the Crooks . . . the proud Babel of religion, knowledge, authority, in the enticement and weakening which undermine and ruin it, turns into the wretched and joyful Babel of the people. (Introduction to *Notre-Dame de Paris*)

Festival and madness. The feminine figure who crystallizes around herself the swirling glances of a threatened culture. And not far away—revolutionary myths, the figure of liberty.

The Child, the Savage

Freud, contributing the idea of *polymorphous pervisity*, returns to this figure and cancels the image of childhood innocence. But also, by describing the tortures of a child who is cruelly trapped between the signifiers, Mother and Father, Freud overturns the image of childhood as paradise and transforms it into hell. All the same, the experience of madmen and deviants shows that overturning does not mean destroying; and, in fact, childhood hell is recovered in desire's paradise because polymorphous perversity is also the stage of something lost too soon, the period when any desire is attainable by the child. Not that the child can realize all desires—far from it—in fact, one of the causes of children's suffering is in the disproportion between the desires and the gigantic things they want to reach. But the child can formulate them all, explore the surface of the body's surface through all its orifices, set up its "erogenous zones," and go through all the stages leading to procrustean normality. The Elsewhere of childhood revelry is just that: "No longer any way to reduce this Elsewhere to the imaginary form of a nostalgia, of a lost or future Paradise; what one finds there is the paradise of childish loves, where, By Baudelaire! things are pretty hot!" (Lacan, *Du traitement possible de la psychose*).

Thus, what is important about the festival elements of childhood is to be found in an adult projection. Rousseau, a model of these projective procedures, fantasizes, while surrounded by children for whom he is giving the sort of little party he likes. "Besides, the party did not cost a fortune, and for the thirty cents that it cost me at most, there were more than 100 crowns of happiness." Spontaneity, an economy of money, an economy of words, a restricted exchange, a limited expenditure. And then, at the heart of it, the pleasure of being the demiurge creating childish pleasures. "Then I watched one of the sweetest scenes that can charm a man's heart, seeing joy united with the innocence of that age spread out all around me. Because, seeing it, even the spectators shared it, and I, who had such a bargain sharing this joy, had moreover the pleasure of feeling that it was my creation." The child is the mirror of the adult; the fairy-mirror that gives the right answer. It is the same process for the witch-woman, who gives the inquisitor the answer that is prompted by a common desire. All celebrations, even if they seem to be wild and demented, are geographic and temporal representations of this identification between Self and Others, among every one, among all the others: identification, sexual identity, exchange—but calculated exchange. Calculated in cents and crowns by Rousseau. The economy of monetary signs is repeated in the economy of the signs of language: not speaking, communicating with gestures, tears, smiles, singing—preferably a capella to avoid even that distancing caused by the use of instruments, preferring melody to harmony, preferring nursery rhyme, and preferring speech reduced to practically nothing. Rediscovering the time when people met one another by a spring, the time of a language that let nothing be lost, the time of secret games in the middle of the road; rediscovering relationships between men that are at the right distance, relationships in which the most threatening connections are kept at bay, and the most threatening of all these is man's union with woman. Being, as Hugo says, "all together and each one *tête a tète*" (*La Fète Chez Thérèse*). From Rousseau, we shift to Lévi-Strauss, who observes, through the antropological prism of his own philosophemes, the necessity of a right distance between men—the right distance between groups; neither too close, because they fight, eat each other, destroy each other, as in the universe of fantasy described by Melanie Klein, nor too far, because not knowing each other, they also fight. The right distance between Moon and Sun, Man and Woman, kept apart for eternity by the ferryman paddling on the skiff that keeps them encircling the earth and sky endlessly, as Amerindian myths tell it. The right distance which, culturally, can be found only symbolically, through constraint, through order, but which reflects in this constraint the truly ineradicable nostalgia for paradise: "The sweetness, eternally denied to social man, of a world in which one could live with another" (Lévi-Strauss, *Structures élémentaires de la Parenté*).

Living with one another: this state, which Lévi-Strauss finds in amazonian daydreams and in myths, corresponds to the state described by Rousseau in his musings on the origin of inequality. It is the youth of the world. One meets another at the well, finding there the water necessary for the life of the body, the language necessary for the life of the heart, and the woman necessary for the life of the group. The place of origins, the feast, is also the place of exchange. Madman, child, and woman have the word there. Especially, they have the mastery that they do not have in ordinary reality. In this archaic structure, Lévi-Strauss finds the two axes of exchange that make men's cultural law: the exchange of words, the exchange of women. The exchange of words — language; the exchange of women — exogamy. Their development, however, is not the same: language perfects itself to the detriment of the information that it carries and progressively separates itself from the wealth of the original meaning. It "entropies," having been destined to inevitable degeneration, to an apocalypse of language. We have exchanged so many words that we will end up unable to speak: "words have been able to become everybody's thing." The exchange of women, on the other hand, has kept its original value, for women are both sign and value, sign and producer of sign. We know this perfectly well: it happens that women talk, that they step out of their function as sign. This fact still safeguards culture even in this wonderful scientific version of the great Christian myth: woman is in a primitive state; she is the incarnation of origin. "In men's matrimonial dialogue, woman is not just what is being talked about; because, even if women in general represent a certain category of signs, destined for a certain type of communication, each woman keeps a particular value, which comes from her talent before and after the marriage in holding her part in a duet." It is true that it is not yet a question of autonomous language. There is no doubt that woman might speak by herself, from herself; at least she is recognized as a producer of signs, whereas the other function allotted to her, like the linguistic function, strictly concerns the exchange between the groups. Duet, song, representation of a relationship as spectacle: exchange object and theatrical object; object of theater, woman in the initial exchange. Still, it has to be seen that all the wealth of this exchange preserves within woman the intrinsic value of origin. Ultimately one might even think, as we know, that the woman must remain in childhood, in the original primitive state, to rescue human exchange from an imminent catastrophe owing to the progressive and inescapable entropy of language. Words have been able to circulate too much, to lose their information, to strip themselves of their sense. At least let women stay as they were in the beginning, talking little but causing men's talk — stay as guardians, because of their mystery, of all language. Lévi-Strauss calls what they are thus able to retain "affective wealth," "fervor," "mystery," "which at the origin doubtlessly permeated the whole world of human communications." Later, in *Mythologies*, he will rediscover in Amerindian mythic patterns that "women's periods, their uncontrolled flow, too close to nature and therefore threatening," are the *stabilizing* element through which runs the split between nature and culture: simultaneously the rule and the unruly (*règle/règles*). A natural and dangerous order, always open to the possibility of lasting, turning into a cataclysm; hence, perceived by culture, by men who take on its value, as disorder. That is why women, who are still savages, still close to childhood, need good manners—conventions that keep them under control. They have to be *taught how to live*. "If women are particularly in need of education, it is because they are periodic creatures. Because of it they are constantly threatened—as is the entire world by their being so—by two possibilities which we have just mentioned; either that the rhythm of their periods slow down and immobilize the course of events; or else that it speed up and throw the world into chaos. Because the mind can as easily imagine that women cease to give birth and have periods or that they bleed endlessly and give birth on any plot of grass" (*Mythologiques, l'Origine des manières de table*). Two rhythms oppose each other. The rhythm of feminine periodicity, which the myths know—if not on the grounds of real knowledge, with the unconscious knowledge of primitive logic—guarantees the reproduction of the species. The other rhythm, that of the periodicity of culture, imposed by men on nature, a necessary material transformation, is a rhythm that both follows seasons, plants, animals, and women and restrains them. Affective relations, therefore, must keep a certain backwardness which is attributed to women; the necessary archaism and backwardness determine the climate of passion and of paradise. At the heart of the primitive or savage feast, words and women are "exchanged" without speech—on the verge of what will later truly be language—on the verge of exchange as well. Culture, breaking its origins in paradise, introduces the exchange of women, of goods, or of words, which begin to circulate at the expense of that larval exchange, silent and precious, of the primitive matrix, the original womb. "But the hot and moving climate in which began to bloom the symbolic thought and social life which constitute its collective form, still warms our dreams with its mirage. Right up to our own times, humanity has dreamed of grasping and fixing that fugitive moment in which it was permissible to believe one might be clever with with law of exchange—win without losing, enjoy undivided rights." When all is said and done, to keep women, one must keep them in a primitive, wild state. It is hard to know whether Lévi-Strauss, as an interpreter, is projecting or faithfully transcribing the myths, but through him the truth of the original pattern asserts itself. No longer to exchange, that is, no longer to exchange women, to live without women, is outside history: *without history*.

So the right and wrong sides of social life play together; at halftime there is a celebration. On the right side: exchange, dividing up, gain, profit, but also the diminishing of fervor, the loss of communication. On the wrong side, nothing is exchanged anymore according to the mythological versions. And in their conflicts, *jouissance*, fusion, and community take place, both on this side of the community and beyond it. The origin is the reverse side of the present. This genesis of a disgraceful inversion is what Freud describes in the myth of origin; *Totem and Taboo, Moses and Monotheism, Civilization and Its Discontents* take the route of the feast. The cannibal feast, the totem meal. And the feast comes through mourning: from mourning to joy, just as the devil shows his presence during exorcism by a radiant face. "This mourning is followed," writes Freud, "by the most boisterous and joyful celebration, with unleashing of all instincts and acceptance of all gratifications. And here we easily catch sight of the nature of the feast. It is not because, ordered to be in a joyful mood, men commit excesses; the excess is part of the very nature of the celebration; the joyful mood is produced by the permission given to do what is forbidden in normal times." Celebration follows mourning and the father's murder; but the murder is due to the mother's making capital of women, that is to say, it is due to an *absence of exchange*. The sons kill the father—the man who has all the women—and weep for him. But in a memorial gesture where the repressed reappears, where the father lives again in the totem animal, where the parricidal act is again committed, the festival occurs as a repetition of the *absence of exchange*. The cannibal feast dismembers man's body; it is a paradise that celebrates the origin of the distance between man and woman, the origin of regulation of their relations, and it nullifies this distance in the moment of mourning mixed with joy. In the Freudian version of the story, incest takes root on that spot and, at the same time, the institution of generation occurs—the institution of the infinite succession of fathers and sons exchanging daughters. In the celebration, this exchange disappears: "The desire for mother or sister," Lévi-Strauss comments, "the father's murder and son's repentance, doubtlessly do not correspond to any fact or collection of facts that occupy a given place in history. But, perhaps, in a symbolic form they translate a dream that is both ancient and lasting. . . . The symbolic satisfactions, in which, according to Freud, the grief over incest is vented, do not constitute commemoration of an event. They are something else, and more than that: the permanent expression of a desire for disorder or rather for counterorder."

Unless, perhaps, it might be a more roundabout way of finding an ancient order, one no longer valid, though the essential order in its time. Prohibition of incest is present-day law; it is what is currently forbidden ("currently" here must be understood in the context of mythic narrative, the level to which I always confine myself). But Michelet finds a more convincing explanation. At the time of medieval sorcery, incest has such a broad definition that it includes almost all the members of the same village; to take a wife one must actually leave one's hometown and go search outside the regions that this harsh ecclesiastical law would include. Cousins, even in the sixth degree, pals since baptism, kin throughout childhood: just to love in the village is to commit forbidden incest. So on the occasion of the sabbat, the participants commit incest. They rediscover there the objects of their childhood love; there, in this obvious wild state, they rediscover their true order, the order of their first attachments, with neighbors and cousins. "Incest is the serf's universal condition, a condition perfectly manifested in the sabbat which is their only freedom, their true life, in which they show what they are," writes Michelet. Paradoxically, or on the contrary — logically, this reverse side is the truth: "At the sabbat natural attractions bloomed. The young man rediscovered there the one he knew and loved already, the girl whose "little husband" he was called when he was ten. You can be sure he preferred her and scarcely remembered the impediments of church law. . . . A strong conspiracy and faithful mutual agreement which kept love tightly bound up within the family, excluded the stranger." The sabbat, hence, is endogamous love; a repeat of the childish past, it is also anticipation of the future family, restricted and bourgeois, which will succeed the system of extended kinship. The predominant figure chosen by the sorceress is the young cousin and the surrounding women always feel the seductiveness of this ambiguous character, an always pregnant choice. Myths and narratives are good demonstrations of how these endogamous choices that break out on the sabbat are thwarted throughout ordinary existence. Isolde, on her wuthering heights and at Kareol, will achieve the one solution: death. Only there do children raised together rejoin one another. Yet the sabbat is the time and place in which these reunions will happen without obstruction.

This is finally what the sabbat, the witches' celebration, is. Michelet describes it as the apotheosis of woman. "Woman at the witches' sabbat is all-fulfilling. She is priest and altar and she is the host with which all the people take communion. Basically, is she not God?" Later he goes so far as to insinuate that there, and only there, were sexual practices strictly heterosexual. "The disgusting fraternity of Templars was unnecessary and unknown; at the Sabbat woman was all." All: object and subject of this "communion of revolt," the Black Mass, which for all its reversal is very much a mass, a gathering, a festival. Of course there was violence; of course one can contrast the free, poetic, revolutionary celebration described by Michelet and depicted by Goya's old witches who greedily feast on children. Both parts of the myth are equally true. Apparently unnatural — "antinature" — yet deeply bound to nature, which Christianity had repressed. Unnatural: the witches' sabbat is the one place where the sexual act does not result in reproduction. Witches employ effective contraceptive methods (ice water, Michelet seems to suggest), so that the woman-serf "only ventured to attend the night festival on this express and repeated assurance: 'No woman ever came back pregnant.' " Opposing nature, the witch midwife comforts and soothes women who are victims of constant childbirth. *The Witches' Hammer* says a little more. "No one is more harmful to the catholic faith than midwives," for they alone can kidnap children at birth and consecrate them to demons. Hence, all midwives are potentially witches. Because they help to complete a natural act, they go over to the side of antinature: "certain witches, going against natural human instincts and even against the nature of all animals, with the sole exception of the she-wolf, habitually dismember and eat children." Here we have Goya and the cannibal women. The midwife who kidnaps a child and who is invested with the power of passage is dangerous for coming too close, in latent indeterminate meaning, to nature; she will have imputed to her all the death wishes against the child, or more radically, the imminent, fatal significance with which every birth is contaminated. She will pay for terrors yet to come, for the death of the parents of which the child is the sign. Yet, she is the good mother, in the upside-down world of the night; she annuls sexual exchange, renders it ineffective. She mothers the woman, nurses her. Beyond that, as Michelet observes, looms the figure of a sterile woman — sterile in function, but with a sterility that is both saintly and false: the Virgin, "the Woman who is extolled is not the fertile mother adorned with her children. It is the Virgin and Beatrice, who dies young and childless." And it is Isolde as well, a sorceress who switches love-potions and invites Tristan to the love-sabbat where she will lead him to his death; Isolde who tends wounds but cannot cure Tristan's, Isolde who loves the night and dies of love, consumed by Wagner on the romantic pyre where the Liebestod replaces the justice of the Inquisition. In romantic myth, woman is situated at the fissure where norms hang in balance, where values overturn, where medieval exclusion reverses itself and becomes saintliness.

The sabbat is over. It began between heaven and earth, on a knoll, on a heath all lit up for the great feast of the people; the sabbat is over, with its Mass and universal revelry, one luminous scene in which children play a part and another dark scene wrapped in haze to which only adults have access. There was a special dance, a round, the witches' round: "They turned back to back, hands behind and without seeing each other; but often their backs touched. Bit by bit no one knew who he was himself nor whom he had beside him." A mingling, a mixing of bodies, spatial confusion, disorientation: the body turns upside down, as in the hysteric's fantasy of the head-vagina. A body upside down like the rest of the festival. At the end of the sabbat, only the sorceress remains; Satan has disappeared, everyone has gone home. "But *she*, she who made Satan, who made everything — good and evil, who smiled on so many things, on love, sacrifices, crimes . . . ! what becomes of her? There she is, alone on the empty heath. . . . " And that is when she takes off — laughing.

Crossing Over and Contagion

She laughs, and it's frightening — like Medusa's laugh — petrifying and shattering constraint. There she is, facing us. Women-witches often laugh, like Kundry in *Parsifal*. In the first act, Kundry appears as a faithful servant, mute or nearly so, savage, demented, a poor madwoman. The only word she knows is "serve," and indeed, she "serves" the guild of men who tolerate her, in slavery. Every morning she rides off to look for an undiscoverable balm to cure the unfathomable bleeding and rotten wound of the Grail king, Amfortas. That's the first Kundry: helpful and weak. In the second act, she is a witch. Her real master is Klingsor, a magician who has been excluded from the sacred kingdom by performing on himself the radical operation that could make him chaste. Confusing castration and chastity, Klingsor has swung in the direction of Evil, of sorcery, of seduction. He has a tenor voice. Castrated, he has become diabolical. He has subdued Kundry. And she, too, has a long history; we learn that she has been damned ever since, in a mythical time, she laughed at Christ's passage—accursed laughter that she will carry within her until the end of time. She is the feminine counterpart of the Wandering Jew, assigned by Klingsor to the young Parsifal in order to seduce him. She thinks she will succeed in this by speaking the name of his mother, but the other's chastity prevents their coming together and permits him to "save" Kundry at the moment of the spell of Good Friday. Kundry will laugh no more. One supposes she will remain a servant. She is the madwoman who names, who names the mother; she is also the laugh that disperses, that is the symbol of sexuality whose act is what is forbidden in this opera. It is also she who wounded Amfortas; her laugh keeps a wide gash bleeding in the man's breast. Even that way she soils.

All laughter is allied with the monstrous. That is why Baubô, who was able to make the goddess Demeter laugh, is represented as an inverted body; "a woman's body without head or breast, on whose belly a face is drawn; the lifted dress surrounds this sort of face like a crown of hair" (Freud, *A Mythological Parallel to a Visual Obsession*). Laughter breaks up, breaks out, splashes over; Penthesileia could have laughed; instead, she killed and ate Achilles. It is the moment at which the woman crosses a dangerous line, the cultural demarcation beyond which she will find herself excluded. "Each culture has its risks and its specific problems. It attributes a power to some image or another of the body, according to the situation of which the body is the mirror. . . . The things that defile are always wrong one way or another, they are not in their place or else they have crossed a line they never should have crossed and from this shift a danger for someone results" (Mary Douglas, *Purity and Danger*). To break up, to touch the masculine integrity of the body image, is to return to a stage that is scarcely constituted in human development; it is to return to the disordered Imaginary of before the mirror stage, of before the rigid and defensive constitution of subjective armor. It is dangerous, for the giant images then shifting along the single axis of aggressivity, that is, turned toward the exterior or the interior, are only strolling pieces endowed with a destructive power: these bits of body attack, burn, shred. An entire fantastic world, made of bits and pieces, opens up beyond the limit, as soon as the line is crossed. For the witch (the hysteric), breaking apart can be paradise, but for another, it is hell. It is ears that walk armed with a knife, bird-headed bellies open, that once again Hieronymous Bosch, shifting from one place to another in the split, was able to represent so strongly. And for the hysteric, caught in the contradiction between cultural restraint and sorcerous repression, it is hell and pleasure at the same time, suffering and a tacit paradise that is secret, hidden in a little implicit smile through even the most intense pain. Thus the ambiguity of the witch and her daughter, the hysteric, is gradually explained. From her own archaic point of view, it is pleasure in breaking apart; but from the other's point of view, it is suffering, because to break apart is to aggress. The suffering is not originally hers: it is the other's, which is returned to her, by projection. So Freud's strange remark, "Victims and torturers alike recall their earliest youth in the same way," can be explained. Between the two parts of the couple—inquisitor-witch, psychiatrist-hysteric—circulate suffering and pleasure, paradise and hell.

When the line is crossed, contagion is produced. This phenomenon has been located and attested. Witches spread on the surface of the globe "like caterpillars in our gardens," says an inquisitor. Young Greek girls hang themselves. Bitten women begin to dance the tarentella. The witches' madness is contagious and rapidly transmitted. It is an epidemic. Michelet notes that the epidemics of the Middle Ages are epidemics of skin disease. He gives a general interpretation to the succession of these epidemics. "Three dreadful blows in three centuries. In the first there is shocking external metamorphosis—skin diseases, the leper. In the second the evil is internal, strange nervous excitation, epileptic dances. It all calms down but the blood is going bad, the ulcer is preparing for syphilis, the scourge of the 16th century." It all comes down to the sickness of love, which is prepared for by affliction on the surface and then by pathological dancing. Compassionately, Michelet describes the ferment of desire, the painful, swollen breasts, the pimply skin eruptions and sores—all the signs of repressed desire boiling up. The sorceress calms the agony but spreads contagion. The illness is caught on contact, it heads for the surface; consequently, to protect oneself from it, one only needs to break off contact. Jeanne Favret, in an account of work done in Mayenne in the seventies, tells how "the disenchanter acts as insulation for his client, and as a conductor for his client's adversary. Essentially, he teaches the one who is bewitched how to protect himself from the contact by carefully enclosing himself: not only shutting off but also shutting up, not shaking hands, etc. However, to content oneself with the metaphor of an electrical circuit would simplify the description, because no common language exists among those who manipulate the circuit, and one can never identify its diagram. It would be better to say that 'there is always electricity in the air'; at the very least this is what one suspects since no one among the partners ever knows the exact number or identity of the others" (Le malheur biologique et la répétition). One can die this way—from contact as well as from the refusal of contact: from contact, since it is possible for one to "drop dead" after a sorcerer goes by; from

contact in a new encounter when the Papin sisters are too close to being doubled
by their bosses. But also from noncontact, like the woman who, knowing
she was bewitched and also knowing the way to protect herself from an evil
spell, died after a long period of refusing to speak or eat. Getting away safely
means finding the right distance: neither too close, where one can be struck and
stunned by the shock, nor too far away, where one can no longer stay alive. The
hysteric produces these stunning effects: remember Mr. K.'s accident. The electricity is the identification which, circulating from hand to hand, cannot be
imputed to any one female subject but to everyone: "sexual identity," "sexual
community."

In the witch's case, contagion spreads through bits of bodily *waste* and
through *odors*. These signs persist throughout the hysterical tableau, occasionally with important changes; the hysteric weeps whereas the witch does not, she
pours out whereas the other holds back, or vice versa. The hysteric is the
remembrance of the sorceress. Now to track down the causes of contagion.

Wastes: nail clippings, menstrual blood, excrement, a lock of hair, these
scraps of the body are what will act as a charm. As partial objects detached from
the body, they are especially powerful, in the same way that "object a," the part
where the object of desire settles (Shylock's pound of flesh is the typical example), is powerful in its very detachment. The pound of flesh: take it and it is
death. Flesh in round figures, accountable flesh—hence the body can be divided
as in Penthesileia's fantasies about Achilles's desirable body. Partial objects,
bound by bodily geography to orifices; voice, spit, tears, shit, a cry, anything
secreted and emitted. After that we can understand how men could have wanted
to make tears come out of women's eyes; we understand that the refusal to emit
seems a crime to them. Not to cry: refuse *jouissance*, refuse to emit the precious
secretions that are partial objects for the other's desire. Cry to show that I love
you, the man says to the woman, the inquisitor says to the sorceress—and, somewhere, Freud must say to the hysteric. "Contrary to the axiom—*cessante causa,
cessat effectus*—we can without a doubt deduct from these observations that for
years the determining incident continues to act and to do so not indirectly
through intermediate links, but directly as the triggering cause, exactly like a
moral suffering, which when recalled, even long after and with a clear conscience, can cause the secretion of tears." Tears prove what is true: yes, weep,
that's how you'll get well. Weep: you will tell the truth. And if you don't
weep . . . there is a striking instance of this in the series of Freud's beautiful
ladies: this woman never cries right away, at the moment when she should cry,
but a long while after. "Every day, she would go through each impression once
more, would weep over it and console herself—at her leisure, one might say."
Freud is surprised by these "deferred tears" and notes that they coincide with
annual festivals of remembrance which the lady celebrates for each of the private
catastrophes that have affected her. Weeping is like an intimate celebration; the

hysteric keeps her tears for herself and seems to be unfeeling and untouched, closed for use. Has there been enough talk of her "beautiful indifference"? After having interiorized all the stolen objects, she keeps her inner desires for herself, holding back her tears and swallowing her cries. Going out or coming back in: disgust or craving are the same sort of thing. Vomiting, spasms, gestures of rejection are — when reversed — absorption: food's movement deep in the esophagus, pleasure at feeling the bolus move in the body, a pleasure that affects the sphincters and retention at the other end of the body. The hysteric feels disgust at glasses of water, plates full of meat and congealed fat, spitoons: anything like kitchen or body waste. All things the witch would happily use to make charms and love potions. "Retention of huge amounts of excitation," Freud says. The hysteric keeps the secretion of *jouissance* for herself. Sometimes, in therapy, some waste product from a man would cure her; as if the role were reversed and man's emitting something other than semen would constitute a transgression strong enough to restore order. Saint Augustine recounts: "I know a young girl from Hippo who, by rubbing herself with an oil into which a priest who was praying for her shed tears, was immediately released from the demon." The sorceress, with the tears that have been shed, as well as with her sexual parts used like a hot plate to cook the magic cake, *Peau d'ane*, is one who deals in her own culture, does her own cooking, cooks up her affects. She transforms, she acts: the old culture will soon be the new. She is mixed up in dirty things; she has no cleanliness phobia — the proper housecleaning attacks that hysterics sometimes suffer. She handles filth, manipulates wastes, buries placentas, and burns the cauls of newborn babies for good luck. She makes partial objects useful, puts them back in circulation — properly. *What a fine mess!*

A property of both the hysteric and the sorceress is to make the partial object circulate. It circulates even when it seems blocked. Blocked in the unspeakable; blocked for the inquisitor and the psychiatrist but not blocked for them. The sore throats, the pain of gorge rising, the mountainous passes where Dora recognized her desires, run everywhere inside them. And then, the cries, the cries that never come out, silent cries, the mouth opening on nothing; coughing fits, colds that impede communication through the signifying conventions — colds that are produced for that purpose. For these "blockages" — through which circulate the demons that inhabit a body — have a function.

> Nasal, pleural, stifled or barking? The thing that cannot be shut up,
> which is neither yours nor mine but everyone's, widespread; what
> shakes membranes and breaks up one's sleep — those fits that mime the
> unbearable; that which makes the sex be heard in the throat, in the
> sympathetic vibration of organs — is the cough. It rises irrepressibly.
> An attack they say. But on what? On whom? And also, a cough is certainly just on the edge of vomiting, calling it up and echoing it.
> Rehashed or chewed and spewed again, whatever fills up and blocks

my mouth, whatever taps it then cuts it off with the dead bitten-off words that the tongue puts out, is the very object, full and bitter, of repetition. Sick of the rehash.

A wonderful anonymous text (like all of the review *l'Ordinaire du psy-chanalyste*), which connects the hysterical cough to writing. The writer puts his dejecta on paper. But with this difference, radical in its effects: the symbolic inscription of the written wastes is published and passes into another register. That is where the passionate thread of these wandering associations stops. For the hysteric does *not* write, does *not* produce, does nothing—nothing other than make things circulate without inscribing them. "The cough or nothing, All or nothing," nothing is produced in between. The result: the clandestine sorceress was burned by the thousands; the deceitful and triumphant hysteric disappeared. But the master is there. He is the one who stays on permanently. He publishes writings.

Odors: bewitching contagion is also passed through odors. At Loudun, "the charm was a bouquet of musk roses which were on a step in the dormitory. The prioress who picked it up picked up its scent as well, which several others after her did also, and all were forthwith possessed." A sweet-smelling rose circulates among the nuns; devilry smells. The reversal, the evident repression in an oppo-site form: Miss Lucy R . . . is possessed by an unbearable odor of something burned: "This odor follows me, I am always smelling it, and *it becomes stronger when I get excited.*" Others, on the contrary, lose their sense of smell: those bru-tal anosmias, the odd symptoms that keep one from smelling what is burned; that's getting ready to cook up something bad! Not being able to smell anymore means not smelling kitchen smells, smells of burned desserts. And it is being able to burn dishes yourself, or to look down your nose at them. Cooking badly is also being badly married. Where sex is cooking is linked in part to the kitchen. There is a family, household, intimate stench hanging over it all—to be more closely examined.

If the good smell is diabolical the bad smell must be therapeutic, invested with values to be defended. We should also remember that Strindberg's hero, wishing to rid the body of an evil emotion that must be flushed out, chooses "the most repulsive of all drugs." *Assa foetida*, like other substances with a strong, nauseating odor, has the magical power of putting a displaced uterus back where it belongs, and it is a member of the garlic family. Garlic is also used as a remedy against vampires. Garlands of it are hung in windows or garlic flowers are laid on the bed of the young girls who are threatened. In Bram Stoker's *Drac-ula*, a good mother takes an armful of garlic flowers that have a bad smell from the bed of her daughter, who was bitten by a vampire and is still in imminent danger. The vampire is then able to come in.

Marcel Detienne, in *Jardins d'Adonis*, thoroughly formalized the way smells work. At one extreme there are the Lemnians, who smell so bad that their husbands marry Thracian concubines; immediately, all in one night, they slit the throats of their husbands and male children. At the other end are the prostitutes who, on the Festival of Adonis, make lettuce grow in just one hot day, and who perfume themselves. In the middle are the married women who, during their own Thesmophorian celebrations of Demeter, fast and give off a slight odor of fasting, a delicately rotten stench, which correlates with the necessary momentary separation from their spouses. To make certain that this separation is seen as necessary, the Thesmophorian celebrants chew a bit of garlic to keep the amorous husbands away. Garlic, invested with family values, is clearly the odorous plant that will bring the hysteric, who is lost in her desires, back onto the right track.

The Lemnians smell bad, but why? All versions focus on the same point: they are dirty—stinking, because they don't wash. They smell of armpits or of sex. The sorceress Medea threw *pharmaka* as she traveled the length of their island. She tossed *peganon*, "stinking rue," "herb-of-grace," a strong-smelling aromatic with anaphrodisiac qualities. Stinking rue stifles desires, makes pregnant women abort, and coagulates sperm. A witch's plant, good for separating but perhaps in order to reunite; good for breaking apart, for excluding the Lemnians so completely that they have no choice but to kill man, husband, and child. The deep charge of smells, their separating role—acting to divide men and women—points out the collusion between moral and bodily values, down to the most intimate folds of the body. Evil smells good; good smells bad. Conversely, when the saint gets her reward for having taken on other men's moral and sometimes physical excrement, it will be in the beneficial form of the scent of a rose. "Odor di femina," Woman's Smell. Neither the same smells nor the same values for all women; some smell "bad," others smell "good." Don Juan deceives himself about the smell of marriage. The witch's odor recalls bodily pleasures, which is why the hysteric either substitutes a burned smell that occults any other odor or else can't smell anything at all. To Freud, those are disorders of origin, for the sense of smell is the first and most archaic of the human senses. It is also the first to be lost when man gets up on two feet in his move to upright posture and to culture. Freud's explanation for the disorders of the sense of smell that are associated with hysteria takes into acount the importance both of wastes and of odors: "In animals the most important sense (even with regard to sexuality) is the sense of smell which is diminished in man. As long as the sense of smell (and of taste) dominates, then hair, faeces, the whole surface of the body, and blood as well play a sexually exciting role. Perhaps this fact explains the sensitization of the sense of smell in hysteria" (*Origins of Psychoanalysis*). The origin, lost as soon as history begins, is inscribed in sexual excitation. The sense of smell is its signifier. But also hair—body hair. The sorceress: her hair undone, not contained in a bonnet or headdress. All her hair loose because she is nature.

The hysteric will detest hair, like the Caduveos women getting away from nature, the aborters and child killers, who remove all of their hair and instead of hair have painted faces for adornment. The substitution of cultural adornment in curves and angles for the natural adornments: tatooing as opposed to hair. And Victor Hugo's beard comes back—a smiling ghost: an ironic, androgynous choice, a "woman's" choice despite appearances. Hair, like odors, sides with a redeeming "nature." Dora's disgust with kisses, the lumps stuck in her throat— such repulsions signify their opposite, which the sorceress has taken on herself: a desire too great to find satisfaction. The hysteric is trying to *signify* the original eros by every means: the odors she wards off, the headaches which are metaphors for her aching sex, and also, without a doubt, her lying down. It is the standing position, in effect, that makes the sense of smell useless, and it is in a sexual lying down that it can regain its erotic functions. The hysteric, especially, principally, tries to signify eros through all the possible forms of anesthesia. The indifferent hysteric is signaling her difference and marks herself archaic; insensitive, she defies stimulation. A witch in reverse, turned back within herself, she has put all her eroticizing into internal pain. The sorceress also has anesthetized spots which are a diabolical sign; long needles are stuck into certain parts of her body, men are appointed to this task—the "public prickers." No more blood comes out of these holes, no more pain: nothing results from masculine prodding anymore. But that is when the sorceress is the spectacle, tracked down everywhere, forced to defend herself even if it is with somatic insensitivity. That is where the passage is completed. As long as the sorceress is still free, at the sabbat, in the forest, she is a sensitivity that is completely exposed—all open skin, natural, animal, odorous, and deliciously dirty. When she is caught, when the scene of the inquisition is formed around her, in the same way the medical scene later forms around the hysteric, she withdraws into herself, she cries, she has numb spots, she vomits. She has become hysterical. In the same way that Dora's cough is a castrating response to the seducer's kiss and that the sorceress can cast a spell of impotence with a knot, anesthetizing herself, the defensive woman, the castrating woman, takes refuge outside the world of men. It has become a radical overstepping; an irreversible separation.

Seduction and Guilt

The disrupting event acts as moral suffering would; instead of remorse, the hysteric's physical suffering is produced, and it affects the body at the very spot implicated in the occurrence. "What *is* it that turns into physical pain here? A cautious reply would be: something that might have become and should have become *mental* pain" (Freud's *Studies on Hysteria*). The tremendous stakes in the distinction between physical unconscious pain and mental conscious pain begin to be apparent. There is scarcely a doubt that Freud privileges the moral categories of consciousness—remorse, regret, the whole package of guilty feelings. The therapy of hysteria, and consequently of all analytical therapy, consists of locating the pain in the register of conscious morality and getting rid of all the organic substitutions that the psyche is capable of making. It is a huge displacement whose consequences are still in part unknown: suffering is still suffering in every case, but this time it is for guilt rather than for no known reason. A tragic morality, the morality of psychoanalysis according to Freud, prefers the blind and lucid Oedipus at Colonnus to Oedipus the king, blind to his sins. The expelling of the guilty "pharmakon" is always preferable to plague spreading through Thebes, and the hysteric, if anything, is a plague. Far better that she should be reminded of her sins since she is the guilty one. Afterward let her fend for herself: "Admittedly," says Freud to one of his patients who is rather philosophical and worried, "it is unquestionable that it would be easier for fate than for myself to get rid of your pains, you can be convinced of one thing, which is that if this is successful, you will benefit greatly by turning your hysteric misery into everyday unhappiness. With a psyche that is healthy again, you will be more able to fight off this latter" (*Studies on Hysteria*). Freud, in this scene, plays the role of chorus. A witness to misery, powerless to intervene directly, he punctuates the development of the story with his testimony and immutable knowledge. Fate keeps right on with its schemes, and misery — collective, physical, epidemic, murderous, and mad — is transformed by the workings of tragedy into a misfortune attributed to *her*. But misfortune, which in tragedy is exemplary, the sign of a special heroic quality, a distinction belonging to those who surpass the human scale, has become a banality. Both versions are possible for the original sin: hysterical, somatic misery — hidden in vague recollections; banal misfortune — a moral pain in a "lucid" memory.

History of Seduction: First Scene, "The Perverse Fathers"

In Freudian theory, the seduction scene is the point around which he pivots the Real, grasping the fantasy in the very structure of the scene, and thereby introducing the Symbolic and the Imaginary into the position of the subject. Psychoanalysis begins by running into an "obstacle": the hysteric's implausible tale of seduction. For this implausibility Freud substitutes progressively and not without distress an idea that is still more implausible — that of infantile sexuality. It is a history that goes by stages, in which Freud does his best to find someone who is guilty: there is misery, therefore there is fault. Who is going to be in the wrong? It fluctuates widely. From 1892 on, Freud recognizes that the etiological factors of neuroses are "sexual traumas experienced before the age of understanding." But this hypothesis includes perversion, the corruption of the norm. The other etiological factors are: "1) Exhaustion by means of abnormal gratifications 2) Sexual inhibition 3) Affects which accompany these practices" (*Origins of Psychoanalysis*, manuscript A). These factors will be transformed and extended to include all humans and will later be applied to childhood in general. Perversion then disperses itself and spills onto all the children; this is polymorphous and universal perversion, canceling, by its extent, its immorality and anomaly. But first Freud will have had time to cover every point of family structure. Everyone will be a target while he takes a bead on them with guilt; finally there will be yet another accusation stronger than all the others. Here we see it.

The story of the seduction scene unfolds according to a double process. Freud begins by discovering, in the analysis of cases which he or Breuer is treating, that the patients have been victims of early seductions; the narratives accumulate, the patients are telling — more and more; there is an avalanche of seduction. Simultaneously, the gap between the patient's degree of consciousness at the moment of traumatic shock and the aftereffects (*nachträglichkeiten*) experienced as physical suffering is accentuated. The traumas go further and further back into childhood. A vertiginous regression that Freud will only escape by braking sharply — at fantasy. Freud discovers what he calls "the great clinical secret: hys-

teria is the result of a presexual *sexual shock*, obsessional neurosis is the result
of presexual sexual pleasure which is later transformed into a feeling of guilt."
What is wrong is stripped bare; it comes from pleasure. From pleasure that has
been experienced, obtained before puberty, the physiological age of normal sexuality inscribed in culture's apportionment through initiations. "Presexual"
means *before puberty*, before the appearance of sexual secretions that are tied
to reproduction. The incidents in question then act as memories; therefore, it is
necessary to detect in the patient's biography the triggering incident, the traumatic memory, and its affect—initially one of pleasure but later transformed into
suffering. There is, hence, a divorce between the event and the effect produced:
the latter is inadequate to the memory, it is disproportionate, inordinate, and this
excessiveness—is it tragic?—is at the origin of somatic distress. It is a 'defect
of translation',

> the awakening at a much later period of an old sexual memory pro-
> duces in the psyche an excess of sexuality, having an inhibiting effect
> on thought and giving the memory and its consequences its irreducible,
> obsessive character. That which remains "untranslated" into verbal
> images belongs to the period Ia, so that the awakening of a sexual
> scene does not entail psychical consequences but results in realizations
> (of a physical order), in a *conversion*. Sexual excess prevents transla-
> tion (into verbal images). (*Origins of Psychoanalysis*, manuscript A)

The periods or ages mentioned here correspond to a classification of the life span
into four stages: the preconscious, up to age 4(Ia); the infantile, up to age 8(Ib);
prepuberty, up to age 14 (II); maturity up to age N (III). The scene of seduction,
hence, occurs in an age in which translation into verbal images is impossible,
which is to say, in very early childhood. The memory by itself has no effect;
the effect comes from overabundant sexual energy, which is unusable and held
in reserve, a surplus; a zero sexuality, as Lévi-Strauss describes "mana"—having
a zero symbolic value, which makes the series of signifiers possible.

Then a decisive factor intervenes that comes from listening to the patients.
"A person" is part of this trauma of earliest childhood. Therefore, one must seek
out whoever is responsible: "the *troublemakers** in general must be sought
among the patient's closest relations . . . an indispensable condition proven by
the existence of infantile sexual incidents" (*Origins of Psychoanalysis*, manuscript A). Thus the hysterics are accusing; they are pointing—with their paral-
yses, their dyspneas, their knotted limbs. And they point to either the father, a
dreadful figure, or to some other male kin. The *Studies on Hysteria* present a
parade of young (or less young) persons who provocatively—but with provocation addressed to whom?—hide their story of love with an exploiting relative.

*Clément's emphasis.

Katharina, "a tall, heavy girl with an unhappy face," questions Freud and routs him from his daydreams: "Aren't you a doctor, sir?" She is suffering from breathlessness, dizziness, like all the others she is subjected to some intolerable pressure: "At first I feel something pressing against my eyes. . . . I feel a weight on my chest and I can't get my breath." She imagines "that someone is behind me and is going to grab me suddenly." Freud is quick, he is not going to beat around the bush, he is especially interested "to learn that neuroses could thrive so well at an altitude of more than 6000 feet." (Katharina is the daughter of an innkeeper at a refuge in the Tauern Mountains.) Does she see anything as he approaches? "A dreadful face, who looks at her frighteningly." Does she recognize this face? No. Freud insists: "Two years ago you must have seen or heard something that greatly embarrassed you." Illumination! Now she remembers. She breaks in emotionally: "Jesus! that's true. I saw my uncle with this girl . . . " through a window, because the room was locked, it was dark, her uncle was lying on top of her cousin. She can't get her breath . . . she vomits. Then several incidents return to her: it seems her uncle had surprised her several times at night. She woke up feeling his body next to hers: "What are you doing, Uncle? Why don't you stay in your bed?" Another night she awoke and saw a tall, white shape next to the door, lifting the latch. "Oh! Jesus! Uncle, it's you, what are you doing at the door?" etcetera. A fairytale litany, a story built on repetition, which points to the uncle as guilty, perverse, lustful. A note from 1924 is specific: "Many years having gone by since this time, I feel authorized to break the self-imposed rule of discretion and to add that Katharina was not the niece but the daughter of the innkeeper. The girl's illness was caused, therefore, by her own father's approaches." But in 1924, it no longer mattered at all that the father be pointed out as the guilty party by the girl. It had been a long time since Freud believed that.

Rosalie is a singer. She studies singing until the day she loses her voice: choking, a constricted throat, the sound no longer comes out. An unhappy childhood had forced her to live with an aunt who was abused by her husband. A new symptom appears, a certain prickling in her fingertips forces her to twitch her hands rapidly. The scene is reconstructed: "The bad man, who suffered from rheumatism, had demanded that she rub his back and she dared not refuse. He was in bed, and, suddenly, throwing off the covers, he stood up and tried to grab her and throw her down."

Elisabeth suffers leg pains that prevent her from walking and that she calmly endures. One of her thighs is affected by hyperalgesia; at this one spot she feels too much. So much that, when she is pinched at this painful spot, "she cried out as if she were being tickled voluptuously [Freud says to himself], she flushed, threw back her head and torso and shut her eyes." One day Freud discovers a basic point: the girl's thigh was where her father put his swollen foot every morning while she changed his bandages. There are other traumas appearing as well, focusing the conversion onto the legs: she is "nailed to the spot" when her father is brought home stricken with a heart attack; she is immobilized next to her sister's deathbed when she suddenly realizes that the brother-in-law she is fond of will be free. Elisabeth is caught in the erotic network of nursing the sick. Freud underlines the extent to which nurses are in a difficult position: lack of sleep, obsessive worrying, "their own bodily neglect," but especially the habit of forced indifference. "Thus any nurse accumulates many affectively charged impressions, which are barely perceived and which abreaction has not been able to attenuate." The nurse, constantly solicited by the other's body, is constantly forced to repress. Paternal seduction, seduction by a brother-in-law: two guilty parties are named. In one of the first sessions, Elisabeth remembers having had to get out of bed, barefoot, when her father called her.

Lucy is pursued by a burned smell and suffers from a purulent rhinitis. The burned smell disappears when Freud succeeds in drawing out a memory: she gets a letter from her mother, two little girls dance around her to keep her from reading it, and she is torn between wanting to stay where she is, with the little girls, and wanting to return to her mother. Meanwhile, a pudding is burning: the smell became the signifier of this conflict. But another odor is emitted, disguised by the burned smell: a cigar smell is indeed a burned smell but one of something masculine burning. Little girls were cooking pudding, men burn cigars. The memory comes back: her employer, with whom she is in love, suddenly gets up from the table and shouts at the head accountant, "Don't kiss the children!" This phrase hits her like a "thrust to the heart," and the cigar smell sticks. With the memory's return, she completely recovers her sense of smell and her gaiety.

Emmy breaks off every two minutes with exclamations of fear and disgust; she jumps when someone comes into the room; she stutters and clucks when she talks. Bit by bit her story becomes clear. The entreaty "don't touch me" is related to the following incidents: at nineteen, her brother, who had been made very ill by the great amount of morphine he was taking, used to suddenly grab her during his dreadful attacks. Later, a gentleman whom she knew suddenly went crazy at her house and grabbed her arm. Lastly, when she was twenty-eight, she had almost been choked by her younger daughter, who was delirious and held onto her fiercely. "And then a friend also," who liked to sneak into the room and suddenly appear before her; a madman gets into her room by mistake and stands right next to her bed.

The hysteric suffers from Symbolic transgression as much as she suffers from memories. In her kinship relations, she suffers because her father, her brother, and her brother-in-law come to act as sexual aggressors, arousing feelings that will convert to sufferings, to hangups, to aesthetic points—anesthetic or hyperesthetic. So the guilty one is unmasked. This observation leads Freud to set up a schema of the relations between fathers and hysterical daughters: "hysteria seems to me always to result more from the seducer's perversion: heredity follows a seduction by the father. Thus an exchange is established between the generations: 'first generation: perversion, second generation: hysteria, and consequently, sterility. . . . ' In fact, in hysteria it is a question more of a rejection of a *perversion* than of a refusal of sexuality." Thus the perverse generation, accursed as in Greek tragedy or in Judeo-Christian myth, dies out by itself, stricken with sterility. The fathers sin, the daughters are punished in reproduction itself. The figure of the father takes on an importance that it will later have again in Freudian theory, doubtlessly less in the oedipal structure, which is divided between the father and the mother, than in the scientific myth of the primitive horde. The paternal figure, in this first scene of the story of seduction, is described as "prehistoric": "Everything is blamed on someone else but particularly it is blamed on this other person, who is prehistoric, unforgettable, whom later no one will be able to equal." That is why Freud's young hysterics are looking everywhere for an ideal man, are unsuccessful at reconstituting the family, are failures in exogamous exchange. "In the demands formulated by amorous hysterics, in their submission to the beloved object or in their incapacity to marry, as a result of longing after inaccessible ideals, I discern the influence of the paternal figure. Obviously, the cause is located in the stature of the father who condescends to lower himself to the child's level" (*Origins of Psychoanalysis*, letters 52 and 57). Such is the father: at the root of a timeless, ahistorical origin. Correlatively, individual history, like the collective history whose design Freud later will trace, is the infinite repetition of the relations of the original child to the unforgettable, perverse, seductive figure. The "important other person" is the model for all others; he is the foundation for otherness, no longer as an important person but as a *place* in the structure of the subject, the place in relation to which the subject establishes itself in a *dependent position*. The father is the Law; the austerity of the Symbolic, the privileged force of the order, come from the looming, immemorial figure of the prehistoric father. This father is overpossessive: the perverse Law. Thou shalt love none other than me. The hysterics' narratives put into question the social structure in its family roots, in the thread of generations each succeeding the other. The parents ate green grapes and for that the children have their desires set on edge—because of having been eaten in the family when they were green grapes.

History of Seduction: Second Scene, "The Lying Daughters"

At the same time that he puts the seduction scene in place, Freud begins to work on the gap between the reality of this traumatic scene and the fiction of the recollection that is inscribed from it. Indeed, to account for the affective persistence of the traumatic shock, an inscription must take place in the unconscious of the individual involved without his or her knowing it, for "the memory acts as a present event" on the one hand, and, on the other, "the consciousness and the memory are mutually exclusive." Then must there be an unconscious recollection? Reminiscence? Known or unknown? An impasse similar to the aporias of original sin: Adam-Eve—did they or didn't they know, and can one be guilty of an *unknown* sin? "With respect to God we are always wrong," Sören Kierkegaard proposes at the end of *Either . . . Or*. That is the easiest solution: keeping oneself in a state of permanent guilt is to constitute oneself as a subject. For the time being the guilty one is not the hysteric, but the hysteric is also not entirely a subject. Caught up in themes which are not hers, repeating her cues, always somewhere between sleep and wakefulness, between a hypnotic and an excited state, she is not she, but through the play of identifications, she is successively each one of the others. They are going to help her become a subject: they are going to make her guilty. But to do it, it will be necessary, through a process of decomposing hysterical narratives, to introduce doubt, sow the seeds of suspicion onto the reality of what they all are telling. So it begins:

> I have obtained an exact notion of the structure of hysteria. Everything demonstrates that it is a question of the reproduction of certain scenes which sometimes one may reach directly and sometimes only in passing through intervening fantasies. The latter come from things that have been heard but only much later comprehended. Naturally all the materials are real. They represent protective constructions, sublimations, the embellishment of facts that serve at the same time as justification. (*Origins of Psychoanalysis*, letter 61)

The gap between the real and the fictive, an unconscious construction, is deepening; sometimes one can get to the real (later one will no longer be able to), sometimes one only finds fantasy. Doubt begins to weigh heavily over this story of seduction by the father.

The "L" manuscript of 1897 further complicates the combinative:

> *Structure of hysteria*: the aim seems to be to return to the primal scenes. Sometimes one can get there directly, but in certain cases, it is necessary to take roundabout ways, passing through fantasies. These actually erect psychic defenses against the return of those recollections which they must also purge and sublimate. Elaborated with the help of things that have been *heard* and only *later* (nachträglich) utilized, they combine lived events, narratives of past occurrences (concerning their parents' and ancestors' history) and things that the subject himself has seen.

What is left of reality, the dreadful faces framed in a doorway, the shadowy white figures looming at a bedside? Very little: bits of family legend passed from mouth to mouth, ear to ear; fragments of scenes, of understanding, and very little of anything actually seen. So little. From the moment the fantasy is based on what is heard, the spectacular element, which is so powerful in hysterical emotion, moves in the direction of fiction. The mechanism becomes clear. Reality is framed by language, spoken and heard. Somewhat later, in the "M" manuscript, Freud formulates the fantasy as *distortion* and *fusion*, but he particularly attributes an objective to distortion. "These tendencies aim at making recollections, which could or might cause symptoms, inaccessible. . . . This process makes discovery of the original connection impossible." There you have it: one will never know, hence it all risks — how would we know? — being distorted. Falsified? False? The reality of the seduction disappears. From then on two elements make access to the real impossible: on the one hand, the gap between the seen and the heard and, on the other, the fragmentation relating to fantasy.

A few months later, Freud writes again to Fliess, "a great secret." "I must confide in you the great secret which during these past months has slowly been revealed. I no longer believe in my *neurotica*" (the hypothesis of a presexual shock in hysterical structure). He then lays out the reasons that persuaded him to change his tack. "First of all there were the repeated disappointments I experienced during my attempts to push my analyses to their true culmination, the flight of the people whose cases seemed to me to lend themselves best to this treatment." Several times, in fact, the patients ran away, were no longer heard from, disappeared at the very moment when they were going to reveal the secret of the primal scene to him. "One of my proud ships has sunk," says this captain of the expedition, commanding a discoverer's fleet to the Americas of hysteria. . . . They were on the verge of . . . They were just about to . . . The moment of revelation is suspended. Then, since the great secret doesn't want to come out, Freud pursues the questioning of his hypotheses further: Second, "the surprise in observing that in each case it was necessary to accuse the father of perversion, the notion of the unexpected frequency of hysteria in which the same determining cause is met up with again, whereas that perverse acts committed against children be so widespead seems very unlikely." Now the corner's turned, retreat completed. Faced with including paternity in perversion, the spirit recoils. Once again blame will fall on the daughter, then on the child, in the form of the Oedipus complex and of infantile sexuality. Third, "the conviction that no "reality-index" exists in the unconscious so that it is impossible to distinguish truth from fiction that is affectively invested (which is why a solution remains possible, it is provided by the fact that sexual fantasy always plays itself out around the parents)." The trick is played: the perverse father exonerated; guilt disseminated and, at this historical moment, preferably attributed to the one who knew how to fantasize a reality that, it seems, is to remain undecipherable. Throughout the period in which he listened to hysteria, Freud was like a prisoner of the mythology of origins. Pursuing a real cause, he sought to discover a true story. When this discovery became impossible — the patients ran away, were liars, one just didn't know . . . a definitive corner was turned. Once the real had become inaccessible, it passed into the realm of reconstruction, of what was recorded, but also of what was impossible, hence the anxiety as one approached it, always on the borderline. It is the frequency of the seduction scene that remains to be read: its repetition will engender Oedipus, the structure belonging to a childhood caught up in parental sexuality. And then the therapeutic possibilities diminish: "Fourth, I have come to notice that in the most advanced psychoses, the unconscious memory does not burst forth, so that the youthful incident, even in the most frenzied cases, is not revealed. When one remarks that the unconscious never succeeds in conquering conscious resistance, one ceases to hope that, during analysis, the reverse process might take place and result in a complete domination of the unconscious by the conscious." The secret is still inviolate.

The cure's termination becomes more distant, infinitely deferred. If there is no buttress showing the disorder's real foundation, is there no longer anything able to signify the end of the analysis? "Considering this," Freud ends in saying, "I was ready to give up on two things—the total elimination of a neurosis and the exact knowledge of its etiology in childhood."

But from this point on, the hysteric will be accused of lying. In *Project for a Scientific Psychology*, an entire section of the study is devoted to the "first hysterical lie." The story of Emma comes from another reading. Emma is no longer able to go into a shop by herself. This problem stems from when she was thirteen: she went in and two salesmen, seeing her, began to laugh. She interprets it herself: the men laughed at the way she was dressed, and she desired one of them. A second memory makes its appearance: when she was eight she went into a shop to buy some candy, and the shopkeeper pawed her. But she went back several times after this incident, as if she hoped to provoke him. Freud's reading consists of linking the first and second scenes together. The shopkeeper laughed when he touched her: laughter, therefore, and her being alone will be the symbol, the link. The two salesmen actualized once again the first scene, arousing anxiety in the presence of desire. Still, we are no more certain that this was the first scene, was there another one before it?

Finally, there is the circuit of lies where that pearl of hysterics, Dora, is imprisoned. Dora, whose symptoms are the symptoms of emerging desire, at the same time is keeping herself for some obscure circuit: she coughs, she is mute, she writes, she feels pressure. As soon as the couple, referred to as the K.'s, come into Freud's narrative, accusation begins: Dora's accusation against Mr. K.; it seems he declared his love to her beside the lake. "The one accused forcefully denied having done the least thing which might merit such an interpretation." The accusation is turned back against Dora, through the intermediary of

Mrs. K., who claims that Dora is only interested in sexual things and that she reads pornographic books. Because he passed this information on, Freud will see Dora leave half-way through analysis. The circuit is complete: in the first scene—Dora the victim, Dora seduced; Dora, licentious and perverse in the second. Next, Dora accuses her father: he is having an affair with Mrs. K. Immediately afterward, Freud notes: "This way in which patients defend themselves against self-reproach by reproaching someone else for the same thing, is something which is unquestionably automatic. The model for it is found in the replies of children who immediately respond 'Liar! You're one yourself!' when someone has accused them of lying." Freud begins to accuse Dora; Dora would accuse herself. She makes accusations against her father: he gave Dora's mother a venereal disease caught from Mrs. K.—Dora's self-accusation. Freud concludes: She masturbates. Now she's trapped. She turns against Freud, accuses him in turn, since he is the object of the transference.

She runs away; Freud sees it as revenge. In Freud's note added in 1923, in which he recognizes that the flaw in this analysis lies in not recognizing Dora's homosexuality, it seems the only one who emerges intact from the circuit of accusation is Mrs. K. Dora is "protecting" her, even though it was Mrs. K. who encouraged her interest in the bookish erotic secrets. The Nambikwara call homosexuality "the love-lie": let's borrow their expression, just for fun. In the circuit made up of one person or another's lies, it is Dora, nevertheless, who is compromised. Girls are liars. This is a return to moralistic theories on the subject of therapy for hysteria. The celebrated Jules Falret, in *Folie raisonnable ou folie morale (Reasonable Madness or Moral Madness)*, very calmly writes: "These patients are real actresses; they have no greater pleasure than in deceiving the people with whom they have some relationship. . . . In a word, the hysterics' life is nothing but a perpetual lie; they act pious and devoted and succeed in passing themselves off as saints, while in secret they abandon themselves to the most shameful acts, and within themselves make the most violent scenes with their husbands and children, scenes in which they say disgusting and sometimes obscene things and abandon themselves to the most reckless deeds."

Freud will not take these positions, of course, and I am not going to hold it against him merely for having *done as the others* did regarding femininity. Freud faithfully reflects the ideological bedrock that makes the hysteric "the family invalid," as he refers to Elisabeth. Like everyone, he is a captive in the family circus that attempts to charge each member in turn with pathogenic guilt. The circuit of seduction only echoes family structure, which Freud obviously could not change by himself. It is good enough that, even if unwittingly, he has given us the instruments for thinking of these changes, of their limits, and of something else that may break open these limits.

History of Seduction: Third Scene, "The Guilty Mother"

The circuit has not ended. For, if the primal scene concerns the parents' sexual relationship — the problem of generation, the question put to the father must have a homologue in a question put to the mother, who until now has been strangely absent. Having first believed in and then disproved seduction by the father, Freud constructs the Oedipus complex; then keeping on the tortuous track of the first seduction, always with his sights on the first genital pleasure, he begins to talk (he had to), about seduction by the mother. Let's examine the text where Freud doggedly retraces the path.

> During the period in which one was especially preoccupied with discovering the sexual traumas of childhood, almost all my patients told me they had been seduced by their father. I finally concluded from this that these allegations were false and I thus learned that hysterical symptoms did not ensue from real facts, but from fantasies. It was only later that I realized that this fantasy of seduction by the father, was the expression of the typical Oedipus complex in women. In the little girl's pre-oedipal history one also finds this seduction fantasy, but then it is the mother who is the seducer. Here the fantasy borders on reality, for perhaps the mother was really the one who caused, even perhaps aroused the first pleasurable genital sensations, and did so while caring for the child's bodily needs. (*New Introductory Lectures*)

This goes several degrees beyond the period in which the *Studies* were produced: all women, and not just those who 'it's obvious' are struggling with the fantasy of seduction by the father, a normal sign of family structure. What is more, the little girl is seduced by the mother. And if it is the mother, this other possible combination necessarily goes back to an earlier stage, since bodily care is mentioned. The distribution of work within the family, which one must certainly refer to as bourgeois, takes shape here. According to Freud, maids, governesses, and coachmen surround the hysterics, and Freud is careful to mention apropos Katharina that her clothes clearly reveal that she is not a servant at the inn but the daughter of the innkeeper, despite her serving him his dinner. Mothers take care of the bodies, Fathers intervene as law. Dirtiness and cleanliness are women's prerogative, even daughters' prerogative, in their function as nurses for their old and sick fathers. The only mention made of Dora's mother depicts her as "uneducated" and suffering from "housewife's psychosis." Dora doesn't get along with her anymore because she refuses to integrate herself into the household tasks that her mother demands of her. Cleanliness of the (proper-tied) body, a crud hunt that turns back on the family: beneficial, well done. So, in caring for the youngest children, the mother handles bodies, sexual organs, fools around in the folds of the body, fondles: that, according to Freud, is her seduction. But the trap is even fuller than that; for if one looks at the analysis of little Hans, what does one see? There it is the child himself who is the seducer. "Hans is four years three months old. This morning his mother gives him his daily bath and, after his bath she dries and powders him. While she is powdering around his penis, carefully not touching it, Hans asks: "Why don't you put your finger on it?"

Mother: Because it's nasty.
Hans: What's that? Nasty? Why?
Mother: Because it's not proper, not nice.
Hans (*laughing*): But lots of fun!

In a note, a little girl, about Hans's age, plays the same game, closing her thighs on her mother's hand. Whether she steers clear of it or not, whether she goes around the penis, the genitals, or handles them, whether she follows the law or transgresses it, she is caught: seductress. A seductress in the apprenticeship of proper cleanliness: dirty despite herself, right down to the physical techniques which she is made culturally responsible for transmitting. Proper. *What a fine mess.*

Indeed, Michelet had noted the *child's* seduction: neither girl nor boy, androgynous rather, sexual every which way. The serf's wife loved sprites and goblins, who came into the house with the children and made the cradle rock gently. The fireside goblin hides—in a butter jar, in a rose, in the sparkling embers. "He is nimble and daring, and if one didn't hold onto him, perhaps he would get away. He watches and hears too much. . . . And, with all that, there is something of the lover about him. More intrusive than anyone else, and so small, he slips around everywhere." He invades her, possesses her, then grows up to be a demon. She is the very devil with him in her body. "Something makes her skin crawl strangely, making her toss and turn, unable to sleep. She sees weird figures. The Spirit who was so little and so sweet seems to have become imperious. He is presumptuous. She is worried and indignant, wants to get up. She stays but she moans, feels she is becoming dependent, says to herself: 'So now I don't belong to myself anymore!' " The Devil emerges through the seductive child, but at least the poor serf-woman is cleared of any seduction.

On the other hand, there is the terrifying mother figure described by Melanie Klein. Here the guilt for seduction and the resulting anxiety, whether one is object or subject of this seduction, are pushed to extremes. All because the breast is taken away. "I consider the loss of the breast as the most fundamental cause of conversion toward the father. Identification with the father is less charged with anxiety than identification with the mother." In the earlier stages of oedipal conflict, the figure of a castrating mother is found, one who is powerful and devouring and at the same time seductive.

Fear of the mother is so crushing because it is combined with an intense fear of castration by the father. The destructive tendencies whose object is the belly-womb are aimed equally, with their full intensity of oral and anal sadism, at the father's penis which must—according to the child's idea—be there. During this period the fear of castration by the father is concentrated on the penis. The feminine phase is therefore characterized by an anxiety linked to the mother's belly and the father's penis, and this anxiety subjects the boy to the tyranny of a superego which devours, dismembers and castrates, and which is formed of maternal and paternal images at the same time. (Klein, *Essais de Psychanalyse*)

Now she is a *penis thief*: the father's penis must certainly be in her belly. Let's return to *The Witches' Hammer*: "What [asks the Inquisitor] is to be thought of these witches who collect this way [by taking away the male organ], sometimes collecting a great number of them [20 or 30] and who then go around putting them in birds' nests or shutting them up in boxes, where they keep on moving like living organs, eating oats or other things as some have seen and as they are generally believed to do?" ("How witches can take the male organ from a man.") The sorceress takes men's penes, as, from the child's point of view, the mother takes the father's penis. We find ourselves in a kind of primal scene, which is internalized to the space within the body. The center of that space is opaque and organic: there the father-penis encounters the mother-belly. One can't see any more. But one well imagines the dreadful encounter from which these excrement-children will again emerge. The fact remains that in this phantasmic mythology the sorceress and mother come together again—are one and the same. Guilty. The hysteric is indeed the witch's daughter.

History of Seduction: Epilogue, "A Family Affair"

Thus it is displaced from father to mother via the daughter. The sons are not left out; their guilt will be the object of the great myth of the primitive horde: "One day, the brothers who had been driven away came back together, killed and ate the father, which put an end to the paternal horde's existence." Humanity's first lie, therefore, is the repression of the initial traumatic act, which will give rise, as Freud says, to "so many things: social organizations, moral restrictions, religions." Guilt is their basic motivation, just as it is the motivation of the hysterical scene of seduction; it proceeds from the same reversal. In the seduction scene causing the hysteric's illness, Freud believes, at first, that he perceives the father's guilt; later he notices that this guilt is projective. As it is represented in the primitive horde, guilt circulates between the fathers and sons in the same way: but the first repression reverses the relationship, and it is the sons who, in their turn, take the guilt upon themselves. But what is the consequence of this charge? "What the father had at one time prevented by the very fact of his existence, the sons forbade to themselves in the present, by virtue of that 'retrospective obedience' which is characteristic of a psychological situation made familiar to us by psychoanalysis. They deny their act, forbidding that the totem, the father substitute, be put to death, and they refuse to reap the fruit of these deeds, refusing to have sexual relations with the women they have set free. It is thus that the son's feeling of guilt has given birth to the two fundamental taboos of totemism which, for this reason had to be confused with the two repressed desires of the Oedipus Complex." Hence, the exchange of women derives from guilt; and their guilt—women's guilt—comes from the transgression of this exchange, and so forth. *The woman must circulate, not put into circulation.* But the hysteric puts into circulation, as does the sorceress in her own manner; both of them violate exogamous exchange and transgress kinship. The transgressions of kinship: the unconscious erotic unions of Emmy, Lucy, Elisabeth, Dora with members. Family members. Transgressions—the choice of too close an object, the brother-in-law, the brother, the father, or even Mr. K., linked to the father by Mrs. K., or even Mrs. K., the father's mistress. Transgressions turned into arrests: this forbidden, endogamous circulation of desire within the realm of kinship is signified by the knots tied in the places it might get through; it can no longer come out. If "it" came out it would immediately embrace the forbidden man or woman. Remember the plot of Dreyer's *Dies Irae*: there is a young girl whose mother, a witch, died at the stake, an old shepherd-husband, a young son-in-law in the house. A love story, not concealed, weaves itself between the two young people; during the night, incest, to which the girl, at least, consents in the full light of knowledge. She makes a straightforward wish for the death of her old husband; at that moment, he dies, stricken by an attack. Then the old mother, the mother-in-law, emerges from her hole and accuses the young woman of sorcery; and she herself comes to believe it. She can believe nothing else; she has come out with her desire, she has disobeyed the rules, and besides, isn't she the witch's daughter, and didn't her husband die at the very moment she formulated the hope—just like Mr. K. before Dora's eyes? Wasn't her affliction caused because she went too far with her desire?

And always, everywhere in the hysterical sagas, there is the feminine character to whom Freud gives the role of homosexual object; the character with whom the hysteric "identifies." The feminine Other, solidly in place, a reference point without which transgression, whether real or fictive, in actions or focused on the body, cannot be carried out. In the story told by Dreyer, an old witch, who was her mother's friend, burns before the young girl's eyes; for Dora—Mrs. K., for Katharina—cousin Francisca, whom her father slept with; for Rosalie—the "aunt," mistreated by the "uncle" (the mother, the father); for Elisabeth—the dead sister, before whom she stands frozen; for Lucy—the two little girls who, above all, must not be kissed; for Emmy – her sick daughter, who hugs her "until she smothers." Everywhere, the other woman. "Thus," writes Lacan,

> The hysteric experiences herself in hommages which are addressed to another woman, and offers the woman in whom she adores her own mystery to the man whose role she is taking without fully being able to enjoy it. Seeking endlessly for what it is to be a woman, she cannot help but betray her desire, since this desire is the desire for the other, for want of having made a satisfactory narcissistic identification which would have prepared her to satisfy both the one and the other in the position of an object. (*La psychanalyse et son enseignement*)

A fine description of masculine mastery and the aporias it gives rise to: the hysteric "experiences herself" at what price? – in "hommages," and in doing this, betrays her woman desire. Implicit in the very ambiguity of the expression "woman desire" is her desire both to be and to have. Imaginary transition, incompatible synthesis, impossible compromise; a dreamed-of transgression, which through Michelet's pen is successful, the imaginary sorceress of whom no one has any trace; except in rediscovering the desire that this figure and her acts of violence awaken in ourselves, women.

For the sorceress, the one Michelet described, this repressed which he reinvented, has no family, gets out of the family, engenders no family. She is born, or rather, she appears by dint of repression, pressed, like grapes, by the feudal system of exploitation: "the appalling mechanics of crushing, flattening out, the cruel press for soul breaking. From turn of the screw to turn of the screw, breathing no longer and coming apart she flows out of the machine and falls on the unknown earth." There she is, sprung up like a wolf-child, a feminine Gaspard Hauser. "It's a monster, an aerolith, come from who knows where. Good God! Who would dare come near it?" Later we will learn that there is no sorceress worth her salt who is not born of the love between a mother and her son – at a time when sons stayed home longer with their mothers. Thus, born of incest, she is without a family: "At her appearance, the sorceress has neither father, nor mother, nor son, nor husband, nor family." There is no question of being a daughter; in Michelet's desire, femininity cuts through.

The family apparatus, crushing not the sorceress but all other women, does not include daughters. Since she is without family, she lives nowhere, in the places that signify "nowhere": "in impossible places, in bramble forests, on the heath where entangled thorns and thistles do not permit *passage*." What is important is that it does not permit *passage*; from this isolation she will open up forbidden passages and she will contort the cruel rites of passage of Christian culture. From this position outside the family, she will derive two gifts which are the very opposite of the Oedipus: "the illuminism of lucid madness, which, depending on its extent is poetry, second sight, a sharp penetration, speech both

innocent and cunning, and above all the ability to believe all one's own lies."
This is what settles the problem of what is true: she is true because she believes
her own lies. She deceives "herself," she doesn't deceive anybody. But she does
not deceive herself, she repeats, she anticipates, she is not in the present, she
is the obscure past of paganism, shaking up the present to arrive at science.
"From this gift comes another, the sublime power of *solitary conception*, the
parthenogenesis that our physiologists now recognize in the physical fertility of
the females of numerous species, and which is no less sure for conceptions of
the mind."

Solitary conception: "Alone she conceived and gave birth." To whom? a burst
of laughter, a Robin Hood who plays truant; it is the Doctor. (A slipup: the doctor has not lived up to the hopeful image which Michelet invested in him.) However, knowledge is transgression: "The transgressor is knowledgeable, the man
of knowledge transgresses: to go over the boundary, he turns the cultural space
inside out like the finger of a glove, but it is still the same space which remains
mythical" (Michel Serres, *Hermès ou la Communication, Dictionnaire*). Michel
Serres marks here the return of knowledge to reality; because in fact the "knowledge" Michelet talks about is completely mythical, for him the idea of science
is romantic. It is the same game when Lacan speaks of the relationship of the
hysteric and "knowledge"; the "knowledge" of the master, whether he be the
father of the family or the university professor: "the hysteric is the divided subject, in other words the unconscious in practice, who puts the master up against
a wall to produce a knowledge." In the circus of transference it is easy to speak
of the hysteric's "challenge," the master's "defeat," of the pathetic figure of the
academic who reproduces the master. It all takes place in the hysteric's imaginary room, transformed into an amphitheater. It's the *Armchair Real*: the limits
of psychoanalysis. I prefer to say that the hysteric, following where the sorceress
leads, is split between man and woman, between the two figures of her bisexuality. She is between the family walls, which she does not leave, and a *jeune naissance* (a new young birth), the I-nnascence that is not yet accomplished.

Taking Flight

While the sorceress is parthenogenetic and the hysteric demonstrates the
desire to escape a family the sorceress never had, they inaugurate and prefigure
in a myth that is reread and reconstructed, something that has never taken place.
There has always been bisexuality. But it is always dominated by masculinity,
always coming back to the same. It is the sequence that moves from hermaphrodite to phoenix, from the fusion of masculine and feminine to immortality.
Hermaphrodite—the fusion of a young shepherd jealous of his virility and a
young nymph in heat; Dionysus wearing long robes and in a ritual gesture lifting
his skirts to uncover the phallus; the girl-Kainis becoming Kaineus—the invul-

nerable giant. . . . It all comes back to man who goes through woman to reach immortality. Let's examine the sequence: one moves from hermaphrodite to phoenix (according to Marie Delcourt's schema). The phoenix who engenders himself, like the eagle, or the vulture, or even the heliodrome, burns his father on an aromatic pyre or carries the body to the sources of the Nile. There he is reborn from his own ashes. The Roman emperors use eagles as the symbol of immortality attained in apotheosis; Christ is to be baptized "phoenix," perched on a sacred palm branch, the Christian syncretism seeking to unite images. . . . This history, locked up tight between father and son, includes nothing that touches woman; moreover, it is invented to get rid of her. One dresses up as woman, one fuses together, one turns into a hermaphrodite, and one becomes immortal. One finally escapes giving birth and being born, escapes from the flood of water, blood, and other substances that come out of woman when she bears the child.

The sorceress engenders without a father. She emerges, pressed out by the "soul press," a living product of psychological crushing. The hysteric is bisexual: which means what? In severe hysterical attacks, she is simultaneously "woman" and "man," says Freud: "the patient with one hand holds her dress tightly against her body (as a woman) while with the other hand she is trying (as a man) to rip it off" (*The Relation of Hysterical Fantasies to Bisexuality*). She plays the role of "woman" and of "man": man the aggressor, woman keeping her dress on. Cultural enactments, pathetically symbolized in two gestures, two hands, one dress. The hysteric's *bisexuality*, like the sorceress's *nature*, is doubt-lessly greater if one leaves hysteria behind; departs from the roles helplessly denounced by the hysteric. Quits the show. Ends the circus in which too many women are crushed to death. Is done with the couple: perversion and hysteria, inquisitor and sorceress.

Bisexual women: women in their responses to masculine demands for specta-cle and suffering and, at the same time, men in the misdirected, stammering and bound up initiative of an attack that goes beyond spectacle and turns its back upon the voyeur. *Bisexual women*: anticipating in incompatible and contradic-tory gestures that are not yet possible, that, perhaps, anticipate the impossible. But they are also the women who are most imprisoned. The hysteric, metaphor of the petite bourgeoisie, is a prisoner; the sorceress, metaphor of the people, is a prisoner. And neither one has liberating powers other than the ability to reread the past, other than mythical effectiveness *now*. Now, they no longer exist. Physically they are no more, neither sorceress nor hysteric; and if some-one dresses up as one it is an impersonation. They are old and worn-out figures, awakened only to throw off their shackles. I have dearly loved them but they no longer exist.

Of the mythical bisexuality that gets man immortality which is a far cry from being born of woman, let us keep the bird's wings. Let's keep—it's the same thing—the witch's broom, her taking off, her being swept away, her taking flight. Rather than toward incompatible syntheses and imaginary transitions, let us go toward real transitions and compatible syntheses, a status that is not contradictory. Rather than looking at the spectacle of attacks, let us turn this look, this look that isn't ours, elsewhere, and let it see. Let it see both what it was looking at before and us. Let's borrow from a philosopher what we need to prepare our departure: "The parthenogenetic virgin remains the living matrix of last night's philosophy: the girl, a minor, is hesitating before the troubling, free space of her majority."

She has loosed herself from the looks fixed upon her in her attacks; she has loosed herself from the ties that bound her to those showmen of she-bears: Simon Magus, Jean Bodin, Charcot, a certain Freud . . . all the masters. She, like the sorceress, is going to fly away. But this time, one will know what she becomes.

Bibliography

English editions are mentioned when available; however, page references in the text correspond to the French editions used by Clément.

Bachelard, Gaston. *La Formation de l'esprit scientifique*. PUF.

de Certeau, Michel. *La Possession de Loudun*. Archives, Julliard, 1970.

Detienne, Marcel. *Les jardins d'Adonis*. Bibliothèque des histoires. Gallimard, 1972.

Douglas, Mary. *De la souillure*. Bibliothèque d'Anthropologie. Maspero, 1971 (*Purity and Danger: An Analysis of Concepts of Pollution and Taboo*. Routledge and Kegan Paul, 1984).

Falret, Jules. *Folie raisonnable et Folie morale*. 1866.

Favret, Jeanne. *Le malheur biologique et sa répétition*, special issue of "Histoire et Structure." d'Annales, 1971.

Flaubert, Gustave. *La Tentation de Saint-Antoine* (*The Temptation of St. Anthony*. Translated by Kitty Mrosovsky. Cornell, 1981).

Freud, Sigmund. *Totem et Tabou* [*Totem and Taboo*]. Payot, 1951; *Cing Psychanalyses* ["Analysis of a Phobia in a Five-Year-Old Boy"]. PUF, 1954; *Études sur l'hystérie* [*Studies on Hysteria*]. PUF, 1956; *Naissance de la psychanalyse* [*Origins of Psychoanalysis*]. PUF, 1956; *Ma Vie et la psychanalyse* [*Autobiographical Writings*]. Gallimard, 1968; *Nouvelles conferences sur la psychanalyse* [*New Lectures on Psychoanalysis*]. Idées. Gallimard, 1971; *Névrose, psychose, perversion* [*Neurosis and Psychosis*]. PUF, 1973.

Hugo, Victor. *Notre-Dame de Paris*. Livre de Poche, 1972 (*Notre-Dame of Paris*. Translated by John Sturrock. Penguin, 1978).

Klein, Melanie. *Essais de psychanalyse*. 1967.

Lacan, Jacques. "L'aggressivité en psychanalyse," "La psychanalyse et son enseignement," "Du traitement possible de la psychose" ["Aggressivity in Psychoanalysis," "Psychoanalysis and Teaching It," "Of the Possible Treatment of Psychosis"] in *Écrits*. Seuil, 1966; *Premiers écrits sur la paranoia*. Seuil, 1975.

Laplanche, Jean, and J. Pontalis. *Vocabulaire de la psychanalyse*. PUF, 1967 (*The Language of Psychoanalysis*. Translated by Donald Micholson-Smith. Norton, 1974).

Lévi-Strauss, Claude. *Structures élémentaires de la parenté*. Mouton, 1972 (*Elementary Structures of Kinship*. Edited by R. Needham. Beacon Press, 1969); *Introduction à l'oeuvre de Marcel Mauss*. PUF, 1966; *L'origine des manières de table*, *Mythologiques* 3. Plon (*The Origin of Table Manners*. Harper and Row, 1979).

de Martino, Ernesto. *La Terre du remords*. Bibliothèque des Sciences Humaines. Gallimard, 1966.

Mauss, Marcel. *Sociologie et Anthropologie*. PUF, 1966.

Maurel, Jean. *Introduction à Notre-Dame de Paris*. Livre de Poche, 1972.

Michelet, Jules. *La Sorcière* (*Satanism and Witchcraft*. Citadel Press, 1983).

L'Ordinaire du psychanalyste no. 2 (Novembre 1973). Les Mains libres.

Sartre, Jean-Paul. *L'Idiot de la Famille*. Gallimard, 1971 (*The Family Idiot*, vol. 1. Translated by Carol Cosman. Johns Hopkins, 1983).

Serres, Michel. *Hermès ou la Communication*. Dictionnaires. Éditions de Minuit, 1968.

Sprenger et Institoris. *Le Marteau des Sorcières*. Civilisations et mentalités. Translated into French in 1974 by Armand Danet. Plon.

Veith, Ilza. *Histoire de l'hysterie*. Psychologie contemporaine. Seghers, 1972 (*Hysteria: The History of a Disease*. University of Chicago, 1970).

Sorties
Out and Out
Attacks/Ways Out/Forays

Sorties: Out and Out:
Attacks/Ways Out/Forays

Where is she?
Activity/passivity
Sun/Moon
Culture/Nature
Day/Night

Father/Mother
Head/Heart
Intelligible/Palpable
Logos/Pathos.
Form, convex, step, advance, semen, progress.
Matter, concave, ground – where steps are taken, holding and dumping-ground.
Man
Woman

Always the same metaphor: we follow it, it carries us, beneath all its figures, wherever discourse is organized. If we read or speak, the same thread or double braid is leading us throughout literature, philosophy, criticism, centuries of representation and reflection.
Thought has always worked through opposition,
Speaking/Writing
Parole/Écriture
High/Low

Through dual, hierarchical oppositions. Superior/Inferior. Myths, legends, books. Philosophical systems. Everywhere (where) ordering intervenes, where a law organizes what is thinkable by oppositions (dual, irreconcilable; or sublatable, dialectical). And all these pairs of oppositions are *couples*. Does that mean something? Is the fact that Logocentrism subjects thought—all concepts, codes and values—to a binary system, related to "the" couple, man/woman?

Nature/History
Nature/Art
Nature/Mind
Passion/Action

Theory of culture, theory of society, symbolic systems in general—art, religion, family, language—it is all developed while bringing the same schemes to light. And the movement whereby each opposition is set up to make sense is the movement through which the couple is destroyed. A universal battlefield. Each time, a war is let loose. Death is always at work.
Father/son   Relations of authority, privilege, force.
The Word/Writing   Relations: opposition, conflict, sublation, return.
Master/slave   Violence. Repression.
We see that "victory" always comes down to the same thing: things get hierarchical. Organization by hierarchy makes all conceptual organization subject to man. Male privilege, shown in the opposition between *activity* and *passivity*, which he uses to sustain himself. Traditionally, the question of sexual difference is treated by coupling it with the opposition: activity/passivity.
There are repercussions. Consulting the history of philosophy—since philosophical discourse both orders and reproduces all thought—one notices[1] that it is marked by an absolute *constant* which orders values and which is precisely this opposition, activity/passivity.
Moreover, woman is always associated with passivity in philosophy. Whenever it is a question of woman, when one examines kinship structures, when a family model is brought into play. In fact, as soon as the question of ontology raises its head, as soon as one asks oneself "what is it?," as soon as there is intended meaning. Intention: desire, authority—examine them and you are led right back . . . to the father. It is even possible not to notice that there is no place whatsoever for woman in the calculations. Ultimately the world of "being" can function while precluding the mother. No need for a mother, as long as there is some motherliness: and it is the father, then, who acts the part, who is the mother. Either woman is passive or she does not exist. What is left of her is unthinkable, unthought. Which certainly means that she is not thought, that she does not enter into the oppositions, that she does not make a couple with the father (who makes a couple with the son).
There is Mallarmé's tragic dream,[2] that father's lamentation on the mystery

of paternity, that wrenches from the poet *the* mourning, the mourning of mournings, the death of the cherished son: this dream of marriage between father and son. — And there's no mother then. A man's dream when faced with death. Which always threatens him differently than it threatens a woman.

"a union
a marriage, splendid   And dreams of filiation
— and with life   that is masculine, dreams
still in me   of God the father
I shall use it   issuing from himself
for . . .   in his son — and
so not mother then?"   no mother then

She does not exist, she can not-be; but there has to be something of her. He keeps, then, of the woman on whom he is no longer dependent, only this space, always virginal, as matter to be subjected to the desire he wishes to impart.

And if we consult literary history, it is the same story. It all comes back to man — to *his* torment, his desire to be (at) the origin. Back to the father. There is an intrinsic connection between the philosophical and the literary (to the extent that it conveys meaning, literature is under the command of the philosophical) and the phallocentric. Philosophy is constructed on the premise of woman's abasement. Subordination of the feminine to the masculine order, which gives the appearance of being the condition for the machinery's functioning.

Now it has become rather urgent to question this solidarity between logocentrism and phallocentrism — bringing to light the fate dealt to woman, her burial — to threaten the stability of the masculine structure that passed itself off as eternal-natural, by conjuring up from femininity the reflections and hypotheses that are necessarily ruinous for the stronghold still in possession of authority. What would happen to logocentrism, to the great philosophical systems, to the order of the world in general if the rock upon which they founded this church should crumble?

If some fine day it suddenly came out that the logocentric plan had always, inadmissibly, been to create a foundation for (to found and fund) phallocentrism, to guarantee the masculine order a rationale equal to history itself.

So all the history, all the stories would be there to retell differently; the future would be incalculable; the historic forces would and will change hands and change body — another thought which is yet unthinkable — will transform the functioning of all society. We are living in an age where the conceptual foundation of an ancient culture is in the process of being undermined by millions of a species of mole (Topoi, ground mines) never known before.

When they wake up from among the dead, from among words, from among laws.

Once upon a time . . .

One cannot yet say of the following history "it's just a story." It's a tale still true today. Most women who have awakened remember having slept, *having been put to sleep*.

Once upon a time . . . once . . . and once again.

Beauties slept in their woods, waiting for princes to come and wake them up. In their beds, in their glass coffins, in their childhood forests like dead women. Beautiful, but passive; hence desirable: all mystery emanates from them. It is men who like to play dolls. As we have known since Pygmalion. Their old dream: to be god the mother. The best mother, the second mother, the one who gives the second birth.

She sleeps, she is intact, eternal, absolutely powerless. He has no doubt that she has been waiting for him forever.

The secret of her beauty, kept for him: she has the perfection of something finished. Or not begun. However, she is breathing. Just enough life—and not too much. Then he will kiss her. So that when she opens her eyes she will see only *him*; him in place of everything, all-him.[3]

—This dream is so satisfying! Whose is it? What desire gets something out of it?

He leans over her . . . Cut. The tale is finished. Curtain. Once awake (him or her), it would be an entirely different story. Then there would be two people, perhaps. You never know with women. And the voluptuous simplicity of the preliminaries would no longer take place.

Harmony, desire, exploit, search—all these movements are preconditions—of woman's arrival. Preconditions, more precisely, of her *arising*. She is lying down, he stands up. She arises—end of the dream—what follows is sociocultural: he makes her lots of babies, she spends her youth in labor; from bed to bed, until the age at which the thing isn't "woman" for him anymore.

"Bridebed, childbed, bed of death": thus woman's trajectory is traced as she inscribes herself from bed to bed in Joyce's *Ulysses*. The voyage of Ulysses with Bloom standing constantly at the helm as he navigates Dublin. Walking, exploring. The voyage of Penelope—Everywoman: a bed of pain in which the mother is never done with dying, a hospital bed on which there is no end to Mrs. Purefoy's labor, the bed framing endless erotic daydreams, where Molly, wife and adulteress, voyages in her memories. She wanders, but lying down. In dream. Ruminates. Talks to herself. Woman's voyage: as a *body*. As if she were destined—in the distribution established by men (separated from the world where cultural exchanges are made and kept in the wings of the social stage when it is a case of History)—to be the nonsocial, nonpolitical, nonhuman half of the living structure. On nature's side of this structure, of course, tirelessly listening to what goes on inside—inside her belly, inside her "house." In direct contact with her appetites, her affects.

And, whereas he takes (after a fashion) the risk and responsibility of being an agent, a bit of the public scene where transformations are played out, she represents indifference or resistance to this active tempo; she is the principle of consistency, always somehow the same, everyday and eternal.

Man's dream: I love her—absent, hence desirable, a dependent nonentity, hence adorable. Because she isn't there where she is. As long as she isn't where she is. How he looks at her then! When her eyes are closed, when he completely understands her, when he catches on and she is no more than this shape made for him: a body caught in his gaze.

Or woman's dream? It's only a dream. I am sleeping. If I weren't asleep, he wouldn't look for me, he wouldn't cross his good lands and my badlands to get to me. Above all, don't wake me up! What anguish! If I have to be entombed to attract him. And suppose he kissed me? How can I will this kiss? Am I willing?

What does she want? To sleep, perchance to dream, to be loved in a dream, to be approached, touched, almost, to almost come (*jouir*). But not to come: or else she would wake up. But she came in a dream, once upon a time.

And once again upon a time, it is the same story repeating woman's destiny in love across the centuries with the cruel hoax of its plot. And each story, each myth says to her: "There is no place for your desire in our affairs of State." Love is threshold business. For us men, who are made to succeed, to climb the social ladder, temptation that encourages us, drives us, and feeds our ambitions is good. But carrying it out is dangerous. Desire must not disappear. You women represent the eternal threat, the anticulture for us. We don't stay in your houses; we are not going to remain in your beds. We wander. Entice us, get us worked up—that is what we want from you. Don't make us stretch out, soft and feminine, without a care for time or money. Your kind of love is death for us. A threshold affair:[4] it's all in the suspense, in what will soon be, always differed. On the other side is the fall: enslavement for the one and for the other, domestication, confinement in family and in social function.

By dint of reading this story-that-ends-well, she learns the paths that take her to the "loss" that is her fate. Turn around and he's gone! A kiss, and he goes. His desire, fragile and kept alive by lack, is maintained by absence: man pursues. As if he couldn't have what he has. Where is she, where is woman in all the spaces he surveys, in all the scenes he stages within the literary enclosure?

We know the answers and there are plenty: she is in the shadow. In the shadow he throws on her; the shadow she is.

Night to his day—that has forever been the fantasy. Black to his white. Shut out of his system's space, she is the repressed that ensures the system's functioning.

Kept at a distance so that he can enjoy the ambiguous advantages of the distance, so that she, who is distance and postponement, will keep alive the enigma, the dangerous delight of seduction, in suspense, in the role of "eloper," she is Helen, somehow "outside." But she cannot appropriate this "outside" (it is rare that she even wants it); it is his outside: outside on the condition that it not be entirely outside, the unfamiliar stranger that would escape him. So she stays inside a domesticated outside.

Eloper: carried away with herself and carried off from herself.

—Not only is she the portion of strangeness—*inside* his universe where she revives his restlessness and desire. Within his economy, she is the strangeness he likes to appropriate. Moreover, the "dark continent" trick has been pulled on her: she has been kept at a distance from herself, she has been made to see (= not-see) woman on the basis of what man wants to see of her, which is to say, almost nothing. She has been forbidden the possibility of the proud "inscription above my door" marking the threshold of The Gay Science. She could never have exclaimed:

> The house I live in is my own,
> I never copied anyone . . .

She has not been able to live in her "own" house, her very body. She can be incarcerated, slowed down appallingly and tricked into apartheid for too long a time—but still only for a time. One can teach her, as soon as she begins to speak, at the same time as she is taught her name, that hers is the dark region: because you are Africa, you are black. Your continent is dark. Dark is danger- ous. You can't see anything in the dark, you are afraid. Don't move, you might fall. Above all, don't go into the forest. And we have internalized this fear of the dark. Women haven't had eyes for themselves. They haven't gone exploring in their house. Their sex still frightens them. Their bodies, which they haven't dared enjoy, have been colonized. Woman is disgusted by woman and fears her.

They have committed the greatest crime against women: insidiously and vio- lently, they have led them to hate women, to be their own enemies, to mobilize their immense power against themselves, to do the male's dirty work.

They have committed an antinarcissism in her! A narcissism that only loves itself if it makes itself loved for what is lacking! They have created the loathsome logic of antilove.

The "Dark Continent" is neither dark nor unexplorable: It is still unexplored only because we have been made to believe that it was too dark to be explored. Because they want to make us believe that what interests us is the white conti- nent, with its monuments to Lack. And we believed. We have been frozen in our place between two terrifying myths: between the Medusa and the abyss. It would be enough to make half the world break out laughing, if it were not still going on. For the phallo-logocentric *aufhebung* is there, and it is militant, the reproducer of old schemes, anchored in the dogma of castration. They haven't changed a thing: they have theorized their desire as reality. Let them tremble, those priests; we are going to *show* them our *sexts!*

Too bad for them if they collapse on discovering that women aren't men, or that the mother doesn't have one. But doesn't this fear suit them fine? Wouldn't the worst thing be—isn't the worst thing that, really, woman is not castrated, that all one has to do is not listen to the sirens (because the sirens were men) for history to change its sense, its direction? All you have to do to see the Medusa is look her in the face: and she isn't deadly. She is beautiful and she laughs.

They say there are two things that cannot be represented: death and the female sex. Because they need femininity to be associated with death; they get a hard-on when you scare their pants off! For their own sake they need to be afraid of us. Look at the trembling Perseuses, with their advance, armor-clad in apotropes as they back toward us! Pretty backs. There's not a minute to lose. Let's get out of here.

They, the feminine ones, are coming back from far away, from forever, from "outside," from the heaths where witches stay alive; from underneath, from the near side of "culture;" *from their childhoods*, which men have so much trouble making women forget, and which they condemn to the *in-pace*. Walled in— those little girls with their "bad-mannered" bodies. Preserved, safe from themselves and intact, on ice. Frigified. But the signs of unrest down there! How hard the sex cops have to work, always having to start over, to block women's threatening return. So many forces have been deployed on both sides that the struggle has been stuck for centuries, balanced in a shaky standstill.

We, coming early to culture, repressed and choked by it, our beautiful mouths stopped up with gags, pollen, and short breaths; we the labyrinths, we the ladders, we the trampled spaces; the stolen and the flights—we are "black" *and* we are beautiful.

A Woman's Coming to Writing:
Who
Invisible, foreign, secret, hidden, mysterious, black, forbidden
Am I . . .

Is this me, this no-body that is dressed up, wrapped in veils, carefully kept distant, pushed to the side of History and change, nullified, kept out of the way, on the edge of the stage, on the kitchen side, the bedside?
For you?

Is that me, a phantom doll, the cause of sufferings and wars, the pretext, "because of her beautiful eyes," for what men do, says Freud, for their divine illusions, their conquests, their havoc? Not for the sake of "me," of course. But for my "eyes," so that I will look at you, so that he will be looked at, so that he will see himself seen as he wants to be. Or as he fears he is not. Me, nobody, therefore, or else the mother that the Eternal Male always returns to when seeking admiration.

Men say that it is for her that the Greeks launched a thousand ships, destroyed, killed, waged a fabulous war for ten-times-ten years—among men! For the sake of her, yonder, the idol, carried off, hidden, lost. Because it is for-her and without-her that they live it up at the celebration of death that they call their life.

Murder of the Other:

I come, biographically, from a rebellion, from a violent and anguished direct refusal to accept what is happening on the stage on whose edge I find I am placed, as a result of the combined accidents of History. I had this strange "luck": a couple of rolls of the dice, a meeting between two trajectories of the diaspora,[5] and, at the end of these routes of expulsion and dispersion that mark the functioning of western History through the displacements of Jews, I fall. —I am born—right in the middle of a scene that is the perfect example, the naked model, the raw idea of this very process: I learned to read, to write, to scream, and to vomit in Algeria. Today I know from experience that one cannot imagine what an Algerian French girl was; you have to have been it, to have gone through it. To have seen "Frenchmen" at the "height" of imperialist blindness, behaving in a country that was inhabited by humans as if it were peopled by nonbeings, born-slaves. I learned everything from this first spectacle: I saw how the white (French), superior, plutocratic, civilized world founded its power on the repression of populations who had suddenly become "invisible," like proletarians, immigrant workers, minorities who are not the right "color." Women.[6] Invisible as humans. But, of course, perceived as tools—dirty, stupid, lazy, underhanded, etc. Thanks to some annihilating dialectical magic. I saw that the great, noble, "advanced" countries established themselves by expelling what was "strange"; excluding it but not dismissing it; enslaving it. A commonplace gesture of History: there have to be *two* races—the masters and the slaves.

We know the implied irony in the master/slave dialectic: the *body* of what is strange must not disappear, but its force must be conquered and returned to the master. Both the appropriate and the inappropriate must exist: the clean, hence the dirty; the rich, hence the poor; etc.

So I am three or four years old and the first thing I see in the street is that the world is divided in half, organized hierarchically, and that it maintains this distribution through violence. I see that there are those who beg, who die of hunger, misery, and despair, and that there are offenders who die of wealth and pride, who stuff themselves, who crush and humiliate. Who kill. And who walk around in a stolen country as if they had had the eyes of their souls put out. Without seeing that the others are alive.

Already I know all about the "reality" that supports History's progress: everything throughout the centuries depends on the distinction between the Selfsame, the ownself (—what is mine, hence what is good) and that which limits it: so now what menaces my-own-good (good never being anything other than what is good-for-me) is the "other." What is the "Other"? If it is truly the "other," there is nothing to say; it cannot be theorized. The "other" escapes me. It is elsewhere, outside: absolutely other. It doesn't settle down. But in History, of course, what is called "other" is an alterity that does settle down, that falls into the dialectical circle. It is the other in a hierarchically organized relationship in which the same is what rules, names, defines, and assigns "its" other. With the dreadful simplicity that orders the movement Hegel erected as a system, society trots along before my eyes reproducing to perfection the mechanism of the death struggle: the reduction of a "person" to a "nobody" to the position of "other"—the inexorable plot of racism. There has to be some "other"—no master without a slave, no economico-political power without exploitation, no dominant class without cattle under the yoke, no "Frenchmen" without wogs, no Nazis without Jews, no property without exclusion—an exclusion that has its limits and is part of the dialectic. If there were no other, one would invent it. Besides, that is what masters do: they have their slaves made to order. Line for line. They assemble the machine and keep the alternator supplied so that it reproduces all the oppositions that make economy and thought run.

The paradox of otherness is that, of course, at no moment in History is it tolerated or possible as such. The other is there only to be reappropriated, recaptured, and destroyed as other. Even the exclusion is not an exclusion. Algeria was not France, but it was "French."

Me too. The routine "our ancestors, the Gauls" was pulled on me. But I was born in Algeria, and my ancestors lived in Spain, Morocco, Austria, Hungary, Czechoslovakia, Germany; my brothers by birth are Arab. So where are we in history? I side with those who are injured, trespassed upon, colonized. I am (not) Arab. Who am I? I am "doing" French history. I am a Jewish woman. In which ghetto was I penned up during your wars and your revolutions? I want to fight. What is my name? I want to change life. Who is this "I"? Where is my place? I am looking. I search everywhere. I read, I ask. I begin to speak. Which language is mine? French? German? Arabic? Who spoke for me throughout the generations? It's my luck. What an accident! Being born in Algeria, not in France, not in Germany; a little earlier and, like some members of my family, I would not be writing today. I would anonymiserate eternally from Auschwitz. Luck: if I had been born a hundred years earlier, I told myself, I would have been part of the Commune. How?—you? Where are my battles? my fellow soldiers? What am I saying . . . the comrades, women, my companions-in-arms?

I am looking everywhere. A daughter of chance. One year earlier. A miracle. I know it; I hate it: I might never have been anything but dead. Yesterday, what could I have been? Can I imagine my elsewhere?

—I live all of my childhood in this knowledge: several times I have miraculously survived. In the previous generation, I would not have existed. And I live in this rebellion: it is impossible for me to live, to breathe, to eat in a world where my people don't breathe, don't eat, are crushed and humiliated. My people: all those that I am, whose same I am. History's condemned, the exiled, colonized, and burned.

Yes, Algeria is unliveable. Not to mention France.
Germany! Europe the accomplice! . . .

   —There has to be somewhere else, I tell myself. And everyone knows that to go somewhere else there are routes, signs, "maps"—for an exploration, a trip. —That's what books are. Everyone knows that a place exists which is not economically or politically indebted to all the vileness and compromise. That is not obliged to reproduce the system. That is writing. If there is a somewhere else that can escape the infernal repetition, it lies in that direction, where *it* writes itself, where *it* dreams, where *it* invents new worlds.

And that is where I go. I take books; I leave the real, colonial space; I go away. Often I go read in a tree. Far from the ground and the shit. I don't go and read just to read, to forget—No! Not to shut myself up in some imaginary paradise. I am searching: somewhere there must be people who are like me in their rebellion and in their hope. Because I don't despair: if I myself shout in disgust, if I can't be alive without being angry, there must be others like me. I don't know who, but when I am big, I'll find them and I'll join them, I don't yet know where. While waiting, I want to have only my true ancestors for company (and even at that I forgive the Gauls a great deal, thanks to their defeat; they, too, were alienated, deceived, enslaved, it's true)—my true allies, my true "race." Not this comical, repulsive species that exercises power in the place where I was born.

And naturally I focused on all the texts in which there is struggle. Warlike texts; rebellious texts. For a long time I read, I lived, in a territory made of spaces taken from all the countries to which I had access through fiction, an antiland (I can never say the word "patrie," "fatherland," even if it is provided with an "anti-") where distinctions of races, classes, and origins would not be put to use without someone's rebelling. Where there are people who are ready for anything—to live, to die for the sake of ideas that are right and *just*. And where it was not impossible or pathetic to be generous. I knew, I have always known, what I hated. I located the enemy and all his destructive figures: authority, repression, censorship, the unquenchable thirst for wealth and power. The ceaseless work of death—the constant of evil. But that couldn't last. Death had to be destroyed. I saw that reality, history, was a series of struggles, without which we would have long ago been dead. And in my mental voyage, I gave great importance to battlefields, conflicts, the confrontation between the forces of death and the forces of life, between wrong ideas and right ideas. Actually, I have always wanted war; I did not believe that changes would be made except through revolutionary movements. I saw the enormity of power every day. Nazism, colonialism, centuries of violent inequality, the massacre of peoples, religious wars. Only one answer—struggle. And without theorizing any of that, of course—I forged through the texts where there was struggle.

I questioned might—its use, its value; through a world of fiction and myths, I followed closely those who had it and who used it. I asked everywhere: where does your strength come from? What have you done with your power? What cause have you served? I watched the "masters" especially closely—the kings, chiefs, judges, leaders, all those who I thought could have changed society; and then the "heroes": that is to say, the persons endowed with an individual strength but without authority, those who were isolated, eccentric, the intruders: great, undaunted, sturdy beings, who were at odds with the Law.

I have not read the Bible: I took short cuts, I lingered with Saul and with David. The rise and fall of men spoiled by power.

I liked Hercules very much, because he did not put his muscles to work for death, until the day I began to discover he was not a revolutionary but a gullible policeman.

I fought the Trojan war my own way: on neither one side nor the other. I loathed the chiefs' stupid, petty, and sanctifying mentality. What did they serve? A narcissistic glory. What did they love? Their royal image. The masculine code, squared: not only the masculine value but the essence of virility as well, that is undisputed power. Now onto the stage comes the species of men-kings. Vile patterns. Villainous bosses. Wily. Guilty consciences. The Agamemnon type. I despised the species.

And I pushed ahead into all the mythical and historical times.

And what would I have been then? Who? — A question that didn't come to me until later. The day when suddenly I felt bad in every skin I had ever worn.

Indeed, in Homeric times I was Achilles. I know why. I was the antiking. And I was passion. I had fits of rage that made History difficult. I didn't give a damn for hierarchy, for command, and I know how to love. I greatly loved women and men. I knew the value of a unique person, the beauty, the sweetness. I didn't ask myself any petty questions, I was unaware of limits, I enjoyed my bisexuality without anxiety: that both kinds harmonized within me seemed perfectly natural to me. I never even thought it could be otherwise. Had I not lived among women for a long time? And among men I gave up nothing of the tender, feminine intensities. Prohibition didn't come near me. I was far above stupid superstitions, sterile divisions. And I always loved wholly: I adored Patroclus with all my might; as a woman I was his sister, his lover, his mother; as a man, his brother, his husband, and himself. And I knew better than any man how to love women because of having been their companion and their sister for so long. I loved and I loved love. I never went back on love.

But sometimes I was ashamed: I was afraid of being Ulysses, and wasn't I sometimes? As Achilles I was uncompromising. But when I changed weapons? When I used the weapons of the crafty one, the one who knew too much about mediocrity and human weakness and not enough about true unbending strength—? "Silence, exile and cunning" are the tools of the young man-artist with which Stephen Dedalus arms himself to organize his series of tactical retreats while he works out in "the smithy of his soul the uncreated conscience of his race." A help to a loner, of course. But I didn't like to catch myself being Ulysses, the artist of flight. The Winner: the one who was saved, the homecoming man! Always returning to himself—in spite of the most fantastic detours. The Loaner: loaning himself to women and never giving himself except to the ideal image of Ulysses, bringing his inalterable resistance home to his hot-shot little phallic rock, where, as the crowning act of the *nostos*—the return, which was so similar, I said to myself, to the Jewish fantasy (next year in Jerusalem)— he produced a remarkable show of force. I didn't analyze the bowshot, of course, but I did suspect it contained some "male" symbolic values that made it repugnant to me. How banal! To resist the Sirens, he ties himself up! to a mast! a little phallus and a big phallus too. . . . Later on Ulysses becomes a radical socialist. Noteworthy. I was bitter for a long time about having believed I was this resourceful man when I tried to get out of threatening situations by lying or subterfuge (which happened two or three times in my childhood). I was furious that I had been on the defensive. And, at that time, I didn't have the knowledge, the intellectual means that would have allowed me to understand and forgive myself. Thus from hero to hero went my armor, my sword, my shield.

Then the day comes—rather late for that matter—when I leave childhood. My anger is unmollified. The Algerian war approaches. Societies falter, I feel—the smell of my blood, too, is changing—a real war is coming, coming to a boil. And I quit being a child who is neuter, an angry bundle of nerves, a me seething with violent dreams, meditating widespread revenge, the overthrow of idols, the triumph of the oppressed.

No longer can I identify myself simply and directly with Samson or inhabit my glorious characters. My body is no longer innocently useful to my plans. (breasts) I am a woman.

Then everything gets complicated. I don't give up on war. That would be suicide: struggle is more necessary than ever. For in reality, the offense is also against me, as a woman, and the enemy is all over the place: not only are there class enemies, colonialists, racists, bourgeois, and antisemites against me— "men" are added to them. Or rather, the enemy becomes twice as formidable and more hated. But the worst of it is that among my brothers, in my own imaginary camp, some aggressors appear who are as narrow-minded, crude, and frightening as the ones confronting me. In some way I always knew, always saw this glaring, sexual brutishness surrounding me. But it never becomes intolerable to me until it hurts me as it passes through my own body and drags me into this spot of insoluble contradictions, impossible to overcome, this place I have never been able to get out of since: the friend is also the enemy. All women have lived that, are living it, as I continue to live it. "We" struggle together, yes, but, who is this "we"? A man and beside him a thing, somebody — (a woman: always in her parenthesis, always repressed or invalidated as a woman, tolerated as a non-woman, "accepted"!) — someone you are not conscious of, unless she effaces herself, acts the man, speaks and thinks that way. For a woman, what I am saying is trite. It has often been said. It is that experience that launched the front line of the feminist struggle in the U.S. and in France: discovering discrimination, the fundamental unconscious masculine racism in places where, theoretically, it should not exist! A political irony: imagine fighting against racism with militants who *are* racist!

I, revolt, rages, where am I to stand? What is my place if I am a woman? I look for myself throughout the centuries and don't see myself anywhere. I know now that my fighters are masculine and that their value almost inevitably is limited: they are great in the eyes of men and for each other. But only on the condition that a woman not appear and make blind and grotesque tyrants of them, marred by all the flaws that I want them to be free of — exposing them to be miserly, inhuman, small, fearful . . .

Where to stand? Who to be? Who, in the long continuing episodes of their misfortune — woman's abundance always repaid by abandonment? Beginning Medea's story all over again, less and less violently, repeating more and more tenderly, sadly, the gift, the fervor, the passion, the alienation, the stunning discovery of the worst (which isn't death): that total love has been used by the loved one for his base ambitions. "The one who was everything for me, I know only too well, my husband has become the worst of men." (Euripides, *Medea*).

Vast — this procession of mistreated, deceived, devastated, rejected, patient women, dolls, cattle, cash. Stolen swarms. Exploited and plundered to such an extent. They give everything. That, doubtless, is their offense. For example — Ariadne, without calculating, without hesitating, but believing, taking everything as far as it goes, giving everything, renouncing all security — spending without a return — the anti-Ulysses — never looking back, knowing how to break off, how to leave, advancing into emptiness, into the unknown. But as for Theseus, he ties himself tightly to the line the woman holds fast to make him secure. While she, she takes her leap without a line. I read the *Life of Theseus* in Plutarch.

A model destiny! Two lines weave the elevation of man and the simultaneous debasement of woman. All the figures of a rise to power are inscribed in the route Theseus takes. The still unacknowledged son comes to be recognized by his father, Aegeus, who has won Medea as wife. (Here is an irony of history: with Medea, at the end of a career of successive exiles, once and for all the stage is cleared where the first version of male cultural organization will install itself!) Then the splendid moment in which the mystery of filiation is revealed: father and son recognize each other by the signs of their order, which are the sword (. . . and the sandals: for Theseus [his name recalls] is the one who was able to lift the boulder under which Aegeus stashed his sandals. What is a son? The man who can lift the rock . . . to tie on the inherited shoes).

Then a triumphant career is woven: the crossing of feminine bodies with the thread of a pitiless soul, and a huge territory is accumulated as he passes from woman to woman. Through Ariadne, Antiope, Hippolyta, Phaedra, hecatombs of numberless, loving women and amazons; with Theseus the last great flames die. And so on, down to Helen, abducted at the age of ten (this is how she got started or, rather, got "started.") At that point no more is known, because Theseus evaporates, at the end of the road of abduction and consummation/consumption . . . and he is still running. Moreover, after his father's death, he gathered the inhabitants of the whole province of Attica into one city and reduced them to a town body. Plutarch recounts that there were some in favor of submitting to Theseus's management and others who gave in anyhow, for fear of his strength. Centralization, destruction of all the little units of local administration: the birth of Athens. Afterward he lived happily, invented coins which he had hammered in the image of the Marathon bull, and had lots of money.

I could not have been Ariadne: it's all right that she gives herself out of love. But to whom? Theseus doesn't tremble, doesn't adore, doesn't desire; following his own destiny, he goes over bodies that are never even idealized. Every woman is a means. I see that clearly.

But I would have dared to be Dido. This is where I begin to suffer in a woman's place. Reading Virgil again, in the *Aeneid* (Books 3 and 4); one sees how the venerable Aeneas, who is destined to found a city, is kept from the feminine danger by the gods.

Less of a bastard than Jason, less "pure" in plain, brute *jouissance* than Theseus, more moral; there is always a god or a cause to excuse or explain Aeneas's skill at seeding and shaking off his women, dropping them. Act I, Exodus from Troy. Theseus is armed with his father on his shoulders and his son in his arms:

> for, my wife Creuse is taken away from me while I run, taking the
> wrong roads and straying from my usual direction. Did she stop as the
> result of any unfortunate fate, or did she take the wrong road, or did
> she succumb to fatigue? I don't know, but I have never seen her again.
> I didn't notice she was lost and didn't think about her until the moment

at which we arrived at the burial mound, at the sacred habitation of ancient Ceres.

Second book:

> It was only there, when we were all together again that I saw that she alone was missing and had disappeared without her companions, her son or husband's knowing. Who then, both men and gods, did I not accuse in my distraction?

Horror! The venerable one looks all over and everywhere. Death herself comes to justify him before History.

> Then she spoke thus to me and took away my cares with these words "Why let yourself go on so in such an insane grief, oh my loving husband? These things don't happen unless the gods will them; and they do not allow you to take Creuse as your companion: a flourishing fortune, a kingdom, a royal wife are reserved for you; stop shedding tears for your darling Creuse. No I will not see the splendid homes of the Myrmidons and Dolops; I will not go, as a slave, to serve Greek women, I a Dardanadide and the daughter-in-law of divine Venus. The powerful mother of the gods keeps me on her shores. Farewell, and always love our common son.[7]

Act I. Theme: "a woman's slave?" No! Mercury who is sent by Jupiter intervenes in the name of the league of empire builders: so you are building a beautiful city for a woman and forgetting your kingdom and your own destiny? Thus pious Aeneas will be saved from shame. The next scenes would have been unbearable for him; grief, love, and Dido's beauty are mingled in heartrending songs, and Aeneas doubtless would have weakened. But "the fates are against it, and a god closes the hero's serene ears." He hurts, but he has his law, and that is what he espouses: and his law is clear, because, by dying, Creuse is giving him a sublime strength. The good love for man is his country, the fatherland. A masculine land to hand down from father to son. For Ascanias then . . .

In Dido's place. But I am not Dido. I cannot inhabit a victim, no matter how noble. I resist: detest a certain passivity, it promises death for me. So, who shall I be? I have gone back and forth in vain through the ages and through the stories within my reach, yet find no woman into whom I can slip. My sympathy, my tenderness, my sorrow, however, are all hers. But not me, not my life. I can never lay down my arms. Of course, Joan of Arc is someone; but for me, a Jew and suspicious of anything related to the Church and its ideological rule, she is totally uninhabitable. But otherwise I am with her—for her energy, her unique confidence, the stark simplicity of her action, her clear-cut relationship with men—and for her trial and her stake. But apart from her who I never was, there was nobody. For a long time I continued to be a sort of secret Achilles, profiting from his sexual ambiguity which permitted me mine. But you can't be Achilles every day. And I want to become a woman I can love. I want to meet women who love themselves, who are alive, who are not debased, overshadowed, wiped out. I read—now driven by the need to confirm whether or not there is, on the other side of the world, this relationship between beings that alone merits the name of love. For a springboard, there are some ideas—or rather, beliefs, premonitions—that I do not theorize and that stay more or less unconscious for quite a long time. Everywhere I see the battle for mastery that rages between classes, peoples, etc., reproducing itself on an individual scale. Is the system flawless? Impossible to bypass? On the basis of my desire, I imagine that other desires like mine exist. If my desire is possible, it means the system is already letting something else through. All the poets know that: whatever is thinkable is real, as William Blake suggests. And it's true. There have to be ways of relating that are completely different from the tradition ordained by the masculine economy. So, urgently and anxiously, I look for a scene in which a type of exchange would be produced that would be different, a kind of desire that wouldn't be in collusion with the old story of death. This desire would invent Love, it alone would not use the word love to cover up its opposite: one would not land right back in a dialectical destiny, still unsatisfied by the debasement of one by the other. On the contrary, there would have to be a recognition of each other, and this grateful acknowledgment would come about thanks to the intense and passionate work of knowing. Finally, each would take the risk of *other*, of difference, without feeling threatened by the existence of an otherness, rather, delighting to increase through the unknown that is there to discover, to respect, to favor, to cherish.

This love would not be trapped in contradictions and ambivalences entailing the murder of the other indefinitely. Nor would it be caught up again in the huge social machinery taking individuals back to the family model. It would not collapse in paradoxes of relationship to the other like the ones whose pitiless vicious circle Hegel based on the idea of *Physical Property*.

The Empire of the Selfsame
(Empirically from Bad to Worse)

—For, unfortunately, Hegel isn't inventing things. What I mean is that the dialectic, its syllogistic system, the subject's going out into the other *in order to come back* to itself, this entire process, particularly described in the *Phenomenology of the Mind*, is, in fact, what is commonly at work in our everyday banality. Nothing is more frightening or more ordinary than Society's functioning the way it is laid out with the perfect smoothness of Hegelian machinery, exhibited in the movement through which one passes, in three stages, from the family to the State.

A historical process dynamized by the drama of the Selfsame (*Propre*). Impossible to conceive of a desire that does not entail conflict and destruction. We are still living under the Empire of the Selfsame. The same masters dominate history from the beginning, inscribing on it the marks of their appropriating economy: history, as a story of phallocentrism, hasn't moved except to repeat itself. "With a difference," as Joyce says. Always the same, with other clothes.

Nor has Freud (who is, moreover, the heir of Hegel and Nietzsche) made anything up. All the great theorists of destiny or of human history have reproduced the most commonplace logic of desire, the one that keeps the movement toward the other staged in a patriarchal production, under Man's law.

History, history of phallocentrism, history of propriation: a single history. History of an identity: that of man's becoming recognized by the other (son or woman), reminding him that, as Hegel says, death is his master.

It is true that recognition, following the phallocentric lead, passes through a conflict the brunt of which is borne by woman; and that desire, in a world thus determined, is a desire for appropriation. This is how that logic goes:

1) Where does desire come from? From a mixture of difference and *inequality*. No movement toward, if the two terms of the couple are in a state of equality. It is always a difference of forces which results in movement. (Reasoning that is, therefore, based on "physical" laws.)

2) A little surreptitious slippage: the *sexual* difference with an *equality* of force, therefore, does not produce the movement of desire. It is *inequality* that triggers desire, as a desire—for appropriation. Without inequality, without struggle, there is inertia—death.

It is on this level of analysis (more or less conscious, depending on the supposed masters) that what I consider to be the great masculine imposture operates:

One could, in fact, imagine that difference or inequality—if one understands by that noncoincidence, asymmetry—lead to desire without negativity, without one of the partner's succumbing: we would recognize each other in a type of exchange in which each one would keep the *other* alive and different. But in the (Hegelian) schema of recognition, there is no place for the other, for an equal other, for a whole and living woman. She must recognize and recuntnize the male partner, and in the time it takes to do this, she must disappear, leaving him to gain Imaginary profit, to win Imaginary victory. The good woman, therefore, is the one who "resists" long enough for him to feel both his power over her and his desire (I mean one who "exists"), and not too much, to give him the pleasure of enjoying, without too many obstacles, the return to himself which he, grown greater—reassured in his own eyes, is making.

All women have more or less experienced this cuntditionality of masculine desire. And all its secuntdary effects. The fragility of a desire that must (pretend to) kill its object. Fantasizing rape or making the transition to the act of rape. And plenty of women, sensing what is at stake there, cuntsent to play the part of object . . .

Why did this comedy, whose final act is the master's flirtation with death, make Bataille laugh so hard, as he amused himself by pushing Hegel to the edge of the abyss that a civilized man keeps himself from falling into? This abyss that functions as a metaphor both of death and of the feminine sex.

All history is inseparable from economy in the limited sense of the word, that of a certain kind of savings. Man's return—the relationship linking him profitably to man-being, conserving it. This economy, as a law of appropriation, is a phallocentric production. The opposition appropriate/inappropriate, proper/improper, clean/unclean, mine/not mine (the valorization of the selfsame), organizes the opposition identity/difference. Everything takes place as if, in a split second, man and being had propriated each other. And as if his relationship to woman was still at play as the possibility—though threatening, of the not-proper, not-clean, not-mine: desire is inscribed as the desire to reappropriate for himself that which seems able to escape him. The (unconscious?) stratagem and violence of masculine economy consists in making sexual difference hierarchical by valorizing one of the terms of the relationship, by reaffirming what Freud calls *phallic primacy*. And the "difference" is always perceived and carried out as an opposition. Masculinity/femininity are opposed in such a way that it is male privilege that is affirmed in a movement of conflict played out in advance.

And one becomes aware that the Empire of the Selfsame is erected from a fear that, in fact, is typically masculine: the fear of expropriation, of separation, of losing the attribute. In other words, the threat of castration has an impact. Thus, there is a relationship between the problematic of the not-selfsame, not-mine (hence of desire and the urgency of reappropriation) and the constitution of a subjectivity that experiences itself only when it makes its law, its strength, and its mastery felt, and it can all be understood on the basis of masculinity because this subjectivity is structured around a loss. Which is not the case with femininity.

What does one give?

All the difference determining history's movement as property's movement is articulated between two economies that are defined in relation to the problematic of the gift.

The (political) economy of the masculine and the feminine is organized by different demands and constraints, which, as they become socialized and metaphorized, produce signs, relations of power, relationships of production and reproduction, a whole huge system of cultural inscription that is legible as masculine or feminine.

I make a point of using the *qualifiers* of sexual difference here to avoid the confusion man/masculine, woman/feminine: for there are some men who do not repress their femininity, some women who, more or less strongly, inscribe their masculinity. Difference is not distributed, of course, on the basis of socially determined "sexes." On the other hand, when I speak of political economy and libidinal economy, connecting them, I am not bringing into play the false question of origins—a story made to order for male privilege. We have to be careful not to lapse smugly or blindly into an essentialist ideological interpretation, as both Freud and Jones, for example, risked doing in their different ways. In the quarrel that brought them into conflict on the subject of feminine sexuality, both of them, starting from opposite points of view, came to support the formidable thesis of a "natural," anatomical determination of sexual difference-opposition. On that basis, both of them implicitly back phallocentrism's position of strength.

We can recall the main lines of the opposing positions: Jones (in *Early Feminine Sexuality*) in an ambiguous move attacks the Freudian theses that make woman out to be a flawed man.

For Freud:

1) The "fate" of the feminine situation is an effect of an anatomical "defect."

2) There is only one libido and it is male in essence; sexual difference is inscribed at the beginning of the *phallic phase* that both boys and girls go through. Until that point, the girl will have been a sort of little boy: the genital organization of the infantile libido is articulated through the equivalence activity/masculinity. The vagina has not yet been "discovered."

3) Since the first object of love, for both sexes, is the mother, it is only in the boy that the love of the opposite sex is "natural."

For Jones: femininity is an autonomous "essence."

From the beginning (starting at the age of six months) the girl has a "feminine" desire for her father; analysis of the little girl's most primitive fantasies would show, in fact, that in place of the breast, which is perceived as disappointing, the penis or (by an analogical shift) an object shaped like it is desired. One is already in the chain of substitutions, which means that the child, in the series of partial objects, would come to take the place of the penis . . . for, to counter Freud, Jones obediently reenlists in Freudian territory. And overdoes it! He concludes from the equation breast-penis-child that the little girl feels a primary desire toward her father. (And the desire to have the father's child would be primary also.) He concludes that, of course, the girl has a primary love for the opposite sex as well. Therefore, she too has a right to her own Oedipus complex as a primary formation and to the threat of mutilation by the mother. In the end—a woman, that is what she is and with no anatomical defect: her clitoris is not a minipenis. Clitoral masturbation is not, as Freud claims, a masculine practice. And seeing the early fantasies, it would seem that the vagina is discovered extremely early.

In fact, by affirming that there is a specific femininity (all the while preserving orthodox theses elsewhere), Jones is still reenforcing phallocentrism under the pretext of taking femininity's side (and God's too, who, he reminds us, created them male and female!). And bisexuality disappears in the unbridged abyss separating the opponents here.

As for Freud, if one subscribes to what he says in his article on the *Disappearance of the Oedipus Complex (1933)* in which he identifies himself with Napoleon: "anatomy is destiny," one participates in condemning woman to death. And in wrapping up all of History.

It is undeniable that there are psychic consequences of the difference between the sexes. But they certainly cannot be reduced to the ones that Freudian analysis designates. Starting from the relationship of the two sexes to the Oedipus complex, the boy and the girl are steered toward a division of social roles such that women "inevitably" have a lesser productivity because they "sublimate" less than men and that symbolic activity, hence the production of culture, is the work of men.[8]

Elsewhere, Freud starts from what he calls the *anatomical* difference between the sexes. And we know how that is represented in his eyes: by the difference between having/not having the phallus. By reference to those precious parts. Starting from what will take shape as the transcendental signifier with Lacan.

But *sexual difference* is not determined simply by the fantasized relation to anatomy, which depends to a great extent on catching *sight* of something, thus on the strange importance that is accorded to exteriority and to that which is specular in sexuality's development. A voyeur's theory, of course.

No, the difference, in my opinion, becomes most clearly perceived on the level of *jouissance*, inasmuch as a woman's instinctual economy cannot be identified by a man or referred to the masculine economy.

For me, the question asked of woman "What does she want?"—is a question that woman asks herself, in fact, because she is asked it. It is precisely because there is so little room for her desire in society that, because of not knowing what to do with it, she ends up not knowing where to put it or if she even has it. This question conceals the most immediate and most urgent question: "How do I pleasure?" What is it—feminine *jouissance*—where does it happen, how does it inscribe itself—on the level of her body or of her unconscious? And then, how does it write itself?

One can ramble on for a long time about hypothetical prehistory and a matriarchal epoch. Or, like Bachofen,[9] one can attempt to prefigure a gynarchic society, drawing from it poetic and mythical effects, which have a powerfully subversive impact regarding the history of family and male power.

All the ways of differently thinking the history of power, property, masculine domination, the formation of the State, and the ideological equipment have some effect. But the change that is in process concerns more than just the question of "origin." There is phallocentrism. History has never produced or recorded anything else—which does not mean that this form is destinal or natural. Phallocentrism is the enemy. Of everyone. Men's loss in phallocentrism is different from but as serious as women's. And it is time to change. To invent the other history.

There is "destiny" no more than there is "nature" or "essence" as such. Rather, there are living structures that are caught and sometimes rigidly set within historicocultural limits so mixed up with the scene of History that for a long time it has been impossible (and it is still very difficult) to think or even imagine an "elsewhere." We are presently living in a transitional period—one in which it seems possible that the classic structure might be split.

It is impossible to predict what will become of sexual difference—in another time (in two or three hundred years?). But we must make no mistake: men and women are caught up in a web of age-old cultural determinations that are almost unanalyzable in their complexity. One can no more speak of "woman" than of "man" without being trapped within an ideological theater where the proliferation of representations, images, reflections, myths, identifications, transform, deform, constantly change everyone's Imaginary and invalidate in advance any conceptualization.[10]

Nothing allows us to rule out the possibility of radical transformation of behaviors, mentalities, roles, political economy—whose effects on libidinal economy are unthinkable—today. Let us simultaneously imagine a general change in all the structures of training, education, supervision—hence in the structures of reproduction of ideological results. And let us imagine a real liberation of sexuality, that is to say, a transformation of each one's relationship to his or her body (and to the other body), an approximation to the vast, material, organic, sensuous universe that we are. This cannot be accomplished, of course, without political transformations that are equally radical. (Imagine!) Then "femininity" and "masculinity" would inscribe quite differently their effects of difference, their economy, their relationship to expenditure, to lack, to the gift. What today appears to be "feminine" or "masculine" would no longer amount to the same thing. No longer would the common logic of difference be organized with the opposition that remains dominant. Difference would be a bunch of new differences.

But we are still floundering—with few exceptions—in Ancient History.

The Masculine Future

There are some exceptions. There have always been those uncertain, poetic persons who have not let themselves be reduced to dummies programmed by pitiless repression of the homosexual element. Men or women: beings who are complex, mobile, open. Accepting the other sex as a component makes them much richer, more various, stronger, and—to the extent that they are mobile— very fragile. It is only in this condition that we invent. Thinkers, artists, those who create new values, "philosophers" in the mad Nietzschean manner, inventors and wreckers of concepts and forms, those who change life cannot help but be stirred by anomalies—complementary or contradictory. That doesn't mean that you have to be homosexual to create. But it does mean that there is no *invention* possible, whether it be philosophical or poetic, without there being in the inventing subject an abundance of the other, of variety: separate-people, thought-/people, whole populations issuing from the unconscious, and in each suddenly animated desert, the springing up of selves one didn't know—our women, our monsters, our jackals, our Arabs, our aliases, our frights. That there is no invention of any other I, no poetry, no fiction without a certain homosexuality (the I/play of bisexuality) acting as a crystallization of my ultrasubjectivities.[11] I is this exuberant, gay, personal matter, masculine, feminine or other where I enchants, I agonizes me. And in the concert of personalizations called I, at the same time that a certain homosexuality is repressed, symbolically, substitutively, it comes through by various signs, conduct-character, behavior-acts. And it is even more clearly seen in writing.

Thus, what is inscribed under Jean Genêt's name, in the movement of a text that divides itself, pulls itself to pieces, dismembers itself, regroups, remembers itself, is a proliferating, maternal femininity. A phantasmic meld of men, males, gentlemen, monarchs, princes, orphans, flowers, mothers, breasts gravitates about a wonderful "sun of energy"—love,—that bombards and disintegrates these ephemeral amorous anomalies so that they can be recomposed in other bodies for new passions.

She is bisexual:

What I propose here leads directly to a reconsideration of *bisexuality*. To reassert the value of bisexuality;[12] hence to snatch it from the fate classically reserved for it in which it is conceptualized as "neuter" because, as such, it would aim at warding off castration. Therefore, I shall distinguish between two bisexualities, two opposite ways of imagining the possibility and practice of bisexuality.

1) Bisexuality as a fantasy of a complete being, which replaces the fear of castration and veils sexual difference insofar as this is perceived as the mark of a mythical separation—the trace, therefore, of a dangerous and painful ability to be cut. Ovid's Hermaphrodite, less bisexual than asexual, not made up of two genders but of two halves. Hence, a fantasy of unity. Two within one, and not even two wholes.

2) To this bisexuality that melts together and effaces, wishing to avert castration, I oppose the *other bisexuality*, the one with which every subject, who is

not shut up inside the spurious Phallocentric Performing Theater, sets up his or her erotic universe. Bisexuality—that is to say the location within oneself of the presence of both sexes, evident and insistent in different ways according to the individual, the nonexclusion of difference or of a sex, and starting with this "permission" one gives oneself, the multiplication of the effects of desire's inscription on every part of the body and the other body.

For historical reasons, at the present time it is woman who benefits from and opens up within this bisexuality beside itself, which does not annihilate differences but cheers them on, pursues them, adds more: in a certain way *woman is bisexual*—man having been trained to aim for glorious phallic monosexuality. By insisting on the primacy of the phallus and implementing it, phallocratic ideology has produced more than one victim. As a woman, I could be obsessed by the scepter's great shadow, and they told me: adore it, that thing you don't wield.

But at the same time, man has been given the grotesque and unenviable fate of being reduced to a single idol with clay balls. And terrified of homosexuality, as Freud and his followers remark. Why does man fear *being* a woman? Why this refusal (*Ablehnung*) of femininity? The question that stumps Freud. The "bare rock" of castration. For Freud, the repressed is not the other sex defeated by the dominant sex, as his friend Fliess (to whom Freud owes the theory of bisexuality) believed; what is repressed is leaning toward one's own sex.

Psychoanalysis is formed on the basis of woman and has repressed (not all that successfully) the femininity of masculine sexuality, and now the account it gives is hard to disprove.

We women, the derangers, know it only too well. But nothing compels us to deposit our lives in these lack-banks; to think that the subject is constituted as the last stage in a drama of bruising rehearsals; to endlessly bail out the father's religion. Because we don't desire it. We don't go round and round the supreme hole. We have no *woman's* reason to pay allegiance to the negative. What is feminine (the poets suspected it) affirms: . . . and yes I said yes I will Yes, says Molly (in her rapture), carrying *Ulysses* with her in the direction of a new writing; I said yes, I will Yes.

To say that woman is somehow bisexual is an apparently paradoxical way of displacing and reviving the question of difference. And therefore of writing as "feminine" or "masculine."

I will say: today, writing is woman's. That is not a provocation, it means that woman admits there is an other. In her becoming-woman, she has not erased the bisexuality latent in the girl as in the boy. Femininity and bisexuality go together, in a combination that varies according to the individual, spreading the intensity of its force differently and (depending on the moments of their history) privileging one component or another. It is much harder for man to let the other come through him. Writing is the passageway, the entrance, the exit, the dwelling place of the other in me—the other that I am and am not, that I don't know how to be, but that I feel passing, that makes me live—that tears me apart, disturbs me, changes me, who?—a feminine one, a masculine one, some?—several, some unknown, which is indeed what gives me the desire to know and from which all life soars. This peopling gives neither rest nor security, always disturbs the relationship to "reality," produces an uncertainty that gets in the way of the subject's socialization. It is distressing, it wears you out; and for men this permeability, this nonexclusion is a threat, something intolerable.

In the past, when carried to a rather spectacular degree, it was called "possession." Being possessed is not desirable for a masculine Imaginary, which would interpret it as passivity—a dangerous feminine position. It is true that a certain receptivity is "feminine." One can, of course, as History has always done, exploit feminine reception through alienation. A woman, by her opening up, is open to being "possessed," which is to say, dispossessed of herself.

But I am speaking here of femininity as keeping alive the other that is confided to her, that visits her, that she can love as other. The loving to be other, another, without its necessarily going the rout of abasing what is same, herself.

As for passivity, in excess, it is partly bound up with death. But there is a nonclosure that is not submission but confidence and comprehension; that is not an opportunity for destruction but for wonderful expansion.

Through the same opening that is her danger, she comes out of herself to go to the other, a traveler in unexplored places; she does not refuse, she approaches, not to do away with the space between, but to see it, to experience what she is not, what she is, what she can be.

Writing is working; being worked; questioning (in) the between (letting oneself be questioned) of same *and of* other without which nothing lives; undoing death's work by willing the togetherness of one-another, infinitely charged with a ceaseless exchange of one with another—not knowing one another and beginning again only from what is most distant, from self, from other, from the other within. A course that multiplies transformations by the thousands.

And that is not done without danger, without pain, without loss—of moments of self, of consciousness, of persons one has been, goes beyond, leaves. It doesn't happen without expense—of sense, time, direction.

But is that specifically feminine? It is men who have inscribed, described, theorized the paradoxical logic of an economy without reserve. This is not contradictory; it brings us back to asking about their femininity. Rare are the men able to venture onto the brink where writing, freed from law, unencumbered by moderation, exceeds phallic authority, and where the subjectivity inscribing its effects becomes feminine.

Where does difference come through in writing? If there is difference it is in the manner of spending, of valorizing the appropriated, of thinking what is not-the-same. In general, it is in the manner of thinking any "return," the relationship of capitalization, if this word "return" (*rapport*) is understood in its sense of "revenue."

Today, still, the masculine return to the Selfsame is narrower and more restricted than femininity's. It all happens as if man were more directly threatened in his being by the nonselfsame than woman. Ordinarily, this is exactly the cultural product described by psychoanalysis: someone who still has something to lose. And in the development of desire, of exchange, he is the en-grossing party: loss and expense are stuck in the commercial deal that always turns the gift into a gift-that-takes. The gift brings in a return. Loss, at the end of a curved line, is turned into its opposite and comes back to him as profit.

But does woman escape this law of return? Can one speak of another spending? Really, there is no "free" gift. You never give something for nothing. But all the difference lies in the why and how of the gift, in the values that the gesture of giving affirms, causes to circulate; in the type of profit the giver draws from the gift and the use to which he or she puts it. Why, how, is there this difference?

When one gives, what does one give oneself?

What does he want in return—the traditional man? And she? At first what *he* wants, whether on the level of cultural or of personal exchanges, whether it is a question of capital or of affectivity (or of love, of *jouissance*)—is that he gain more masculinity: plus-value of virility, authority, power, money, or pleasure, all of which reenforce his phallocentric narcissism at the same time. Moreover, that is what society is made for—how it is made; and men can hardly get out of it. An unenviable fate they've made for themselves. A man is always proving something; he has to "show off," show up the others. Masculine profit is almost always mixed up with a success that is socially defined.

How does she give? What are her dealings with saving or squandering, reserve, life, death? She too gives *for*. She too, with open hands, gives herself—pleasure, happiness, increased value, enhanced self-image. But she doesn't try to "recover her expenses." She is able not to return to herself, never settling down, pouring out, going everywhere to the other. She does not flee extremes; she is not the being-of-the-end (the goal), but she is how-far-being-reaches.

If there is a self proper to woman, paradoxically it is her capacity to depropriate herself without self-interest: endless body, without "end," without principal "parts"; if she is a whole, it is a whole made up of parts that are wholes, not simple, partial objects but varied entirety, moving and boundless change, a cosmos where eros never stops traveling, vast astral space. She doesn't revolve around a sun that is more star than the stars.

That doesn't mean that she is undifferentiated magma; it means that she doesn't create a monarchy of her body or her desire. Let masculine sexuality gravitate around the penis, engendering this centralized body (political anatomy) under the party dictatorship. Woman does not perform on herself this regionalization that profits the couple head-sex, that only inscribes itself within frontiers. Her libido is cosmic, just as her unconscious is worldwide: her writing also can only go on and on, without ever inscribing or distinguishing contours, daring these dizzying passages in other, fleeting and passionate dwellings within him, within the hims and hers whom she inhabits just long enough to watch them, as close as possible to the unconscious from the moment they arise; to love them, as close as possible to instinctual drives, and then, further, all filled with these brief identifying hugs and kisses, she goes and goes on infinitely. She alone dares and wants to know from within where she, the one excluded, has never ceased to hear what-comes-before-language reverberating. She lets the other tongue of a thousand tongues speak—the tongue, sound without barrier or death. She refuses life nothing. Her tongue doesn't hold back but holds forth, doesn't keep in but keeps on enabling. Where the wonder of being several and turmoil is expressed, she does not protect herself against these unknown feminines; she surprises herself at seeing, being, pleasuring in her gift of changeability. I am spacious singing Flesh: onto which is grafted no one knows which I—which masculine or feminine, more or less human but above all living, because changing I.

I see her "begin." That can be written—these beginnings that never stop getting her up—can and must be written. Neither black on white nor white on black, not in this clash between paper and sign that en-graves itself there, not in this opposition of colors that stand out against each other. This is how it is:

There is a ground, it is her ground—childhood flesh, shining blood—or background, depth. A white depth, a core, unforgettable, forgotten, and this ground, covered by an infinite number of strata, layers, sheets of paper—is her sun (*sol . . . soleil*). And nothing can put it out. Feminine light doesn't come from above, doesn't fall, doesn't strike, doesn't go through. It radiates, it is a slow, sweet, difficult, absolutely unstoppable, painful rising that reaches and impregnates lands, that filters, that wells up, that finally tears open, wets and spreads apart what is dull and thick, the stolid, the volumes. Fighting off opacity from deep within. This light doesn't plant, it spawns. And I see that she looks very closely with this light and she sees the veins and nerves of matter. Which he has no need of.

Her rising: is not erection. But diffusion. Not the shaft. The vessel. Let her write! And her text knows in seeking itself that it is more than flesh and blood, dough kneading itself, rising, uprising openly with resounding, perfumed ingredients, a turbulent compound of flying colors, leafy spaces, and rivers flowing to the sea we feed.

So! Now she's her sea, he'll say to me (as he holds out to me his basin full of water from the little phallic mother he doesn't succeed in separating himself from). Seas and mothers.

But that's it—our seas are what we make them, fishy or not, impenetrable or muddled, red or black, high and rough or flat and smooth, narrow straits or shoreless, and we ourselves are sea, sands, corals, seaweeds, beaches, tides, swimmers, children, waves . . . seas and mothers.

More or less vaguely swelling like wavesurge indistinctly sea-earth-naked, and what matter made of this naked sea-rth would deter us? We all know how to finger them, mouth them. Feel them, speak them.

Heterogenous, yes, to her joyful benefit, she is erogenous; she is what is erogenous in the heterogenous; she is not attached to herself, the airborne swimmer, the thieving flyer. Stunning, extravagant, one who is dispersible, desiring and capable of other, of the other woman she will be, of the other woman she is not, of him, of you.

Woman (I) have no fear of elsewhere or of same or of other. My eyes, my tongue, my ears, my nose, my skin, my mouth, my body for (the) other, not that I desire it to stop up some hole, to overcome some flaw of mine, not because I am fatefully hounded by "feminine" jealousy, not because I am caught up in the chain of substitutions that reduces the substitutes to one ultimate object. It's all over for the stories of Tom Thumb and of the *Penisneid* that the old grandmothers whispered to us, those ogresses serving their son-fathers. Let them believe what they need to make themselves feel important—believe we are dying of envy, that we are this hole edged with penis envy; that's their age-old deal. Undeniably (we confirm this at a cost to us but also to our amusement), men are structured only for the feathering of their shafts to let us know they have a hard-on; so we will assure them (we, the motherly mistresses of their little pocket signifier) that they are something, that they still have them. It is not the penis that woman desires in the child, it is not that hot-shot piece around which every man gravitates. Except within the historical *limits* of the Ancient world, gestation doesn't come down to coincidences, to those mechanical substitutions that the unconscious of an eternally "jealous woman" puts in place, or to the *Penisneid*, or to narcissism, or to a homosexuality linked to the always-there-mother.

The relation borne to the child must also be rethought. One trend of current feminist thought tends to denounce a trap in maternity that would consist of making the mother-woman an agent who is more or less the accomplice of reproduction: capitalist, familialist, phallocentrist reproduction. An accusation and a caution that should not be turned into prohibition, into a new form of repression.

Will, you, too, discounting everyone's blindness and passivity, be afraid the child might *make* a father and hence that the woman making a kid plays herself more than one dirty trick, engendering the child—the mother—the father—the family all at the same time? No, it's up to you to break the old circuits. It will be the task of woman and man to make the old relationship and all its consequences out-of-date; to think the *launching* of a new subject, into life, with de-familialization. Rather than depriving woman of a fascinating time in the life of her body just to guard against procreation's being recuperated, let's de-mater-paternalize. Let's defetishize. Let's get out of the dialectic that claims that the child is its parents' death. The child is the other but the other without violence. The other rhythm, the pure freshness, the possibles' body. Complete fragility. But vastness itself. Let's be done with repeating the litany of castration that transmits and pedigrees itself. We're not going to back up to go forward anymore. Let's not repress something as simple as wanting to live life itself. Oral drive, anal drive, vocal drive, all drives are good forces, and among them the gestational drive — just like wanting to write: a desire to live oneself within, wanting the belly, the tongue, the blood. We are not going to refuse ourselves the delights of a pregnancy, which, moreover, is always dramatized or evaded or cursed in classical texts. For if there is a specific thing repressed, that is where it is found: the taboo of the pregnant woman (which says a lot about the power that seems invested in her). It is because they have always suspected that the pregnant woman not only doubles her market value but, especially, valorizes *herself* as a *woman* in her own eyes, and undeniably takes on weight and sex. There are a thousand ways of living a pregnancy, of having or not having a relationship of another intensity with this still invisible other.

Really experiencing metamorphosis. Several, other, and unforeseeable. That cannot but inscribe in the body the good possibility of an alteration. It is not only a question of the feminine body's extra resource, this specific power to produce some thing living of which her flesh is the locus, not only a question of a transformation of rhythms, exchanges, of relationship to space, of the whole perceptive system, but also of the irreplaceable experience of those moments of stress, of the body's crises, of that work that goes on peacefully for a long time only to burst out in that surpassing moment, the time of childbirth. In which she lives as if she were larger or stronger than herself. It is also the experience of a "bond" with the other, all that comes through in the metaphor of bringing into the world. How could the woman, who has experienced the not-me within me, not have a particular relationship to the written? To writing as giving itself away (cutting itself off) from the source?

There is a bond between woman's libidinal economy — her *jouissance*, the feminine Imaginary — and her way of self-constituting a subjectivity that splits apart without regret, and without this regretlessness being the equivalent of dying, of the exhaustion described by Valéry as the Young Fate — answering herself with anomalies, without the ceaseless summoning of the authority called Ego.

Unleashed and raging, she belongs to the race of waves. She arises, she approaches, she lifts up, she reaches, covers over, washes a shore, flows embracing the cliff's least undulation, already she is another, arising again, throwing the fringed vastness of her body up high, follows herself, and covers over, uncovers, polishes, makes the stone body shine with the gentle undeserting ebbs, which return to the shoreless nonorigin, as if she recalled herself in order to come again as never before . . .

She has never "held still"; explosion, diffusion, effervescence, abundance, she takes pleasure in being boundless, outside self, outside same, far from a "center," from any capital of her "dark continent," very far from the "hearth" to which man[13] brings her so that she will tend his fire, which always threatens to go out. She watches for him, but he has to keep an eye on her; for she can be his storm as well: "will I die by a storm? Or will I go out like a light that doesn't wait to be blown out by the wind, but which dies tired and self-satisfied? . . . or: will I extinguish my own self in order not to burn down to the end?"[14] Masculine energy, with its limited oil reserves, questions itself. Whereas, the fact that feminine energy has vast resources is not without consequences — still very rarely analyzed — for exchange in general, for love-life, and for the fate created for woman's desire. Exasperating: he's afraid she "goes too far." And the irony of her fate has her either be this "nothing," which punctuates the Dora case — ("You know my wife is nothing to me") — or this too-much, too-much reversed into not-enough, the "not how it should be" that reminds her that her master is on the limited side.

She doesn't hold still, she overflows. An outpouring that can be agonizing, since she may fear, and make the other fear, endless aberration and madness in her release. Yet, vertiginous, it can also be intoxicating — as long as the personal, the permanence of identity is not fetishized — a "where-am-I," a "who-enjoys-there," a "who-I-where-delight": questions that drive reason, the principle of unity, mad, and that are not asked, that ask for no answer, that open up the space where woman is wandering, roaming (a rogue wave), flying (thieving).

This power to be errant is strength; it is also what makes her vulnerable to those who champion the Selfsame, acknowledgment, and attribution. No matter how submissive and docile she may be in relation to the masculine order, she still remains the threatening possibility of savagery, the unknown quantity in the household whole.

"Mysterious"[15] — the incalculable with which they must be counted. — Mysterious, yes — but she is blamed for that even if pleasure is derived from always wanting to expose her. And mysterious to herself, something she has been disturbed by for a long time, made to feel guilty for "not understanding herself" (taking herself in) or knowing herself (cunt-born), because all around her they valorized a "knowledge" (cunt-birth) as ordained, as a mastery, a "control" (cunt-role) (of knowings! cunt-births!) established on repression and on "capture," arrest, sub-poenis, confinement.

Writing femininity tranformation:
And there is a link between the economy of femininity — the open, extravagant

subjectivity, that relationship to the other in which the gift doesn't calculate its influence—and the possibility of love; and a link today between this "libido of the other" and writing.

At the present time, *defining* a feminine practice of writing is impossible with an impossibility that will continue; for this practice will never be able to be *theorized*, enclosed, coded, which does not mean it does not exist. But it will always exceed the discourse governing the phallocentric system; it takes place and will take place somewhere other than in the territories subordinated to philosophical-theoretical domination. It will not let itself think except through subjects that break automatic functions, border runners never subjugated by any authority. But one can begin to speak. Begin to point out some effects, some elements of unconscious drives, some relations of the feminine Imaginary to the Real, to writing.

What I have to say about it is also only a beginning, because right from the start these features affect me powerfully.

First I sense femininity in writing by: a privilege of *voice: writing and voice* are entwined and interwoven and writing's continuity/voice's rhythm take each other's breath away through interchanging, make the text gasp or form it out of suspenses and silences, make it lose its voice or rend it with cries.

In a way, feminine writing never stops reverberating from the wrench that the acquisition of speech, speaking out loud, is for her—"acquisition" that is experienced more as tearing away, dizzying flight and flinging oneself, diving. Listen to woman speak in a gathering (if she is not painfully out of breath): she doesn't "speak," she throws her trembling body into the air, she lets herself go, she flies, she goes completely into her voice, she vitally defends the "logic" of her discourse with her body; her flesh speaks true. She exposes herself. Really she makes what she thinks materialize carnally, she conveys meaning with her body. She *inscribes* what she is saying because she does not deny unconscious drives the unmanageable part they play in speech.

Her discourse, even when "theoretical" or political, is never simple or linear or "objectivized," universalized; she involves her story in history.

Every woman has known the torture of beginning to speak aloud, heart beating as if to break, occasionally falling into loss of language, ground and language slipping out from under her, because for woman speaking—even just opening her mouth—in public is something rash, a transgression.

A double anguish, for even if she transgresses, her word almost always falls on the deaf, masculine ear, which can only hear language that speaks in the masculine.

We are not culturally accustomed to speaking, throwing signs out toward a scene, employing the suitable rhetoric. Also, it is not where we find our pleasure: indeed, one pays a certain price for the use of a discourse. The logic of communication requires an economy both of signs—of signifiers—and of subjectivity. The orator is asked to unwind a thin thread, dry and taut. We like uneasiness, questioning. There is waste in what we say. We need that waste. To write is always to make allowances for superabundance and uselessness while slashing the exchange value that keeps the spoken word on its track. That is why writing is good, letting the tongue try itself out—as one attempts a caress, taking the time a phrase or a thought needs to make oneself loved, to make oneself reverberate.

It is in writing, from woman and toward woman, and in accepting the challenge of the discourse controlled by the phallus, that woman will affirm woman somewhere other than in silence, the place reserved for her in and through the Symbolic. May she get out of booby-trapped silence! And not have the margin or the harem foisted on her as her domain!

In feminine speech, as in writing, there never stops reverberating something that, having once passed through us, having imperceptibly and deeply touched us, still has the power to affect us—song, the first music of the voice of love, which every woman keeps alive.

The Voice sings from a time before law, before the Symbolic took one's breath away and reappropriated it into language under its authority of separation. The deepest, the oldest, the loveliest Visitation. Within each woman the first, nameless love is singing.

In woman there is always, more or less, something of "the mother" repairing and feeding, resisting separation, a force that does not let itself be cut off but that runs codes ragged. The relationship to childhood (the child she was, she is, she acts and makes and starts anew, and unties at the place where, as a same she even others herself), is no more cut off than is the relationship to the "mother," *as it consists of* delights and violences. Text, my body: traversed by lilting flows; listen to me, it is not a captivating, clinging "mother"; it is the equivoice that, touching you, affects you, pushes you away from your breast to come to language, that summons *your* strength; it is the rhyth me that laughs you; the one intimately addressed who makes all metaphors, all body(?)—bodies(?)—possible and desirable, who is no more describable than god, soul, or the Other; the part of you that puts space between yourself and pushes you to inscribe your woman's style in language. Voice: milk that could go on forever. Found again. The lost mother/bitter lost. Eternity: is voice mixed with milk.

Not the origin: she doesn't go back there. A boy's journey is the return to the native land, the *Heimweh* Freud speaks of, the nostalgia that makes man a being who tends to come back to the point of departure to appropriate it for himself and to die there. A girl's journey is farther—to the unknown, to invent.

How come this privileged relationship with voice? Because no woman piles up as many defenses against instinctual drives as a man does. You don't prop things up, you don't brick things up the way he does, you don't withdraw from pleasure so "prudently." Even if phallic mystification has contaminated good relations in general, woman is never far from the "mother" (I do not mean the role but the "mother" as no-name and as source of goods). There is always at least a little good mother milk left in her. She writes with white ink.

Voice! That, too, is launching forth and effusion without return. Exclamation, cry, breathlessness, yell, cough, vomit, music. Voice leaves. Voice loses. She leaves. She loses. And that is how she writes, as one throws a voice — forward, into the void. She goes away, she goes forward, doesn't turn back to look at her tracks. Pays no attention to herself. Running breakneck. Contrary to the self-absorbed, masculine narcissism, making sure of its image, of being seen, of seeing itself, of assembling its glories, of pocketing itself again. The reductive look, the always divided look returning, the mirror economy; he needs to love himself. But she launches forth; she seeks to love. Moreover, this is what Valéry sensed, marking his Young Fate in search of herself with ambiguity, masculine in her jealousy of herself: "seeing herself see herself," the motto of all phallocentric speculation/specularization, the motto of every Teste; and feminine in the frantic descent deeper deeper to where a voice that doesn't know itself is lost in the sea's churning.

Voice-cry. Agony — the spoken "word" exploded, blown to bits by suffering and anger, demolishing discourse: this is how she has always been heard before, ever since the time when masculine society began to push her offstage, expulsing her, plundering her. Ever since Medea, ever since Electra.

Voice: unfastening, fracas. Fire! She shoots, she shoots away. Break. From their bodies where they have been buried, shut up and at the same time forbidden to take pleasure. Women have almost everything to write about femininity: about their sexuality, that is to say, about the infinite and mobile complexity of their becoming erotic, about the lightning ignitions of such a minuscule-vast region of their body, not about destiny but about the adventure of such an urge, the voyages, crossings, advances, sudden and slow awakenings, discoveries of a formerly timid region that is just now springing up. Woman's body with a thousand and one fiery hearths, when — shattering censorship and yokes — she lets it articulate the proliferation of meanings that runs through it in every direction. It is going to take much more than language for him to make the ancient maternal tongue sound in only one groove.

We have turned away from our bodies. Shamefully we have been taught to be unaware of them, to lash them with stupid modesty; we've been tricked into a fool's bargain: each one is to love the other sex. I'll give you your body and you will give me mine. But which men give women the body that they blindly hand over to him? Why so few texts? Because there are still so few women winning back their bodies. Woman must write her body, must make up the unimpeded tongue that bursts partitions, classes, and rhetorics, orders and codes, must inundate, run through, go beyond the discourse with its last reserves, including the one of laughing off the word "silence" that has to be said, the one that, aiming for the impossible, stops dead before the word "impossible" and writes it as "end."

In body/Still more: woman is body more than man is. Because he is invited to social success, to sublimation. More body hence more writing. For a long time, still, bodily, within her body she has answered the harassment, the familial conjugal venture of domestication, the repeated attempts to castrate her. Woman, who has run her tongue ten thousand times seven times around her mouth before not speaking, either dies of it or knows her tongue and her mouth better than anyone. Now, I-woman am going to blow up the Law: a possible and inescapable explosion from now on; let it happen, right now, in language.

When "*The* Repressed" of their culture and their society come back, it is an explosive return, which is *absolutely* shattering, staggering, overturning, with a force never let loose before, on the scale of the most tremendous repressions: for at the end of the Age of the Phallus, women will have been either wiped out or heated to the highest, most violent, white-hot fire. Throughout their deafening dumb history, they have lived in dreams, embodied but still deadly silent, in silences, in voiceless rebellions.

And with what force in their fragility: "fragility," a vulnerability to match their matchless intensity. Women have not sublimated. Fortunately. They have saved their skins and their energy. They haven't worked at planning the impass of futureless lives. They have furiously inhabited these sumptuous bodies. Those wonderful hysterics, who subjected Freud to so many voluptuous moments too shameful to mention, bombarding his mosaic statue/law of Moses with their carnal, passionate body-words, haunting him with their inaudible thundering denunciations, were more than just naked beneath their seven veils of modesty—they were dazzling. In a single word of the body they inscribed the endless vertigo of a history loosed like an arrow from all of men's history, from biblicocapitalist society. Following these yesterday's victims of torture, who anticipate the new women, no intersubjective relationship will ever be the same. It is you, Dora, you, who cannot be tamed, the poetic body, the true "mistress" of the Signifier. Before tomorrow your effectiveness will be seen to work—when your words will no longer be retracted, pointed against your own breast, but will write themselves against the other and against men's grammar. Men must not have that place for their own any more than they have us for their own.

If woman has always functioned "within" man's discourse, a signifier referring always to the opposing signifier that annihilates its particular energy, puts down or stifles its very different sounds, now it is time for her to displace this "within," explode it, overturn it, grab it, make it hers, take it in, take it into her women's mouth, bite its tongue with her women's teeth, make up her own tongue to get inside of it. And you will see how easily she will well up, from this "within" where she was hidden and dormant, to the lips where her foams will overflow.

It is not a question of appropriating their instruments, their concepts, their places for oneself or of wishing oneself in their position of mastery. Our knowing that there is a danger of identification does not mean we should give in. Leave that to the worriers, to masculine anxiety and its obsessional relationship to workings they must control—knowing "how it runs" in order to "make it run." Not taking possession to internalize or manipulate but to shoot through and smash the walls.

Feminine strength is such that while running away with syntax, breaking the famous line (just a tiny little thread, so they say) that serves men as a substitute cord, without which they can't have any fun (*jouir*), to make sure the old mother really is always behind them watching them play phallus, she goes to the impossible where she plays the other, for love, without dying of it.

De-propriation, depersonalization, because she, exasperating, immoderate, and contradictory, destroys laws, the "natural" order. She lifts the bar separating the present from the future, breaking the rigid law of individuation. Nietzsche, in *The Birth of Tragedy*, said that this is the privilege of divinatory, magical forces. What happens to the subject, to the personal pronoun, to its possessives when, suddenly, gaily daring her metamorphoses (because from her within—for a long time her world, she is in a pervasive relationship of desire with every being) she makes another way of knowing circulate? Another way of producing, of communicating, where each one is always far more than one, where her power of identification puts the same to rout. —And with the same traversing, dispersing gesture with which she becomes a feminine other, a masculine other, she breaks with explanation, interpretation, and all the authorities pinpointing localization. She forgets. She proceeds by lapse and bounds. She flies/steals.

To fly/steal is woman's gesture, to steal into language to make it fly. We have all learned flight/theft, the art with many techniques, for all the centuries we have only had access to having by stealing/flying; we have lived in a flight/theft, stealing/flying, finding the close, concealed ways-through of desire. It's not just luck if the word "voler" volleys between the "vol" of theft and the "vol" of flight, pleasuring in each and routing the sense police. It is not just luck: woman partakes of bird and burglar, just as the burglar partakes of woman and bird: hesheits pass, hesheits fly by, hesheits pleasure in scrambling spatial order, disorienting it, moving furniture, things, and values around, breaking in, emptying structures, turning the selfsame, the proper upside down.

What woman has not stolen? Who has not dreamed, savored, or done the thing that jams sociality? Who has not dropped a few red herrings, mocked her way around the separating bar, inscribed what makes a difference with her body, punched holes in the system of couples and positions, and with a transgression screwed up whatever is successive, chain-linked, the fence of circumfusion?

A feminine text cannot not be more than subversive: if it writes itself it is in volcanic heaving of the old "real" property crust. In ceaseless displacement. She must write herself because, when the time comes for her liberation, it is the invention of a *new, insurgent* writing that will allow her to put the breaks and indispensable changes into effect in her history. At first, individually, on two inseparable levels: — woman, writing herself, will go back to this body that has been worse than confiscated, a body replaced with a disturbing stranger, sick or dead, who so often is a bad influence, the cause and place of inhibitions. By censuring the body, breath and speech are censored at the same time.

To write — the act that will "realize" the un-censored relationship of woman to her sexuality, to her woman-being giving her back access to her own forces; that will return her goods, her pleasures, her organs, her vast bodily territories kept under seal; that will tear her out of the superegoed, over-Mosesed structure where the same position of guilt is always reserved for her (guilty of everything, every time: of having desires, of not having any; of being frigid, of being "too" hot; of not being both at once; of being too much of a mother and not enough; of nurturing and of not nurturing . . .). Write yourself: your body must make itself heard. Then the huge resources of the unconscious will burst out. Finally the inexhaustible feminine Imaginary is going to be deployed. Without gold or black dollars, our naphtha will spread values over the world, un-quoted values that will change the rules of the old game.

In the Selfsame Empire, where will the displacement's person find somewhere to lose herself, to write her not-taking-place, her permanent availability.

But somewhere else? There will be some elsewhere where the other will no longer be condemned to death. But has there ever been any elsewhere, is there any? While it is not yet "here," it is there by now — in this other place that disrupts social order, where desire makes fiction exist. Not any old fiction, for, of course, there is classical fiction caught in the oppositions of the system, and literary history has been homogeneous with phallocentric tradition, to the point of being phallocentrism-looking-at-itself, taking pleasure in repeating itself.

But I move toward something that only exists in an elsewhere, and I search in the thought that writing has uncontrollable resources. That writing is what deals with the no-deal, relates to what gives no return. That something else (what history forbids, what reality excludes or doesn't admit) can manifest itself there: some other. With the desire to keep this other alive — hence some living feminine — some difference — and some love; for example a desire, like the one that can unleash a woman, that goes all the way and does not let itself be subjugated by anything. That imposes its necessity as a value without letting itself be intimidated by cultural blackmail, the sacrosanction of social structures. That does not organize life around the threat of death; because a life that has given up can no longer call itself life.

Hence, a "place" of intransigence and of passion. A place of lucidity where no one takes what is a pretense of existence for life. Desire is clearly there like a stroke of fire, it shoots the night through with something. Lightning! that way! I don't have it wrong. Life is right here. Afterward, it's death.

Sometimes I find where to put the many-lifed being that I am. Into elsewheres opened by men who are capable of becoming woman. For the huge machine that ticks and repeats its "truth" for all these centuries has had failures, or I wouldn't be writing. There have been poets who let something different from tradition get through at any price—men able to love love; therefore, to love others, to want them; men able to think the woman who would resist destruction and constitute herself as a superb, equal, "impossible" subject, hence intolerable in the real social context. Only by breaking the codes denying her could the poet have desired that woman. Her appearance causing, if not a revolution, harrowing explosions. Sometimes, moreover, it is in the fissure made by an earthquake, when material upheaval causes radical change in things, when all structures are momentarily disoriented and a fleeting savagery sweeps order away, that the poet lets woman pass through for a brief interval. Kleist did so to the point of dying wishing that women who never lowered their heads—lover-sisters, maternal-daughters, mother-sisters—live. After it's over, as soon as the magistrates' courts are back in place, someone must pay: immediate and bloody death for these uncontrollable elements. (Only for poets, not for novelists who stick with representation. Poets because poetry exists only by taking strength from the unconscious, and the unconscious, the other country without boundaries, is where the repressed survive—women or, as Hoffmann would say, fairies.)

There was Kleist: all was passion then. Passions sweeping beyond the individual, on all levels. No more barriers. Michael Koolhaas is wonderful, going off to war against the moral and social universe, against the political and religious stronghold, against the State because of a tariff barrier. For a tariff barrier is enough to prevent any life that thinks it is beyond being a subjugated human. One gets beyond everything with Kleist and it is not called transgression. Because passion suddenly flares up in the world where that idea does not exist.

There was that being-of-a-thousand-beings called Shakespeare. I lived all the characters of his worlds: because they are always either alive or dead, because life and death are not separated by any pretense, because all is stunningly joined to nothing, affirmation to no, because, from one to the next, there is only one kiss, one phrase of bliss or tragedy, because every place is either abyss or summit, with nothing flat, soft, temperate. There man turns back into woman, woman into man—a slaveless world: there are villains, powers of death. All the living are great, more than human.

And because compromise cannot take place on their boundless territories, and because only excessively does one venture there, those are elsewheres that put politics on trial: a universe of becoming where power and its snares can never be calmly inscribed. Through the lives profusing there, an endless, tragic struggle continues against false ideas, codes, "values," mastery's ignoble and murderous stupidity.

Kleist, Shakespeare. There are others. But I have never known an equal to such generosity. That is where I have loved. And felt I was loved. Now, from there, I will set forth my ideas about the future. Thanks to a few who were fools about life, I myself stayed alive, at the time when there was no place anywhere for the whole-me (though there was a place for little bits of me). When I wasn't writing. I was Kleist's Penthesileia, not without being Achilles, I was Antony for Cleopatra and she for him; I was also Juliet, because with Romeo I went beyond the father cult. I was Saint Teresa of Avila, that madwoman who knew a lot more than all the men. And who knew how to become a bird on the strength of loving.

Moreover, I have always been a bird. A bit vulture, a bit eagle: I have looked the sun in its face. Born several times — dead several times so that I could be reborn from my ashes; I am mysteriously related to a tree found only in Arabia. I have always practiced flight/theft, and as a thief/who-flies, I got away, flew away, moved away from lands and seas (I never crawled, burrowed, dug, trudged; but I swam a lot). And as a thief, for a long time, I inhabited Jean Genêt.

The hysterics are my sisters. As Dora, I have been all the characters she played, the ones who killed her, the ones who got shivers when she ran through them, and in the end I got away, having been Freud one day, Mrs. Freud another, also Mr. K . . . , Mrs. K   — and the wound Dora inflicted on them. In 1900, I was stifled desire, its rage, its turbulent effects. I kept the merry-go-round of bourgeois-conjugal pettiness from going around without squeaking horribly. I was everything, I sent each "person"/nobody back to his little calculations, each discourse to its lie, each cowardice to its unconscious, I said nothing but made everything known. I stole their little investments, but that's nothing. I slammed their door. I left. But I am what Dora would have been if woman's history had begun.

It is then that writing makes love other. It is itself this love. Other-Love is writing's first name.

At the beginnings of *Other-Love* there are differences. The new love dares the other, wants it, seems in flight, be-leaves, does some stealing between knowing and making up. She, the one coming from forever, doesn't stand still, she goes all over, she exchanges, she is desire-that-gives. Not shut up inside the paradox of the gift-that-takes or in the illusion of onely uniting. She enters, she betweens—she mes and thees between the other me where one is always infinitely more than one and more than me, without fearing ever to reach a limit: sensualist in our be-coming. We'll never be done with it! She runs through defensive loves, motherings and devourings. She runs her risks beyond stingy narcissism, in moving, open, transitional space. Beyond the back-to-bed of war-love that claims to represent exchange, she mocked the dynamics of Eros which is fed by hate—hate: an inheritance, a leftover, a deceiving subservience to the phallus—to love, to regard-think-seek the other in the other, to de-specularize, to de-speculate. She doesn't enter where history still works as the story of death. Still, having a present does not prevent woman's beginning the story of life elsewhere. Elsewhere, she gives. She doesn't measure what she is giving, but she gives neither false leads nor what she doesn't have. She gives cause to live, to think, to transform. That "economy" can no longer be expressed as an economic term. Wherever she loves, all the ideas of the old management are surpassed. I am for you what you want me to be at the moment in which you look at me as if you have never before seen me so: every moment. When I write, all those that we don't know we can be write themselves from me, without exclusion, without prediction, and everything that we will be calls us to the tireless, intoxicating, tender-costly-search for love. We will never lack ourselves.

The Dawn of Phallocentrism:

Freud:

Under the influence of external conditions—which we need not follow up here and which in part are also not sufficiently known—it happened that the matriarchal structure of society was replaced by a patriarchal one. This naturally brought with it a revolution in the existing state of the law. An echo of this revolution can still be heard, I think, in the *Oresteia* of Aeschylus. This turning from the mother to the father, however, signifies above all a victory of spirituality over the senses— that is to say, a step forward in culture, since maternity is proved by the senses whereas paternity is a surmise based on a deduction and a premiss. This declaration in favour of the thought-process, thereby raising it above sense perception, has proved to be a step with serious consequences. (*Moses and Monotheism*, p. 153)

Joyce:

Fatherhood, in the sense of conscious begetting, is unknown to man. It is a mystical estate, an apostolic succession, from only begetter to only begotten. On that mystery and not on the madonna which the cunning Italian intellect flung to the mob of Europe the church is founded and refounded irremovably because founded, like the world, macro- and microcosm, upon the void. Upon uncertitude, upon unlikelihood. *Amor matris*, subjective and objective genitive, may be the only true thing in life. (*Ulysses*, p. 204)

What is a father? "Fatherhood is a legal fiction," said Joyce. Paternity, which is a fiction, is fiction passing itself off as truth. Paternity is the lack of being which is called God. Men's cleverness was in passing themselves off as fathers and "repatriating" women's fruits as their own. A naming trick. Magic of absence. God is men's secret.

> Among the precepts of Mosaic religion is one that has more sig-
> nificance than is at first obvious. It is the prohibition against making
> an image of God, which means the compulsion to worship an invisible
> God. I surmise that in this point Moses surpassed the Aton religion in
> strictness. Perhaps he meant to be consistent; his God was to have nei-
> ther a name nor a countenance. The prohibition was, perhaps, a fresh
> precaution against magic malpractices. If this prohibition was accepted,
> however, it was bound to exercise a profound influence. For it signi-
> fied subordinating sense perception to an abstract idea; it was a tri-
> umph of spirituality over the senses; more precisely, an instinctual
> renunciation accompanied by its psychologically necessary conse-
> quences. (*Moses and Monotheism*, p. 152)

Jewoman:

And in the same story, as Kafka told it,[16] the man from the country, the one-who-doesn't-know-but-believes, comes before the law. A doorkeeper stands before the law. And the gullible man asks to go into the law. But even though the door opens, one doesn't go in. Maybe later. Nothing keeps the poor fellow from entering. Except everything: the doorkeeper, the way he looks, his black beard, the door, the fact of its being open; the fact that nothing keeps him from *entering the law*, except what the law is; except that it is what it is. And waiting.

> In the first years he curses his evil fate aloud; later, as he grows old,
> he only mutters to himself. He grows childish, and since in his
> prolonged watch he has learned to know even the fleas in the door-
> keeper's fur collar, he begs the very fleas to help him and to persuade
> the doorkeeper to change his mind. Finally his eyes grow dim and he
> does not know whether the world is really darkening around him or
> whether his eyes are only deceiving him. But in the darkness he can
> now perceive a radiance that streams immortally from the door of the
> Law. Now his life is drawing to a close. Before he dies, all that he
> has experienced during the whole time . . . condenses into one ques-
> tion, which he has never yet put to the doorkeeper. He beckons the
> doorkeeper, since he can no longer raise his stiffening body. The
> doorkeeper has to bend far down to hear him, for the difference in

size between them has increased very much to the man's disadvantage. "What do you want to know now?" asks the doorkeeper, "you are insatiable." "Everyone strives to attain the Law," answers the man, "how does it come about, then, that in all these years no one has come seeking admittance but me?" The doorkeeper perceives . . . that his hearing is failing, so he bellows in his ear: "No one but you could gain admittance through this door, since this door was intended only for you. Now I am going to shut it. (Pp. 63–65)

And no one is there now to learn what the man devoted his whole life just to begin to think, no one to reap the discovery that could come about only at the price of a whole life, at the moment of death. There is never anyone there when what has never been not-open or open closes, the door, the threshold of the law. What law? The law where? who? whose?

But the Real has very clearly crystallized in the relationship of forces between the petitioner "outside-the-law" and the doorkeeper, the first in a series of representatives of the L− −, the cop, the first level of a power with a thousand laws. "Outside" law? What is inside law? Is there an "inside" to law? A place? A country maybe? A city, a kingdom? As long as he lived, that is what he believed.

Was he ever outside in relation to the desired inside that is reserved for every man—that place, that L− −, which he believed was his good, his right, his "accessible" object. *Into* which he would enter and which he was going to enjoy.

So it is the L− − that will have served as "life" for him, will have assigned him his place before the L− −, permanently. Immobilized, shriveled. And no one will have been there to learn from the dying man, from the dead man, what he began to think maybe at the last second: that the law isn't within, it has no place, it has no place other than the gullible man's body that comes to rot in front of the door, which has always been in the L− −, and the L− − has only existed to the extent that it appears before what he doesn't see it is behind, around, before, *inside him* that it is nothing without him, that its apparently absolute power is inexhaustible, because like Moses's God, it doesn't exist; it is invisible; it doesn't have a place to take place; it doesn't have anything. It "is" hence it is only if he makes it; it is nothing more than the tremendous power of the invisible.

Exploited by thousands of its representatives—supposed-to-represent-it, who draw their dissuasive, repressive power, their calm and absolute violence from this nothing that is out of sight.

You will not pass. You will not see me. A woman is before the door of the law. And the bearded watchman—his beard so pointed, so threatening—warns her not to go through. Not to go, not to enjoy. And by looking toward, and look-ing in, and feeling herself looked at without knowing where the L− −'s look is coming from, she gets it to come, she believes she sees a glimmer radiating, which is the little flame that the constant flow of her gaze keeps burning in emptiness, in nothing. But from always being looked at without seeing, she pales, she shrinks, she grows old, she is diminished, sees no more, lives no more. That is called "internalizing." She is full of this nothing that she imagines and that she pines for. Sublimation? Yes, but negative, turning the power—whose source she is without knowing it—back against herself. Her powerlessness, her paralysis, her feebleness? They are the measure of her power, her desire, her resistance, her blind confidence in their L — —. Suppose she "entered?" Why not have taken this step? Not even the first step? Does she fear the other doors? Or does she have forebodings? Or is it the choice between two mockeries of life inscribing themselves in the nothingness that she embodies and that rivets her in the visible, on the lowest level, in relation to her nearest interlocutor: fleas in the doorkeeper's coat, a flea herself.

Or maybe there is an L — — and it is the petrifying result of not-knowing reinforced by power that produces it.

And they told her there was a place she had better not go. And this place is guarded by men. And a law emanates from this place with *her* body for its locus. They told her that inside her law was black, growing darker and darker. And a doorkeeper preached prudence to her, because beyond it was even worse.

And she doesn't enter her body; she is not going to confirm the worst, it is not even properly hers. She puts it in the hands of the doorkeeper.

So, the resounding blow of this same trick echoes between Jew and woman. In the tabernacle it is metamorphosed as a box full of nothing that no one would miss. The trick of the "omnipotent." The voice saying "I-am-who-I-say-I-am." My name is "the-one-who-is-where-you aren't." What is a father? The one taken for father. The one recognized as the true one. "Truth," the essence of fatherhood, its force as law. The "chosen" father.

And one day—as Freud sees it still inscribing itself in the *Oresteia*[17]—the matriarchy is done for, the sons stop being sons of mothers and become sons of fathers. The question of filiation swings, changes tack: What is a mother? And they no longer ask themselves which is more certain, but, which is stronger?

On one side there is mother, belly, milk. The bond passing through flesh, blood, and milk, through the life debt. What is owed to her? A debate begins over sperm and milk: does she provide food only, or does she also provide a germ? Who begins?

How hard it all is for Orestes who is at a turning point in time and whose action, a matricide—until now the crime of crimes—marks the end of mothers and inaugurates the sublime era! How do you estimate the value of the mother's murder? What value does blood have? What is the value of words? In the struggle between Blood and Words, the marriage pact—a commitment made with word and will—is stronger, Apollo claims, than the blood-tie. The link to mother loosens. The link to word tightens. We are still in the age of the organic. From now on legality is to come to the assistance of the father's order. A new relationship between body and justice will have to be instituted.

Veils: presented in the *Coephorae*,

divine Vengeance will advance under the veil of illusion, as Agamemnon succumbed under the horrible veil when he was caught in the queen's net. Two gods help the father's children. There is King Apollo or Loxias, who until now has been an oracle who doesn't lie but who, as Zeus's word of advice, "luxates," twists, point obliquely toward the husband. And there is his little lying brother, Hermes, the thief and master of double-talk. But they repeat each other. Zeus and the earth conjoin their efforts on behalf of paternity and its domestic birthplace.

The dead-father, Agamemnon (was he ever anything other than dead, except the day he was killed? Clytemnestra asks, but no one hears the question) is in the strongest position: the position of death. From this impregnable position he secretly leads the final, toppling revolution. "Is it necessary to obey such oracles? Even if I do not obey them, the work must no less be done. Many desires here conspire to the same end: alongside the god's orders there is a father's huge grief; furthermore, there is destitution driving me, and finally the desire that those most illustrious of mortals, the noble-hearted destroyers of Troy, be no longer thus subjected to two women; for he has a woman's heart, and if he doesn't know it, he soon will learn."

Everything follows the commandments of Loxias, the oblique, the god of the ambiguous oracle. He helps the brother—as Phoebus, prompter of deceit: "Alone, by deceit, you will slit the throat. . . . Announce to them and swear on it that Orestes has met his death." An advantageous word could not bring misfortune. Making rumors of his death fly, the brother ensures his life. "Brother."

Helping the sister—nocturnal Hermes, the underground one, the guide, the mediator between the dead and the living, the messenger from the shadowy depths. Bearer of the dead ones' hatred, bearer of strange, violent words. Treacherous Hermes, come from Hell, whispers within cunning Orestes, whom Pheobus rescued. Within Orestes is his other, Pylades, the absent-present, the double with the disturbing name: Pylades, Gate-of-Hell. Stranger-exile-messenger-ghost, set free by the irresistible desire of the dead.

"In the messenger, the twisted word is set straight," says Aeschylus. Orestes's act inscribes wrongs made right by wrenching, torts by torsion. Orestes, clandestine claim-fate, the false, at nightfall commits the more-than-one murder. Hermes, the spirit of limits, chthonian, puts an end to more than one age through Orestes: under the cover of the classic, phallocentric scenario (elimination of the old king—with woman's betrayal and incestuous complexity—); *under* the pretext of duty to avenge (a legitimate duty—brought about with the help of methods contrary to the warrior's head-on, open ethic—); under disguise and deviously hidden-hiding-disclosing in himself more than one nonhuman being, as being more than human, the shifty brother sets time ticking and explodes the feminine nucleus. All the energy still jammed into this end of the after-Medean afternoon, at the twilight of matriarchy, is set free once and for all. Matriarchal shrapnel scatters. The scene soaks up blood diverted from its ancient matrilinear circulation. Orestes, neuter, neither masculine nor feminine, half-active, half-passive, neither criminal nor not-guilty, signs the end of the great reign of mothers. Dawn of phallocentrism.

And then there o-rests upon this earth conquered by man's Law only one last Great Woman, whose days are numbered; she is the one no man could "keep," the age-less eloper—the one who, though scarcely yet a woman, made Theseus retire because of her face, who with a glance lost a thousand ships, inalterable Helen. The combined efforts of the new phallocrats under the leadership of Electra in another setting, do not succeed in robbing her of life. Final, infinite, a seducing leader forever sublimated, she takes off—indomitable but banished by name throughout the centuries.

Who stays behind?

—In the end only sister Electra orests.

This story takes place after midday, in the after-Medea, when the Great Woman has had it, when Theseus cut Ariadne's thread (the one leading men into the unilinear labyrinth of filiations through the mother and keeping them there)—and with a bold stroke, driving the savage, elusive woman's power to the ends of the earth, flushed Medea from her last lair. He puts his sword on the possible-father's table (the stranger, the always uncertain son) and takes power by sheer nerve. Let the sons (and threads) of woman disappear, henceforward the father's son will put his stamp on everything that exists.

At the end of the after-Medea, when the twilight of mothers sinks into a night good for dreams of death, the Electricity comes on: a short period of seeing red.

Soon it will be patriarchy forever.

Electra's ambiguous force: a hellish libido. — Nothing can stop her voice. No justice. Energy.

Not Apollo, lucid god. But Apollo, wolf-hunter, Lykeios "for my heart is like a flesh-eating wolf made unyielding by my mother."

Electra's tongue:

No never will I silence laments nor bitter complaints, as long as I see nights cast fire from all their stars; no—as long as I see the light of day, on the paternal threshold, like a nightingale who has lost her young, I will haunt passersby with my cries.

It is stronger than I, in my sorrow's excess my tongue is carried away, my complaints will forever be numberless. Paternal torture, I see it tirelessly begin again, how can I hold back my flying cries?

The Choir: I see her mouth breathe anger out.
Clytemnestra: What thanks you would earn, stranger, if only you had silenced her inexhaustible cries . . .

A stream of cries, that won't run out, torment's spring that won't go dry: she has to yell, vomit — torrential — this flood that results from paternal torture is bottomless, all the spilled blood, all the lost sperm run, inexhaustible, through this strange gorge, through which from the most distant burial, the father returns. The father, strongest of all, carries off the tongue that calls and projects him. "Viper's tongue!" says Clytemnestra.

The mother's ears are poisoned by this venom. Clytemnestra is already infiltrated: insistent death penetrates the Great Woman through her ears.

Virgin veers into Virago.

The Virago, the woman with sperm, has a tongue that foams. No father without a husband, without children, always I am weeping and weeping. No body, no belly, no breasts, just a tongue. Why are the workings of grief not done? The tongue tightens, stiffens, takes root; it withstands rest and sleep for the sake of the father's non-body.

"These griefs are indissoluble. Mine will neither rest nor cease; my moaning will be forever countless."

Before you — gold-rich Mycenas; before you the gold-rich palace; and before the palace the virgin rich in cries.

Her abounding lips protrude so her voice vibrating will not shatter the mask she uses for a face.

She/the tongue is out front and on the brink. She doesn't go in, doesn't go away, keeps at a distance but near enough for her cries of rage to shake up society, the group. She is on the brink, and she is attached to family social things by this thread — this organ, this extremity. She is pulled extremely tight, stretched between inside and outside. She is both on the threshold herself and on the threshold others cross to go from life to death and from death to life. Tensed, ejaculating, and implacable. She makes things vibrate. The tongue.

Feminine electricity:

— The ancients knew the properties of yellow amber: when the electron is rubbed it attracts light bodies.

The Choir, Clytemnestra, Chrysothemis — light bodies, attracted by magnetic Electra: an intense system of exchange, attraction, particle loss fed by Electra. As soon as she is in the presence of an unstable body whose electrons are easily grabbed, she attracts them — she even releases her own negative particles constantly, stimulating, going over and over the sensitive periphery of her being, this painful skin whose nerves she bares. She does not attract the noble orestian metal that does not give its electrons and does not react to magnetic/loving insistence. She attracts her complement, those feminine bodies that respond to rubbing in the same way, that lose the way she loses, that give the way she gives and depose themselves. A very powerful negative current which, by discharging, makes itself positive in order to wait for the other to come. The voice acts as a physical trap. But she doesn't get anything – she attracts but doesn't take: the magnetic effect must not be done away with. The imbalance must be maintained.

Woman's weapons:

Weeping, crying, poisons, veils, nets. Who cries there?

"What? neither our love, nor the hand we gave each other once can hold you back?"

Who? Medea, Ariadne, Dido,

> How did you moan, when from the heights of your palace, you saw in the distance the effervescent shore and beneath your eyes the whole liquid plain echoing all this clamor? Damned love, how you reduce the heart of mortals! So again she is reduced to tears as her recourse, to trying prayer once more, and to imploring submissively for love, for she does not want to die without having tried everything. . . . Go, my sister, and speak as a supplicant to my proud enemy. . . . Why does he implacably refuse to hear what I have to say? Where is he going so fast? Let him grant his miserable lover the last favor of waiting for favorable winds for the difficult passage. I no longer invoke the old vows of union which he has betrayed, nor his promise to renounce beautiful Latium for me and to abandon his kingdom; I ask a vain delay, a truce, a respite from his rage; I ask him to wait until fortune teaches me to endure my defeat. I beseech the utmost grace . . . and, when he grants it to me, dying, I will give it back to you a hundredfold.
>
> Such were her prayers and such the tears her unhappy sister takes again and again to Aeneas; but he is insensitive to all her tears and remains uncompromising in the face of all he hears. (*Aeneid*, bk. 4, Storm)

All history is thus troubled with her incessant moanings, which insist, die down, come up again, always unheard. For it is a question of life or death for her.

An endless choir swollen by sobs and silences, breathless gasps, hysterics' coughs.

That is the origin of opera. And I say that only men capable of that emission, those tormented ones who give in to their femininity, can love opera.

The others, builders, deny themselves this passion.

> As when Alpine north winds blowing all around vie with one another in striving to topple a sturdy oak whose heart is hardened by the

years, the air whistles, and far off its foliage is strewn on the ground by the blows that shake its trunk; the tree hangs onto the rocks and its head rises as high into the ethereal breezes as its roots dig down into Tartary; so the hero is assailed with ceaseless complaints, and his great heart is swept with sorrow but his will remains unshakable, and her tears flow in vain.

Then ill-fated Dido, in horror at her destiny, calls on death: she is indeed weary of the sight of the sky's vault.

Virgil has pity. Poets know.

What does the philosopher say? Kant, soberly: "Woman has no qualms about domestic war where her tongue is her weapon, and for this purpose, nature has given her the gift of chatter, and passionate volubility which disarms man." Which disarms him? By rearming him: sending him "fleeing" back to his camp.

Can one kill with a tongue?

"Venger of the dead, with cunning steps,/Breaks into the paternal home/where ancient wealth is sleeping."

His fist brandishes freshly sharpened death, "and Maia's son, Hermes,/in treacherous ambushing shadow/guides him to the end . . . it is time!"

"Our men are ready to get down to work." Their men's hands brandishing the masculine weapon. And now, at last, silence.

But I, a woman still wild, soon to be enslaved—at that moment I sheathed my weapon. Did not brandish my tongue.

Electra's tongue, Orestes's tongue, opposite words. A thick flood comes from her, the pain in the ass, a present of poison for the mother: it's obvious, I am giving you my hatred, my shit, my truth, because you ask me for them. I give you what you want. Let Chrysothemis give you her golden silences. I give you what you are afraid of not getting.

"My self, my words, my deeds—you never stop talking about them.

I am not making you say it: your deeds prompt my words."

I am the product of your faults. —But I am the daughter of sperm. The trap starts there, the weave of tricks, the system of obscure words, beginning with the oblique oracle, through the empty urn, the ensnarer tends his nets, the master of lies, of secret, of ambiguous signs, the lock of hair on the tomb, the messenger. Which word kills? the disguised one or the one that is sharp?

"I have paid dearly for the right to speak freely!

—I agree. But use this right sparingly." That's what the brother preaches. I am close by you, but keep quiet. "We had better be quiet. Please, let's drop what it's not essential to say."

It is man's hour, the hour of masculine crime, of deadly calculation. Let's change the economy. Quit wasting yourself.

Patriarchy will know how to manage its possessions, far from excess, close to cunning. Aegisthus, the man of matriarchy, warrior from the women's quarters, is lost: "—Please, a word, just a word"—facing the new man, the one who loses neither his time nor his blood nor his head, the future boss. Hurry and come in, Aegisthus, "it's not a question of verbal sparring: your life is at stake." We are no longer within the circle of women who punch and embrace each other when they fight. Man cuts.

Women's war is ambiguous: there is a bond between enemies that doesn't break; between father's daughter and mother's daughter, between the one bearing the father's noble name and the one with the name of the female parent. And a bond between the ambivalent mother and the inseparable daughter. For woman's fate in history is what is at play here in this wasteful duel. Well-behaved Chrysothemis hesitates between two laws—the law of blood and the law of sperm. But she still belongs to the diminishing matriarchal powers. Electra lights the path, makes way for the patriarchy. The ones who slept on mats have already been left behind. "The ones who are alive are the men who sleep under the earth!"

In this time of reversal everything is two-faced: one face still looks toward the old order; one face envisages the new power. The promised cutting works away on the body of each one. Clytemnestra, haunted by the dreams that take her over, pregnant with a monstrously budding branch, lives by retreating from the fearsome corpse.

She knows what she will know. Split, bearing Electra's violent gift, unable to separate from her. Tongue for tongue. Chrysothemis comes and goes, measuring how the abyss shrinks, how the sides come closer. Orestes himself is more two-timer than one, the man with two fates, a fake dead man for whom they wear mourning. He has his silent shadow in tow—Pylades, what is left of Orestes, a trace of him. Electra, the hybrid, disturbing, unbearable for everyone including Orestes, is simultaneously not-woman and too-much-woman, excess everywhere, excess of excessive logic, mad reason.

It overflows endlessly. Orestes, the male, spattered with a bit too much liquid tenderness must ward her off. And what if he were touched by the dangerous spray? This disorderly force, this "sister," will have to be domesticated.

Remnants of the mother's reign: abundance, excess; the indistinct relationship with death. Woman, the life-giver, has a hard time thinking of death as an end, an erasure. She doesn't bury, she doesn't forget, she keeps the dead alive. A gut-being, a primitive body, yet bound to the sign, to the burial. —Everyone who knows much about the construction of the family has said how woman-family and burial go together, paradoxically: woman who looks after the family and its traces in her bosom and in the earth is the one who guarantees burial. Through earth—woman touches the double nature that she herself is—that gives life and gets it back at its completion. Nocturnal kingdom, mysterious, primitive, not-human, divine. In opposition to the kingdom of the day that man guarantees by making it a political issue. The burial place holding the dead man also inscribes his memory: what does not die — a name, an astounding force, takes cover there. Those who are dead must be preserved as living and dead at the same time. This feminine way of preserving is a way of resisting death.

Clytemnestra, who knows that it is coming, skirts it and escapes it: she knows that death, like life, can get away through some unexpected opening.

Crime will be masculine: the crime, not the wrong; sin is feminine.[18] Does that mean that Aeschylus, too, echoes the masculine/feminine opposition which creates hierarchy, which ordains woman's subservience? In a certain way, yes. *Electra* is a mixed-up, hesitant place: active and passive forces, the forces of life and death, still confront each other there without being absolutely attributed to sexual difference, but their values become more and more emphasized until, in a last electric discharge, what is Orestes wins everything. Electra's force is injected by the father, her vulnerability comes through the mother.

Why doesn't she kill herself? — The nonmurder of the one by the other is obviously overdetermined: not kill Electra so as not to have difficulties with the Gods? — There is no reasonable reason to abstain, either for the daughter or for the mother. But the one does not go without her other, her relay, her mirror, alike and relentless.

And crime — active — is reserved for man. And suppose there is no Orestes anymore? And suppose Electra was going to kill? What if woman took over from man, made off with the scepter, the dagger. That's what she was going to do or else Agamemnon would die a second time. That would mean that there are manly possibilities in woman. That the reign of mothers is therefore not dead, that power could come again from the direction of the maternal hearth? Suspense.

The play's subtle word-play, coined: heads or tails? Battery or surge? Logos and its moderation have to win. From his first entrance, the wise advisor guides and reassures in advance. Orestes arrives in extremis, when all the women are ripe for a radical change. Ripe for death, ripe for domestic subservience.

Crime: active, the male bond, the noble, Promethean deed.

Sin: the feminine, step by step, no by no. Ant's pace. The succession of wrongs is the origin of evil.

But the father dies only to be raised again. All the children have to do is sing the threnody befitting the father loudly enough and the master of the house rises again.

Orestes: — My father, it is to you that I address myself. Come to the aid of those who love you.

Electra: — I too, tears flooding, I call you.

The Choir: — With a common voice our troupe calls you as well. Come to the window, hear us, and be with us against our enemies. He has every interest in returning, the same interest as the son has, who by invoking him legitimates him in order to be legitimatized.

Electra: I too, father, I need you to escape the danger.

Orestes: — Then we will establish solemn feasts in your honor. Otherwise you will be forgotten in the rich banquets.

Electra: — I too, I will bring you libations from the paternal house, from the entire portion of my inheritance, the day of my wedding.

Orestes: — Remember, father, the bath where you perished.

Electra: — Remember the net, how they found a new use for it on you.

Electra: — And the ignominious veil they imagined they could cover you with.

Orestes: — Don't these insults awaken you, father?

Electra: — Are you not lifting your dear head again?

Electra: — Finally, listen to this last outcry, my father; seeing your brood near your tomb, take pity on your female as well as your male descendants, and do not erase this Pelopidean race of ours; it is thus that you will still live, dead though you be.

Orestes: — Yes, children preserve the name of the man who dies, as the cork holds the net up and keeps the linen web from sinking to the bottom. Hear me, it is for you that we moan thus, and you are the one you will save by honoring my prayer.

It is indeed himself he saves, just as he has already been saved, chosen as father from among all possible fathers, "recognized" by his own. And *named* father. For as men have always known, the "father" is never anything but the name of the father. But if the libido is shouting in Electra, in Orestes it negotiates through blackmail: on a fifty-fifty basis. The System, seen by Freud—a more polished, cultured version, is indeed the father-child or god-people "covenant," which is sealed by a cunning, well-tempered "gift."

The father is the restriction, the choice; the first "spiritual" process is to love him: the always uncertain father must be "recognized." Filiation through the mother cannot be denied, but who is sure of the father? It is the son or daughter who affirms the father's paternity. The father is always dependent on the child, who decides whether to recognize or reject him.

Agamemnon rises up again at his offsprings' call, the child of his own blood. He is roused from the tomb by the children's strong voice, roused from the womb of stone.

In a certain way the father is always unknown. Coming from outside, he has to enter and give proof. Outsiders, absolutely other, strangers, ghosts, always capable of coming back, the most fragile and the strongest together. Coming out of the earth to go back into the mother, into the palace, to reappropriate bodies and goods.

That is what is called civilization.

Progress, says Freud, whose logic thus expresses his self-interest in circular performances: "Father, prefer me, so that feeling I am preferred, my self-confidence will grow so that I can call you 'father' all the more loudly." That is also called having an interest. "You have every interest in my greatness. And I in yours." Thus from great man to great man, they make progress in "spirituality." Then there's no need for electricity to circulate to keep the tomblike hearth lit up.

Together a cry from Clytemnestra and the brother's order finally shut off the current: she breathes reason. Healed!

And completely devastated, emptied of people.

No longer will she stand watch, her back to the palace, to face surprise. She enters the long inertia of the foreseen. (If you want to know the sequel, she is done for: a woman gets married to a shade of father-brother, the son-in-law Pylades; a legitimate son reigns and rakes it in; look at the happy times of King Orestes; inheritance is transmitted through the men: patriarchy—political-economy—sexualeconomy—it has all sorted itself out since they checkmated those great screeching females.)

And now the reign of the paternal brother. Recognized by the sister, therefore without the fight to the death that sexual difference always risks triggering, having been careful to rule out the incestuous complications that a raving Electra might have awakened, Orestes, tranquilizing and anesthetic, imposes the law.

Achilles is Penthesileia is Achilles.

I said I owed my life to Kleist. For a long time I lived on the knowledge that he had existed. I owed him not only the will to live but the will to live several lives. To be more than one feminine one or masculine one, to catch fire and burn, to die of life because he caught fire, took on body, pain, and death for me. For anyone wanting his vision of life, a vision unequaled in demands and nobility. Nietzsche says it is enough "to feel the need to transform oneself and to speak through other bodies and other souls, in order to be a poet." That is true. But Kleist goes further. Not only is he capable of these transformations, but he insists on passing through the bodies and souls of those who are stretched to the limit, those closest to the lifesprings and, therefore, closest to life's origins, which is to say, to body, flesh, desire carried away with itself and carrying itself out; and closest to what keeps life going, its extent and its stand against death. And in this approximation, which can work only through love—a total love, without restriction, the way it is when it is the place of all births, when it continually starts over and over in the other a life that knows it is living – it is rare that the individual not run into the thousand obstacles that reality contrives to put up. Ambiguous obstacles, of course, for love's resources are measured against the obstacles and the surmounting of the obstacles. Love's strength is shown, and in the ordeal, doubtless, some part of the effort and the threat are turned back into elation. Why obstacles to love? Accidents maybe. But anyway, in history, the first obstacle, always already there, is in the existence, the production and reproduction of images, types, coded and suitable ways of behaving, and in society's identification with a scene in which roles are fixed so that lovers are always initially trapped by the puppets with which they are assumed to merge. You are not a man, you are not a woman, you are first of all son of, daughter of, you are from such-and-such a class, such-and-such a family, such-and-such a tribe. You are first the anonymous element of a given category, and your fate is set in advance. If you are woman, you will resemble ideal woman; and you will obey the imperatives that mark your line. You will channel your desires, you will address them where, how, and to whom it is proper. You will honor the laws.

But Kleist writes *Penthesileia*. He loves, he is Penthesileia. First, he is this glorious nature, this queen of passion for Achilles, for Love. And then, in return, he is Achilles as he is when under Penthesileia's influence, he really becomes another man: the new lover. How far we are above what is flat and banal, above groveling and self-interest!

A Royal Universe: not reserved for kings. Here royal is a metaphor, although Penthesileia is indeed the queen of the Amazons, the person so designated. Kleist makes the Universe shine – It is royal because he is monarch, the only one, the one for whom, at the same time, there is no substitute, the one out of all the others who is looked at. Because he deals exclusively and vitally with heights, with elevation; and because his whole being is so intense – like forever darting fire – that his entire body wants to rise above kings, kingdoms, laws, the ground, the body really responds to the called and calling soul, and a prodigious strength animates beings, giving them the grace of the Strong. Each lover born of Kleist, whether bourgeois, hero, leader, or young woman, is blessed, in fact, with the tireless energy of the Strong, the raging. Every being born of this love always wants more, higher. And each body is changed by desire into a glorious, radiant body, drawn toward summits, literally pushed headlong, *head up*.

Vision of dazzling Assumptions, flights, self outdoing self, again and again/in body after body, I am not enough, another body must be added to my body, flood of curls winging Penthesileia's head, flood of metaphors that make the main parts of the body glisten, and above the loving forehead, flames, wisps/wicks, rays; above the head a crown – not the sign of power but the poetic wreath, the crown of plants, the sign of creative, transforming power.

All of Kleist's work is a great field for taking off, for flying away in exultation. A field of passion; elation and pain, inextricable joy and sorrow. A wreath of laurels and nettles. How I love it!

The prince of Hombourg, bareheaded, his suit unbuttoned at the top, in Fehr-bellin's garden, sound asleep, busy weaving in his dream a wreath of greenery, of glory or laurel, "a victory wreath with sunflowers." In the dream beloved figures come to put the crown on him, right before his eyes, and they take it a little farther away, and they lift it as if to put it on his brow, and he puts his hands out to take it and to touch, to grab hold of this hand, this dear person, but the wreath floats too high and the dear one fades away. And half-asleep, half-awake, he follows the promised crown: wreaths of roses for young Greek captives: rose chains, iron chains. But there is always that desirable chain, that wedding band, necklace, ring, that says with the same sign: you are lost, you won. Lofty heights, glory, your place, the only one where you can find peace, where you are able to join whatever is unique, whose brilliance calls and guides you. "Such a great undertaking, such a lofty one, rather than not completely accomplishing it—rather than not firmly grasping the crown that lowers onto my brow." Crown of glory? —No, Penthesileia does not want to enjoy symbolic glory. Not the crown, not the figure of glory. But *glory itself*: personified, starred.

The chorus of amazons: What does she want? What more can she want? What can she want more of? —She wants the most! "Him! Him! Who else, if not Him! He crowns the hill like a statue made of brightness. Steel makes him and his horse swim in light. Sapphires and green chalcedony have less brilliance. The surrounding earth, wrapped in the storm's shroud, is no more than mirror's sil-vering that reflects the blinding splendor of the Unique!"

And he, what does he want? "You will be willing to help me reach the one joy surely reserved for me in the future—distant though it may be—I mean, weaving for me the wreath of immortality."[19] He, Kleist, or the Prince.

The love of Beauty in all its figurations, a beauty always more exalted than his—glory, so as to be nobler and more brilliant in order to approach the dear beings who are always worthy of still more, leads him to the brink of the abyss. And that is Kleist. And Kleist is Penthesileia. The same demanding character that cannot remain shut up inside the limitations of one being no matter who; the same erupting glory that wants to appear, mingle its fire with daylight, eclipse light itself, and that cannot be kept inside one's heart; for one who has seen beauty can never stop desiring and can only desire beauty.

Penthesileia was stricken. Wounded. Opened up to Achilles. Through a wound that will never close, light and life flood into her flesh. Here, at the left breast, is the wound, here is Achilles, here is Penthesileia. In the very flesh, yet, he is over there, going faster than the wind. It is *He*. Only He, the one Revealed.

How he desires her! To grasp her, Kleist goes "to places where no human being ever goes," he writes to his sister. And he pursues her a long long time. yet she is in him, always has been in him, like a wound, like his own wound, like the wound he is and that creates him. In him she is the delightful, cruel irruption of the other, of the feminine one he carries, he makes, of whom he is a part, whose place he is, woman—or poetry—woman as the source of creation, part of him. His femininity is that part of him, the man, the lover, the poet, that always *escapes* him. Painfully, deliciously. The radiant wound that after 1806 will be called Penthesileia, in 1805 is already opening its violent way into Kleist: "A year ago, in Dresden, how we flew into each other's arms! How vast was the world that opened up, like an arena before our quivering souls, intoxicated with the desire for combat! And now here we are on the ground, knocked down on top of each other, finishing the race toward the goal with our eyes. Never before did it seem as brilliant as at this moment when we are shrouded in the dust of our fall." Kleist's words to his friend Pfuel: the field is already inscribed where Penthesileia would hurl herself at Achilles for the duel, the pain, the dance.

—Look at this field: it is a solar setting. Around it orbit a series of secondary fields where enemy troops are distributed. Camps and what is behind them revolve around the field where two cultural choices confront each other: men's law and women's law. Greeks and Amazons are defining their relation to sexuality and love in terms of exclusion/inclusion. Ideological interventions from both Laws fall in a shower of gibes, opinions, and discourses onto this field which is (no) more than a battlefield, a field of exchange engagements, an erotic field. At the heart is the social—the sacred place where the confrontation is less between forces or ideas than between loving bodies. There, triggered by increasing reproaches of the subjugated, first slowly, then suddenly—everything is turned upside down. This war is no longer *the* war. This battle to the death is no longer a battle. The telling blows between them are no longer blows.

There is war—but it is elsewhere, occurring on several fronts; it continues but on its same old hackneyed territory, where death tries to conquer life. First there is "true" war, masculine war, whose threat could be forgotten, given the banality of what is at stake (Troy is far away indeed)—if this "true" war did not keep on secreting its desire for death, for corpses, its crude joy. And if the men's camp did not protest against the unsettling transformation of Achilles, into what? into whom? into a player? a warrior who doesn't mean it? It is far worse: Achilles (which brute in the war camp could possibly understand?) is going over to the women's side. Achilles is melting with love, and love gets him mixed up with the woman he lets well up inside him.

No man has the strength, the only true strength that has no need to protect itself, or to flaunt or prove itself, the strength that makes no use of tools or arms and that is secure enough to be a source of peace; not the false strength which is only fear's other face, and which, in order to reassure itself, produces only deeds of death and agression. None except Achilles.

He comes soon, this strong, tender, terrific being, to Penthesileia, as love: his arms laid down. Naked. Like love. Without self defense. Radiant.

Man's war against woman's war: and already war is no longer the same. Because the Amazons don't make war for reasons that men understand. War, for the young women warriors, is a fantastic, ambivalent process to which they are constrained by their mother's invention of a form of manless society. They conduct their war not to kill but to take hold. An astonishing capture of love, putting war at love's mercy and love at the mercy of violence. They have to seize male strength. But they must take it *alive*. The Amazons go around gathering men the way they gather roses for the festivities awaiting the conquered. Defeating, yes, but in order to espouse. It is the invention of a union that is the opposite of rape and masculine abduction; but it takes place on enemy territory. Although the Amazons have broken off from the masculine world and created another State, they are in the minority, they rule only at Themiscyra. And to get what they want from the others, they still must come and conquer, snatch it away; they have to venture onto the other side in an exchange where the terms are still dictated by masculine law, by men's behavior and their codes. For a free woman, there can be no relationship with men other than war. Especially when it is a case of love: the closer one gets to the enemy, the more necessary it is to be violent because of the violence within him, and, paradoxically, the more necessary it is to distance oneself from him. Whence the laws—the prohibitions—weighing heavily on the women warriors, laws of preservation: they marry only the men they have conquered. To be an Amazon is to be faithful to the law of reversal: one must repeat the act that proves or symbolizes that she is not captive or submissive to a man. One has to have won; but this victory does not have the meaning of a masculine triumph. He dominates to destroy. She dominates to not be dominated; she dominates the dominator to destroy the space of domination. Because the one knocked down is helped to his feet. And she leads the one who is "conquered" into her world—a world he has never dared imagine. There waits a festival: a woman who is not a slave. And one produces and celebrates within this universe of queens. Therefore, there is this law of reversal. Another law repeats and upholds it—the law of no-choice. She will not choose the enemy. She will let nothing intervene in her fight, other than the "natural" desire for "a" man, whoever he is, without any preference. For she must not be *attached* to any man. Love for a unique one cannot occur.

Moreover, the unions are only fleeting. Once the Greek men have been loved, they will be sent back to their world. Loved-used. But that does not happen, cannot happen in the world Kleist would have. The army of Amazons slips out from under the law right away, escapes the command of the high priestess, seethes with the ardor of war waiting impatiently to turn into tenderness.

Because these thorny ones are made for roses, and even if they "obey," it is life, in fact, which their obedience obeys; even if they do not "choose," their unconscious chooses, they already love. Prothoé "chooses"—after the fact? who can say?—her prince. Or it is love that chooses the lovers for each other.

But the essence of Penthesileia is pure desire, frenzied desire, immediately outside all law. She is absolutely unbridled: unbounded flight, panicked by any shadow of a boundary-stone. And this pure desire, which has no other law than the need to reach its object, is absolutely, with no uncertainty, the one she wants; she saw it—like lightning she recognized it. A bolt of lightning itself.

> But what I felt, who could tell you, my love, when finally I saw
> you—when you stood before me in the Scamandre valley, surrounded
> by the heroes of your race, like a sun in the center of pale stars. It
> was as if, at the gallop of his white horses, in the crash of thunder,
> Mars himself, the God of war, had come down from Olympus to greet
> his betrothed. Then you vanished and I was left blinded—as when a
> thunderbolt, on a dark night, opens the earth at the traveler's very
> feet—as when the gates of shining Elysium rattle in a storm to greet a
> happy soul and then close up again. At that same moment, Pelides, I
> knew whence came the blow that reached my heart.

Can one imagine a woman thrown by her ardor into the men's zone, and who says: "It's him. It's you. It's the unique one. And I can't make him mine"?

Certainly unimaginable in conventional society, where woman's desire cannot shoot straight like that but must take a thousand detours to express itself, and so often resign itself to the comedy of eloquent silence. Because in ordinary existence, woman does not announce, does not begin things. It is agreed that she will not go after the object of her desire. Courtly love is two-faced: adored, deified, assimilated to the idol that accepts hommage, she has the rank and honors of the Virgin. Conversely, and the same position, in her powerlessness, she is at the disposition of the other's desire, the object, the prostitute. Under these conditions, what is a woman's desire? What is left of it? What shows? What culpable impulse is cut off?

She has acknowledged him as hers. Her brilliant goal, "O Pelides, you were the one, the agonizing worry as I lay awake, like my sleep's endless dream." He is the one, the expected one who does not disappoint expectation, who fulfills it. Who alone can answer her need for everything. For whom she feels she was born, is still being born. Her destiny. The amazon sisters see it thus; for it is on the order of revealed truth. And there is no mistake.

She foresaw him. She sees him. He exists. All that is left to do is to take possession of him. Because—and this is her limit again—prudence soon surmounted, she must try to conquer him: and then let the Amazon be subservient to the woman who loves. And the contest becomes the first battle of love. With iron? But an iron embrace. −Chains, yes, but of flowers. From body to fabulous body dazzling love spurts on impact. Moreover, everything goes on between the lovers, in flesh, organs, blood on the bosom of this stormy battle bed. And suddenly she attacks−now it's the hunt, the flight, the exchange that doesn't tell its names. She guides an animal that she grips with her hard, warrior's thighs, a warrior who, to take pleasure in making himself pursued, becomes feminine; he uses cunning, she confronts, the roles fly. All is approach, cunning and innocent seduction, everything works toward ecstatic violence. "They swoop down on each other like two stars." But bit by bit in this exchange, love draws violence to it and prevails. Achilles lets himself be led among the women. Both are enraptured: each instant is lived at the highest possible level of intensity, at the greatest speed. Dazzling scenes of a race so rapid that their own speed surpasses that of the thought of racing. At that height the very idea of speed is shattered. You can't see them anymore−senses have been eclipsed. The lovers have slipped out of ordinary sight. Clouds. A metaphor also of blind belief. What they become cannot be seen simply with the body's eyes; the eyes of passion, whose glances move faster than light, must also be open.

And in the battle, signs change too: Achilles has understood something not said in ordinary language. This chase, "I certainly know what the divine woman holds against me. She sends me through the air enough feathery kisses that come and whisper their sound of death−and her desire−in my ear."

The whole battle, with its breathless phrases, is a way of making their first love, that love that must pass through fire, very near death: they wound each other, beat each other down, lose their blood, their strength, but never their desire. Everything happens in the most heartrending exchange, as if they had to destroy something to get somewhere else together−that is their tragedy. Before they can bathe in each other's peace, they must mutually destroy the warrior within themselves, the enemy that society has inscribed in their memory; they must kill warring power to liberate loving power−something they are miraculously achieving. Because−they have had their day of eternal life. They pleasure in it. They are coming to it−

Unlike the curse that hangs over similar couples−whether the Homeric Achilles falling in love with Penthesileia, whom he has just killed, or Tancredi passionately reuniting with Clorinda the moment he destroyed her aspect as a warrior. No *jouissance* then; love is condemned in advance to lift its head only in death. The same hopelessness is recalled symbolically like this: a woman warrior is not a woman; it is a woman who has killed the woman in her. Only through death does she return to femininity. To sexual difference.

The heights are there: that is where love is made. Briefly but really. That is where what can happen only in a text by Kleist or in a dream happens. Or on the scene of other love, which is as rare as poetry. Every battle subsides. At the peak of violence, a higher order of time opens up: all emotions have gained velocity, and all desires are raised to the point where Achilles and Penthesileia invent an elsewhere. And for Penthesileia to be at peace, Achilles must move toward her. And Achilles does it. He becomes a flower. And she is the sun:

Penthesileia: Come now, sweet friend, come, put yourself at my feet. Come nearer — even nearer, very close to me. You are not afraid of me? You don't hate me, though I was able to conquer you? Tell me: are you afraid of the one who threw you into the dust?

Achilles (at her feet): As flowers fear a sunbeam.

Penthesileia: Good, well said. So from now on, see me as your sun. . . . Diana, my goddess, he is wounded.

Achilles: Just a scrape on the arm, see, nothing else.

Penthesileia: I beg of you, Pelides, don't believe, never believe that I ever had designs on your life. Yes, I was proud that this arm could get you. But the heart you see here was jealous of the dust welcoming your body when you fell.

Achilles: If you love me, don't talk about it anymore. You see, it is already healed.

Penthesileia: You forgive me then?

Achilles: With all my heart.

The fearsome Achilles stays still as a young dove around whose neck a child is tying a ribbon. He gives himself. She wants to take him: he lets himself be taken. She rules. He lets himself be tamed — but this is no longer the space of mastery. It is the ascent toward a new history, where, having exhausted all anguish and returned all war to its sterility, nothing will remain at stake between queen and king except knowing beauty over and over, no other law than body's insatiable desire.

Achilles: But who are you, descending toward me in an aureole as if the kingdoms of day gaped open? What shall I call you — when my soul asks itself: Whom do you belong to?

Penthesileia: If it asks such questions, just remember my face. Let these eyes and cheeks be the sweet name by which you think of me. In actuality, I give you this gold ring, and the sign it bears will protect you from all evil; just show it, and you will always be brought back to me. A ring, however, can be lost, a name, forgotten. If my name escaped you, if you lost my ring, would you forever recall my face? Can you still see it when you shut your eyes?

Achilles: It is in my memory like a line etched on a diamond.

Yet, it all ends up in the dust. For Kleist, Penthesileia is "at once all the suffering and all the glory of my soul." For horribly, suddenly, peace is torn apart, and weapons are brandished. Love is driven into the abyss. "Now they have knocked each other down and are on the ground, finishing their race to the end with their eyes." The end had never been more shining. This threat had never ceased to exist: how could the one desired be spared? When everything that had always detested desire is in league against it. And how could love succeed in keeping love alive?

On one side the law comes charging back with its two armies; Greeks and Amazons hurtle onto the love scene and tear it to shreds. The power of love must not start muddling clear oppositions. Torn away from each other, the two lovers will not succeed in reuniting, in returning to their heights. Elsewhere is still too fragile, too much of a miracle. God the Desire himself, or Kleist, has a hard time believing in it. The world is too jealous not to put love to death. For Kleist, *too much* is suffering's name. Only that which is excessive is beautiful. Only something that frees itself from all ties, that has no relation to what is known, that rushes out and is lost to sight. The beautiful is always just glimpsed, to become the adored, the too beautiful. Is it you? Yes, it is you. And in the interval between the violent recognition and the moment when you take a name (that, no matter how much your own it is, will bring you back among humans), the abyss is already opening. The no-place opens that will engulf what is, if not lost, at least necessarily always farther away, higher up.

The foreboding of Achilles at the feet of his beloved: "You are thinking of leaving me as well?" "I don't know, my love, don't ask me."

Kleist: "Oh Jesus! If only I can finish *Penthesileia*. Heaven must grant me this one wish, then it can do as it pleases." A heartbreaking paradox: if only I can finish my work so that it will live. yet if it is finished, *completed*, a part of me but departed from me, I lose it alive, living but separate; and if it does not leave me, it is incomplete, insufficient, and half-dead that I keep it. So it was with Achilles and Penthesileia. "Oh gods, you must accord me this victory—this joy—throwing the hero I so ardently desire at my feet in the dust. Grant me him alone, and I will consider you owe me no more of all the happiness allotted to my lifetime." To have him, for a moment, and within that moment an entire life. *Penthesileia*, in Kleist, is Achilles in Penthesileia, the work that must be torn from oneself, that one will die of if it does not live, and if it lives, one dies separated.

It is the most fragile part, the most beautiful, the most desired.

Then Penthesileia weakens, whereas Achilles doesn't: the age-old anguish, Kleist's anguish poisons her.

When Achilles comes back, against his own people—to return, to give himself back to her, having decided to undo the separation, to overcome the threat of death, to pay history the price it requires, having stripped everything away, ready for Penthesileia as she cannot be—he is already lost from sight, has lost her trust. This time she does not hear the message of love, persuaded by appearances, she fears she has gone too far, has been too much a woman. Turned into terror, into madness, multiplied to become a pack of fierce dogs, she "finishes off" the one who was too beautiful, who never left—except for a moment—. While the summit reverses into a bottomless pit of horror, while the savage killing of Achilles turns splendor into intolerable pain, already love is struggling against death. Mutilated by dogs—Penthesileia herself a devouring dog—Achilles dies without hate and within Penthesileia; understanding the error, with sympathy for love. "He drags himself through the crimson of his blood, he gently touches her cheek, he calls her: 'Penthesileia, my betrothed! What are you doing? Is this the Feast of Roses you promised me?' "

And she, Penthesileia, cuts through his armor, and she touches him, she finally takes her shining bird, she loves it mortally, it is not a man that has come in to her bare hands, it is more the very body of love than any man, and its voice as well, which she cruelly makes her own, and she sinks her teeth into the white breast, Oxus and Sphinx on the right, she on the left. Yes, that is their feast gone mad, the feast they devote themselves to desperately. To which he does not refuse to give himself.

She hurls herself wildly toward the end of love; eating Achilles, incorporating him, devouring him with kisses. The space of metaphor has collapsed, fantasies are carried out. Why not? Farther and farther, she herself now able to face the impossible. "There are so many women who hang on their lover's neck and say: I love you so much—oh so much I could eat you up. And the lunatics have scarcely said the word before they are disgusted. But I, my dearest, didn't do that. When I hung around your neck, it was in order to keep my promise—yes—word for word. And you see—I was not as crazy as it seemed." Still further along, where other weddings and another triumph are celebrated: (no more weapons, no more anguish, no more law, no law at all, no threat, no enslaving duty) I no longer follow the law, I am going with him, the one who is there. Is it possible? Without violence? Without killing herself, is she able to stay with Achilles, to become the one who is there?

No more need for arrows, she throws them away. No more need for a dagger; she takes it from her belt. No more need for war. For now she is where love is no longer subjected to failure, where separation separates no more, where blindness no longer blinds.

She goes down into her own breast where the torn Achilles is: "I descend into my breast." She tells the truth, she is following him, she goes where love, unstoppable love can go. Her own body, her own flesh falls for him, for her, entirely wound, and she extracts pure metal from her breast-become-earth, "then I take it to the eternal anvil of hope, and I hone it, I sharpen it into a dagger and finally I hold my bosom to this dagger. There. There. There. And once more." And all is well.

Yes, all is well, beyond History. Where Achilles is comprehended within Penthesileia, whom he comprehends beyond any calculation.

And Kleist—also—dies, from being Penthesileia, from not being able to be Penthesileia without dying,[20] as Penthesileia had to die from being too close to the shadow of the law, from having been afraid of the old ghosts, from having seen life itself get by within reach, within sight, from having brushed against it, from having felt the caress of its flaming hair, from not being able to hold onto it.

How love a woman without encountering death? A woman who is neither doll nor corpse nor dumb nor weak. But beautiful, lofty, powerful, brilliant?

Without history's making one feel its law of hatred?

So the betrothed fall back into dust. Vengeance of castration, always at work, and which the wounded poet can surmount only in fiction.

But on another scene, the jealousy machine breaks down. If I evoke it here too rapidly, it is to plead the case of the Strong and bear it away. There has been a victory of love in history: Shakespeare, who was neither man nor woman but a thousand persons, perpetuates the explosive brilliance of this "inimitable life"—as did Plutarch in his splendid "Life of Antony." So I will only be resounding an echo: the *Gaiety* of the royal couple and its inspired creativity are perfectly sung by texts that should be reread.

The life of Antony—together with Cleopatra—a vision of Cleopatra—some of Antony's words show their scope in a flash.

Cleopatra: I have dreamed of an emperor whose name was Antony. Oh! If only I could sleep again to see again his equal.

His face was like the heavens; the sun and moon shone there, lighting up this little ball, the earth.

His step spanned the ocean; he spread out his arms and shadowed the world; his voice when he spoke to a friend, recalled the music of the spheres; but, in menace, shook the air like thunder. His bounty had no winter; it was a continual autumn growing rich with his gifts. His delicious games seemed those of dolphins lifting waves on their backs; diadems and crowns were eager attendants in his retinue; he let fall islands and continents from the folds of his toga like pieces of gold.

Does such a man exist, *could* he even exist, tell me, one such as the one I dreamed?

But just his being, that he could have been, that is what surpasses the dream and the power of imagining. Nature, for her creation, envies the dream's inexhaustible material, but in conceiving an Antony she outwits the dream, and the dream withdraws in defeat.

Antony: Let Rome be swallowed up by the Tiber; let the orderly empire's immense vault collapse! My space is here. Kingdoms are made of clay; our muddy earth nourishes man and beast indifferently. The nobility of life (he kisses her) when a couple such as ours love each other, two such perfectly matched beings!

The one equal to the other, the one without equal for the other, they have found the secret of embodying Still More. Still More—Encore—Never Enough—though it explodes time and tears a hundred living days from the heart of a minute, still it is nothing, still not enough.

The feisty queen, to whom everything is becoming—scolding, laughing, crying—at every instant another face, at each breath a passion, flesh struggling with a desire for more love, more life, more pleasure, at every moment, the queen with ten tongues; she spoke them all,

> for her beauty alone, according to what they say, was not so incom-
> parable that there might well have been ones as beautiful as she, nor
> such that she enraptured at once those who looked at her; but to fre-
> quent her conversation was so pleasant that it was impossible to escape
> its hold, and along with her beauty, the charm of her talk, the sweet-
> ness and kindness of her nature, that flavored everything she said or
> did, there was a sting which pierced to the quick; and if beyond that,
> there was a great pleasure simply in the sound of her voice and in her
> way of speaking, it was because her tongue was like a musical instru-
> ment with several stops and several registers, which she easily turned
> into whatever language pleased her, to such an extent that she spoke to
> few barbarous nations by interpreter, but she herself replied, at least
> for the most part, whether to the Ethiopians, Arabs, Troglodytes,
> Hebrews, to the Syrians, Medes, and the Parthians, and to many
> others whose languages she had learned; whereas many of her
> predecessors, the kings of Egypt, had scarcely been able to learn
> Egyptian and there had been some who even forgot their Macedonian.
> Thus she captivated Antony with her love. (Plutarch, "Life of
> Antony")

And she also made all the tongues of all the parts of the body speak, and she knew also all the songs of the blood. Wise and innocent, art and nature compos- ing in her the inexhaustible. In the eyes of everyone, populace, kings, enemies or friends, she is the enigma: such a woman, source of beauty, more than plenty—running over. She overfills without saturating. Scarcely has she satisfied before she gives another thing to desire for which she invents another satis- faction.

She is always capable of more, herself the stir. She is extravagance and abundance.

The Romans and Egyptians say that other women cloy the appetite of those nourished by them. "But she makes hungry where most she satisfies." Yet this rare Egyptian, while nourishing the lover famishes him. He who has tasted her, the unequaled one, is forever hungry for her, and she keeps him marvelously, fetes him sumptuously, and every day surpasses the unsurpassable; then there is no longer a place in life for regret. Everything is yet to come, aspiration, vitality. The more you have, the more you give, the more you are, the more you give, the more you have. Life opens up and stretches to infinity. And Antony is not left behind. Although he might have a hard time keeping up with Cleopatra in the realm of invention, he wins in another generosity—the one that for a man consists of daring to strip himself of power and glory and to love and admire a woman enough to take pride happily in rivaling with her in passion.

"And they formed a club for themselves that they called *Amime to bioi*, which is to say, "the inimitable life," a club others would be unable to imitate, celebrating each other in turn, where they spent so much that it exceeded all limits and all reasonable measure."

Right away, moreover, they set themselves outside of ordinary human time, in their admirable relation to the question of age—usually so hard; for both are past youth, both have fully lived, several epochs, other loves. Both of them, knowing this, laughing at themselves, set out anew, beginning their story where most people finish it. Seeing each other—him, black curls mixed with white hair, her, dried skin, wrinkled—as they are: eternal fire and breath.

O thou day o' the world,
Chain mine arm'd neck; leap thou, attire and all,
Through proof of harness to my heart, and there
Ride on the pants triumphing.
Cleopatra: Lord of lords!
O infinite virtue, com'st thou smiling from
The world's great snare uncaught?
Antony: My nightingale,
We have beat them to their beds. What, girl! though grey
Do something mingle with our younger brown, yet ha' we
A brain that nourishes our nerves, and can
Get goal for goal of youth. (Shakespeare, *Antony and Cleopatra*)

Day of this world, light, source of the visible. And he, noblest of men, the crown of the universe, its sense.

By the fire of each facet of these diamond-moments, Shakespeare sparks all the discoveries of this Love unparalleled in History: the one is the source of the other. The one makes or really unmakes, undoes the other.

Is that me, that little girl flying without wings, head down, curls
sweeping the air and feet held by some invisible grasp, the queen with
three crowns and the trappings of Isis? Is it I, when at the thought of
Octavia—because she kept you far from our bed, had all the govern-

ments and thrones been thrown at my feet, and all Asia added to Egypt to spread my power, all the queen's names got away from me, — and a drop of water in the old Nile is what I wanted to be? Is that me, without retinue, without populace, without kingdoms, without outside, who is beating within the bosom of the world? O my husband-mother, how happy I am in your breast! I no longer recognize myself! But now I know myself.

I remember, when kings like jostling children ran to ask you: what is your command? and your name was enough, this magical warcry, to win victories for you in your absence. But all that was nothing! The empires returned to clay. — How much do you love me? Can a love that can be reckoned call itself love? — The Parthians' land, do you want it? If you do, I will give you Media and a hundred other peoples and their lands, but that is nothing — three lives and in each life three other lives, in one smile from your lips. Smile at me! — I want to go to the frontiers: what of you is mine and what does not belong to me? Of your three beds and of your three stories, what part do you give me? I was able to think that. Although surrounded by kings and followed by peoples whose eyes reflected my splendor, I have wept, as Egypt I have envied the drop that is lost in the breast of the Nile. Do you remember? But that was nothing. As Egypt, and you as Antony, we have deranged history's thought and overturned the order of the world. All of the Orient ran through our fingers as our entwinement gave birth to another Nile. To the frontiers! Let's keep going. The space of a kiss, eternity's tongue between our lips. The empire is swallowed up beneath our body. That is where we have given history a lesson it is not about to recover from! But all that you know. Thirty years in three minutes, as in a play by Shakespeare, that is what we have assigned history to do with time that is swollen with pomposity. And to recount three minutes of our body when we peak, thirty years of poetical work will not suffice. As Egypt I already knew that and already I was thinking of the monuments of our eternity. And you too, you knew it. — I want to go to the end and know the limit — I have been able to say that, I remember with pain. — Let's go . . . hunt and if you believe you see another land, I will open it for you under a sky still un-born! (H. C.)

She had to be from the Orient to be so lofty, so free, so much the mistress of herself and *recognized* as such by her contemporaries. She had to be foreign. The "great women" who pass through history or the historical imagination of the western side of the world come, can come only from an elsewhere one expects always to be holding a surprise — good or bad. Queen, entirely radiant, woman, on the condition that she rule from the other side of the world. In Rome, the woman, no matter how high above the common, bows her head before the venerable man, as wife or sister of — king, chief, master — and, jealous or devoted, she follows, she serves. Thus the perfect Octavia, excellent sister and cut out to be an admirable wife—loyal, worthy of an Antony cast as "husband"—but as one is "recast" by the absolute obedience of one's subordinate.

But in the Orient, the Impossible is born; she who is incomprehensible, who exceeds the imagination, who rewards the most powerful desire of the most powerful of men, she who has all, and who is more than all, no existence can contain her, no man has been able to equal her in radiance, in the length of ardor, in passion, yet the greatest ones have adored her, have approached her, she has not fled, it is herself in flesh and in reality who welcomes him, it is herself without making use of the glamour of absence who shows herself, unveiled, given to touch, to taste, but no man has ever equaled her. Except, at the end of her life, Antony.

Unique, greater than than everyone else, for not only is she beauty—that is nothing—but she is also infinite intelligence, completely applied to making life, to making love, to make: to invent, to create, from one emotion to draw out ten thousand forms of beauty, from one joy ten thousand games, from one pain an immense increase of passion. She is life made woman. She is woman made Art: each moment of her story with Antony is created, at the same time ardently lived and immediately multiplied by incessant tensions, transformations, recreations that open and echo the thousands of scenes in which love can infinitely inscribe its need of no limit. All her art in the famous staging of her appearance to Antony's eyes. Entrance that has not ceased repeating itself over the centuries. (Plutarch, Shakespeare, T. S. Eliot—the texts are still mirroring this reflection.)

She knew how to *give herself* to being seen, to bestow unforgettable beauty on seeing, in a representation whose moments rhythm the awakening of desire, its blooming and its delighted satisfaction. Cleopatra's intelligence and strength are remarkably shown in the work she accomplishes—the work of love—on distance, parting, separation: creating a gap only to fill it; never tolerating that a separation wound the loving body.

Thus, priming fascination, by producing herself in an admirable artifice, as if she were herself her work, her painting, her motionless idol, offered, inaccessible—to touch—to description—presenting herself enframed, gliding, in a drift, rising, like beauty with no beginning, passing, like a dream before a speechless people, who beseech the gaze that darts out and never crosses to the shore along which they crowd, blocked by the separating river.

I will tell you: the barge she sat in, dazzling as a throne, set fire to the water; the poop was beaten gold; purple the sails and so perfumed that the winds fainted with love over them; the oars were silver which rhythmically beat the waves to the sound of flutes and made them follow faster beneath the pleasure of their strokes. As for her, her appearance put any description to flight: she lay beneath a pavilion of cloth of gold, even more beautiful than the image of Venus where imagination shames reality; beside her, darling, dimpled boys, like smiling cupids, waved variegated fans, whose breeze seemed to quicken the bloom of her delicate cheeks as if at the same time what they spread both burned and cooled.

Her maids, like Nereids and like mermaids, awaited orders from her eyes, bending over her like decorations. Behind, one would say it was a mermaid at the helm, whose silken lines one saw tighten into prompt service at the touch of her flower fingers. From all the barge an invisible perfumed air exhales, with which the nearest wharves throbbing with the people spilled there by the city, are inebriated. Everyone is running toward her, deserting the public place where Antony is enthroned; he calls but his voice dies out; and if a vacuum were possible, even the air would have left, gone to gaze at Cleopatra itself, leaving a gap in nature.

The barge lands.

And organizing the look's route, by degrees, by a series of postponements, of detours, of approximations that excite and suspend and make souls spin around the fire.

Fabulous fire on the brims, of the river, of the barge, overbrimming of details, of accessories that raise tension and fever to the point of divinity.

Then she, immobile and apparently indifferent, seemingly passive, yields to the looks, which she calls, which she takes.

Separation, reparation. But to Antony, she comes. She does not leave him on the shore, she reaches the land, unites with him, and for thus having opened her to desire, she rewards him, fetes him. Nurses him: she breeds the need to recreate incessantly.

Abundance of fantasies and metaphors that inscribe the dialectic of this desire in figures of nourishment heavenly foods, meats, wines. Everything exchanged between the two boundless lovers is received as the child receives mother's milk: on Antony's word, Cleopatra's ear breakfasts, and that is the right way. We are far from object "a," from the fatality of its absence, from its evasions that only sustain desire by default.

Profusion, energy, exuberance. That is what she is. To be sure, she has at her disposition material reserves from whose magnificence her generosity can draw. Absolute queen of several countries, she can give more than anyone. But also, all the splendor of the life that Antony and Cleopatra make together is commensurate with the fabulous grandeur of their investments, material, fleshly, symbolic, spiritual: not only do they have everything, strength, power – almost absolute – but it is nothing. They do not take all this for something, they reduce it, with a kiss, to the nothing that it has never ceased to be, save in the eyes of beings who know nothing of love, that is to say, everybody. At no moment do all these glories, all these treasures, for which men make peoples kill each other, make them bat an eye.

They have — from the moment Antony saw Cleopatra coming to him — abandoned the minuscule old world, the planet — the shell with its thrones and rattles, its intrigues, its wars, its rivalries, its tournaments of the phallus, so grotesquely represented by the game of penis-check played by the imperialist superpowers of the triumvirate, with the mean solemnity that makes history. And with a leap, it is toward the new land they go to look for an entirely different life. There, all powers are employed, not in diplomacy, or in politics (with which they have no other relation than that which is tragically imposed upon them, because they begin their eternal story right in the middle of an old history that does not let itself just be forgotten like that) but employed to struggle against all the forces of death and to change all the ancient and reductive means of thinking life that would threaten to enclose it, slow it down, deaden it.

How can the wound be closed? How can an economy be created from the abysses that time and history open up in such stormy lives? How make his own, her own, the gaping, the separation, the wrench? When the world and its business wrests me from your breast, how bandage the split? Octavia, the good wife, "will pray" for Antony. But Cleopatra, by force of loving will, masters the lying space, fills the hole in love with her flesh, her extended senses, and however far he may be, it is still in her that he is, that he makes himself felt:

> O Charmion, where do you think he is now? Standing . . . maybe lying down . . . no, he is walking . . . or is he on horseback? O fortunate horse who bears the weight of Antony! Fearless! Flag not! Do you understand whom you are carrying? The one on whom rests half the weight of the world as on Atlas's shoulder. I hear him now speaking, murmuring: "Where, then, is my serpent of the old Nile?" That is what he calls me. . . . Ah! I revel in too delicious a poison.

Truly they have discovered how to suckle together at the wonderful resource of sanctity. Not that they are saints, humble and submissive. On the contrary: human, fallible, tormented, often torn, beaten, jealous, violent, excessive; the signs of weakness are not lacking, but they are hollows between the always higher waves. How high! Vertigo! I am falling! What importance is it if I fall? You pick me up. If she bends, he sets her straight; if he gives in, it will not be long before she recalls his greatness to him. Attached, drawing each other up a difficult ascent, uneven but triumphant. Because Antony is bound to her, Cleopatra's flight by sea makes Antony, altering sail, tack and run so that he is nearly dying from it, being lost and losing her, wanting to hate her, no longer being able to see her.

> *Antony*: Eros! Can you still see me? . . .
> Sometimes, we see a cloud be like a dragon, a lion, a bear, sometimes a wandering vapor offers the image of a tower, a castle, of a crenellated rock, a high mountain, or of a blue promontory covered

with trees, that our deceived eye sees quavering in the air. Have you
sometimes seen these dusky ghosts? . . .

Just now it was a horse, then fleeing like thought, it is no longer
anything; it melts, resorbs, like water in water. . . .

Eros, dear good child, your master is now no more real than these
appearances; here, I am still Antony, but I can no longer keep this
visible form, my child. I went to war for Egypt, for this queen; I
thought I had her heart, for she had mine . . . this heart which when
I could still make use of it, annexed more than a million now lost
hearts, lost. . . . She, Eros, she has played Caesar's game and
tricked me so that my own glory becomes the enemy's
trump. . . . No! don't cry! no, sweet Eros. One still has oneself
when one wants to end oneself.

To the point of being in mourning for his own image. Cleopatra, then, is only
the antiqueen, the Egyptian, the caster of spells: "Come to this! . . . All the
hearts that yapped and wagged at my heels, expecting their food from me, are
going to lick Caesar's feet. They all are carrying incense to his blossoming; the
aging cedar is losing his bark, he who once made shade for all. I am betrayed.
Treacherous soul of the Egyptian, the mortal enchantress whose look armed or
disarmed me, whose breast made my crown, my heaven." She is no more than
the sorceress, a true "gypsy" who strung him along: "at fast and loose she has
beguiled me to the heart of loss." At the game of "guess—if it is knotted or
unknotted," she will have tricked him, led him to the heart of loss.

Is that the end? But where love is the only value, as Antony announced with
his first words, there is no loss that may not be as quickly reversed in victory.
Deeper they descend, tragically deeper, so they can turn abyss into summit. The
nearer death is, the more intense is life, the greater the sorrow, the more
luminous the joy that bursts from it. Nothing, even death, can separate the two
beings in whom life regards and pursues itself. Even death? If there were such.
But it cannot take place for them. And then unwinds, under the staggering display of Shakespeare's language as if beneath a reflecting canopy, a subtle and
glorious erotic agony. Antony does not speak false. "I want to be the bridegroom
of my death, and to run to it as to the lover's bed." For this couple's miracle is
to have captured death at last, to have appropriated the enemy, to have put death
into their enchanted bed, to not be going to die without knowing who awaits in
the bed to which they are going, she, he, unseparated; to have substituted forever for the unlivable absence an absolute embrace. Death, if Cleopatra is there,
is only a threshold open to the other place: "I am coming my queen! —Eros!—
wait for me! On meadows sown with daffodils, hand in hand we will go. Our
passionate approach will make the shades stare. They will leave everything to
follow us. Dido and her lover Aeneas will envy our cortege."

Death? Wedding. And facing him, Cleopatra—having taken refuge in a pyramid — tomb — in which still living, she prepares her departure for a sublime marriage. And love wants them to have their last fete. A beautiful celebration, no one will ever have so sweetly, so ardently written, lived, attained it. It is a fete that unfolds in sorrow, in adoration, the last, the first: Antony, in order to run to his lover death, thinking that Cleopatra already awaits him on the shades' side — has dealt himself the final blow. But Cleopatra is still on the side of time — perched on top of this pyramid, at the point of the phallus in which she resides, which she will make her home forever. And Antony, at the end of his strength, is carried there to the foot of the monument, where the loving woman, one last time, calls him, hails him, makes him come. And breath to breath, scanning an embrace that resembles in its panting all their nights of love, she hoists him up — come, come, come — oh quick, quick, I can't hold back anymore, his soul is escaping — what strange pleasure, what a crazy way to make love, how heavy my lord is, the women are pulling him, come, another try, oh come, come, come! are bringing him to her, and welcome, welcome! Die where you have lived, my kisses revive you, I am dying, Egypt, I am dying — here beneath my lips his breath leaves him, no don't leave him — I can no more — under her lips he yields to love, which no longer leaves him. To die at the top, never to have lost her except to return and be in her arms, to lose breath so that she may take it in.

Nothing is left for her then but to rejoin him, always by the same route, strewn with the signs of their amorous body; as he died in a magnificent erection, she hastens to the wedding bed in a gesture that says also that eros is the name of their couple, giving her breast to an asp: "Peace! Peace! Don't you see my baby at my breast, who sucking puts the nurse to sleep? Sweet as balm, gentle as air, as charming. . . . O Antony! Wait I am going to take you too (she puts another asp to her)."

Even in death, she is the one who nourishes, and nourishing is nourished by love.

And far from kingdoms, from caesars, from brawls, from the cravings of penis and sword, from the unnameable "goods" of this world, far from show and self-love, in harmony with each other, in accord, they live still.

NOTES

1. All Derrida's work traversing-detecting the history of philosophy is devoted to bringing this to light. In Plato, Hegel, and Nietzsche, the same process continues: repression, repudiation, distancing of woman; a murder that is mixed up with history as the manifestation and representation of masculine power.

2. "For Anatole's Tomb" (Seuil, p. 138). This is the tomb in which Mallarmé keeps his son from death and watches over him as his mother.

3. "She only awakens at love's touch and before that moment she is only a dream. But in this dream existence one can distinguish two stages: first love dreams of her, then she dreams of love." Thus Kierkegaard's *Seducer* dreams.

4. The pleasure is preliminary, Freud says. This is a "truth" but only a partial one. It is a point of view, in fact, coming from and upheld by the masculine Imaginary, to the extent that the masculine Imaginary is shaped by the threat of castration.

5. My father, Sephardic—Spain—Morocco—Algeria—my mother, Ashkenazy—Austria—Hungary—Czechoslavakia (her father) and Spain (her mother) passing by chance through a Paris that was short-lived.

6. Women: at that time I wasn't thinking about them. At first, occupying the stage in a way that I could plainly see, the battle to death was the battle pitting colonial power against its victims. Beyond that I perceived that it was the imperialist result of capitalist structure and that it intensified the class struggle by deepening it and making it more monstrous and inhuman: the exploited were not even "workers" but, with racism's assistance, something worse—subhuman; and the universe could pretend to obey "natural" laws. War was on the horizon, partially concealed from me. I wasn't in France. I didn't see betrayal and collaboration with my own eyes. We were living under Vichy: I perceived its effects without knowing their causes. I had to guess why my father couldn't do his work, why I couldn't go to school, et cetera. And I had to guess why, as a little white girl informed me, "all Jews are liars."

7. *Aeneid* 1. 4. 320–65.

8. Freud's thesis is the following: when the Oedipus complex disappears, the *superego* becomes its heir. The moment a boy starts to feel the threat of castration, he begins to overcome the Oedipus complex, with the help of a very harsh superego. For the boy, the Oedipus complex is a primary formation—his first love object is the mother, as it is for the girl. But the girl's history is inevitably constituted under the pressure of a superego that is less harsh: because she is castrated, her superego will not be as strong. She never completely overcomes the Oedipus complex. The feminine Oedipus complex is not a primary formation. The pre-oedipal attachment to the mother entails a difficulty for the girl from which Freud says, she never recovers. It is having to change objects (to love the father) along the way—a painful conversion, which is accompanied by a supplementary renunciation: the passage from pre-oedipal sexuality to "normal" sexuality supposes the abandonment of the clitoris for the vagina. In the terms of this "destiny," women have a reduced symbolic activity: they have nothing to lose, to win, or to defend.

9. J.-J. Bachofen (1815–87), a Swiss historian of "gynocracy," "historian" of a nonhistory. His aim is to show that the various peoples (Greek, Roman, Hebrew) have passed through an age of "gynocracy," the reign of the Mother, before arriving at patriarchy. This age can only be deduced, for it remains without history. This situation, which was humiliating for men, has been repressed, according to Bachofen's theory, and covered by historical oblivion. And he attempts (particularly in *Das Mutterrecht* [*Mother Right*] 1861) to make an archeology of the matriarchal system, which is very beautiful, beginning with a reading of the first historical texts on the level of the symptom, of what is unsaid in them. Gynocracy, he says, is organized materialism.

10. There are encoded paradigms projecting the robot couple man/woman, as seen by contemporary societies that are symptomatic of a consensus of repetition. See the UNESCO issue of 1975, which is devoted to the International Woman's Year.

11. *Prénoms de Personne* [*Nobody's First Names*], Cixous, Editions du Seuil: "Les Comtes de Hoffmann" ["Tales of Hoffmann"], pp. 112ff.

12. See *Nouvelle Revue de Psychoanalyse* no. 7, *Bisexualité et difference des sexes* (Spring 1973).

13. The home manager, according to the definition of the English word "husband," is the "servant of the house," called the "mari."

14. Nietzsche, Aphorism 315, *The Gay Science*.

15. Is it just chance that it is something of woman, a dismembering feminine, which torments the I/Me who is not/is born only to pursue itself, split by Valéry, infinitely dispersed, never really put back together again in the Young Fate?

16.   *Vor dem Gesetz* [*Before the Law*], in Kafka's *Parables and Paradoxes* (Schocken, 1975), is also the key to the end of *The Trial*, in which the riddle is revealed in an "interminable" explication. The necessity for K.'s death is inscribed within it.

17.   Engels reconstitutes the phases of this "revolution" in *The Origin of the Family, Private Property and the State*.

18.   This is Nietzsche's observation. (*Origin of Tragedy*)

19.   Letter to his sister, Ulrike.

20.   In 1811 he actually "descends into his breast," where, watched over by his love, lives a population that is too beautiful. *Penthesileia* dates from 1806 to 1808, when he was in his early 30s.

Exchange

Incautiously we have accepted the challenge of engaging in the following exchange so that the differences, which we certainly perceive less well than would a third person and which have (unconsciously) been at work in this volume, may be apparent. So that by listening to each other, a process of reasoning will emerge that will lead in a direction which, separately, we would not perhaps have taken. And so that we could confront the risks of a dual discourse that does not proceed without reciprocal change, censorship or self-censorship.

Some of our positions hardened immediately. They were also exaggerated by the oral format, which rushes and simplifies concepts. Divergences became entrenched and investments marked. We took a free course together and chose not to "choose." These two parts are the result: one takes off from our social practice, which is teaching, the other from hysterical engagement. We come back together on the ideological battlefield. Constantly and deliberately each subject overflowed and was diverted. So we have not "written" but have let through, trans-scribed clashes and collisions.

A Woman Mistress

If the position of mastery culturally
comes back to men, what will become of
(our) femininity when we find ourselves
in this position?
  When we use a master-discourse?
  Mastery-knowledge, mastery-power:
  ideas demanding an explanation from us.
                                        Other discourses?

C: Let's start out with the difference between our discourses. Yours is a writing
halfway between theory and fiction. Whereas my discourse is, or tries to be,
more demonstrative and discursive, following the most traditional method of
rhetorical demonstration. That doesn't bother me; I accept that method: it is the
method of teaching and of transmitting ideas. We see there can be two women
in the same space who are *differently* engaged, speaking of almost exactly the
same things, investing in two or three different kinds of discourse and going
from one to the other and then on to the spoken exchange.
H: I distrust the identification of a subject with a single discourse. First, there
is the discourse that suits the occasion. I use rhetorical discourse, the discourse
of mastery, orally, for example, with my students, and obviously I do it on purpose; it is a refusal on my part to leave organized discourse entirely in men's
power. I never fell for that sort of bait.
C: There is no reason at all not to steal that discourse from men. . . . Besides,

that doesn't mean anything; we don't steal anything at all—we are within the same cultural system. Granted it is a phallocentric cultural system but trying to make another in advance is unfounded; perhaps we can think that, hypothetically, one day there might be another system but to will that it suddenly be there—at any minute—is utopian.

H: There will not be *one* feminine discourse, there will be thousands of different kinds of feminine words, and then there will be the code for general communication, philosophical discourse, rhetoric like now but with a great number of subversive discourses in addition that are somewhere else entirely. That is what is going to happen. Until now women were not speaking out loud, were not writing, not creating their tongues—plural, but they will create them, which doesn't mean that the others (either men or tongues) are going to die off.

C: In any case, there is no reason for women not to assume the transmission of knowledge. The term causing a problem is the word *mastery* in the phrase "discourse of mastery." If inspired by Lacan, it refers to a relationship between mastery and university, which is such that the master's discourse—from the point of view of its political and economic power—is transferred onto and shapes any discourse dealing with knowledge to be transmitted.

H: I think one has a hard time escaping the discourse of mastery when using, for example, as a teacher, discourse I'll call "objective"; by that I mean a discourse that does not involve an easily located subject of enunciation, that speaks at that particular moment not just in the name of but as universal knowledge itself.

The law does not exist.

In the little chapter "The Dawn of Phallocentrism," I took, on the one hand, a text by Freud on the origin of patriarchy, and I compared it with a Kafka text called *Before the Law*. It is a story that is both extraordinarily clear and as unclear as the question that is its crux: "What is the law?" There is a peasant who was an honest man; he was the only one who could have gone to the other side and seen the law—seen, therefore, that it doesn't exist. Because the door could be opened only for him. He didn't go in there. How could he have gone "there" since the law that doesn't exist was himself? All that was needed was a door and a doorkeeper; he was the one who constantly fabricated the law, and he never saw that the law did not exist.

C: Do you know what that story makes me think of? The mirror stage—the fact that the chimpanzee looks behind the mirror to see who is there, another chimpanzee, itself, or nobody—whereas man identifies and constitutes himself with the mirror. It reflects his image to him, *fixes* it as a subject and subjects it to the law, to the symbolic order, to language, and does it in a way that is both inalienable and alienating. The law exists.

H: Except that the chimpanzee actually is the chimpanzee and we are the result of our relationship to the door. What is the discourse of mastery? There is one. It is what calls itself "the law" but is presented as "the open door" in precisely such a way that you never go to the other side of the door, that you never go to see "what is mastery?" So you never will know that there is no law and no mastery. That there is no master. The paradox of mastery is that it is made up of a sort of complex ideological secretion produced by an infinite quantity of doorkeepers.

Mastery ensures the transmission of knowledge.

C: I wouldn't say that in the same terms. It has to be said straight out: for me mastery is fundamental and necessary. I don't particularly think one can transmit certain knowledges — *the*knowledges — except through mastery. That involves everything having to do with democratic transmission. Paradoxically, information contained in a system of knowledge cannot be transmitted outside of mastery. It is dependent on the "law" of the Symbolic, like the doorkeeper, like the honest man. Subjectivity can be taken in, deluded, by it, of course, but it can also find there an explicit coherence, a certain number of connections shared by all, so that when the statement is transmitted, the receiver has access to it either immediately or through mediation.

Transmitting.

What is at stake is connection and consistency. I know perfectly well you are not about to tell me that truth sticks to what is consistent and that you are going to call into question the existence of other consistencies. As for me, the discourse of mastery exists; of course, it is ambivalent and full of traps as far sub-

---

Culture, which is superstructure, must not be considered as a thing, a good, the result of an evolution, a stock converted into intellectual luxury, but rather as a factor in evolution (which cannot be solely a factor of income) and especially as a process. (Brecht, *Writings on Politics and Society*)

jectivity is concerned: subjectivity finds the positions of psychoanalyst and professor to be almost equally untenable. But despite that, it is through the discourse of mastery that knowledge of the analytic act *is transmitted*. I am not talking about the rest of it.

H: I can't go along with you there. Your position, which I understand, disposes of a problem that is fundamental and primary for me: how is one to think and struggle against what mastery inevitably entails as a form of repression? A mastery's contradiction, if it isn't thought differently, is that, far from transmitting knowledge, it makes it still more inaccessible, makes it sacred. That is Law's dirty trick. Only those people who already have a relationship of mastery, who already have dealings with culture, who are saturated with culture, have ever dared have access to the discourse that the master gives.

C: Now, in this social and cultural system. But certainly you can conceive of societies structured differently, in which the conditions of access to knowledge would be profoundly different.

H: That's why I believe one has to take a thousand precautions. At the present time, it is impossible for me to use the term "mastery" as it is currently used

---

One can say that general culture is what permits the individual to fully feel his solidarity with other men, in space and in time, with the men of his generation as well as with the generations which have preceded him and those yet to follow. To be cultivated, then, is to have received and constantly developed an initiation to different forms of human activity independently of those which correspond to a profession, so as to be able to enter into contact and communion with other men. (Paul Langevin)

because of the repression it implies. Does someone already allied with a certain knowledge want to communicate it to others? Why does one want to communicate it to others? It's the usual question—"what's the use?" Does it serve any purpose? I would say yes, obviously, it has to serve—not serve itself and not serve a superior cause, et cetera. There is a drawback we all know as teachers, which is the almost insurmountable difficulty of occupying a position of mastery.

Giving.

The one who is in the master's place, even if not the master of a knowledge, is in a position of power. The only way to bar that is to execute the master, kill him, eliminate him, so that what he has to say can get through, so that he himself is not the obstacle, so it will be *given*. Something on the order of a personal gift, a subjective one.

C: I don't like that term—personal gift, it tends toward oblation and sacrifice. . . .

What one knows. . . .
What one doesn't know.

H: Giving isn't sacrificing. The person who transmits has to be able to function on the level of knowledge without knowing. I'm not at all referring to Socrates now. Just that one should be in a state of weakness, as we all are, and that *it be evident*. That one have the guts to occupy the position one has no right to occupy and that one show precisely how and why one occupies it. I set my sights high: I demand that love struggle within the master against the will for power.

Mistress woman or woman master?

C: Just the same it will be mastery. When I hear *mastery*, I think of the present meaning of the word, which must come more or less from Hegel. Mastery, in Lacan, is inseparable from something fundamentally bound up with woman, with the hysteric, her referential figure. The hysteric puts the master and the academic, both power and knowledge, in check. What's more, this conjunction "power-knowledge" and this division between the two seem to me to be on the order of myth, with its mythic power and arbitrary nature. Admitting these terms for what they are, would that mean that the hysteric and, hence, somehow, the woman does not have the right to move in the direction of mastery or academics or perhaps even toward the position of analyst? She has only one position, she "puts in check." That is inadmissible—grotesque. But the way you have defined a knowledge expounded with limits and holes is no longer, in effect, entirely mastery. It does correspond just the same to what I meant just now, that is to say, a discourse that—for its own subject, for what concerns knowledge—offers some connections, punctuations, scansions, demonstrations—through which the data of knowledge are transmitted. I see no way to conceive of a cultural system in which there would be no transmission of knowledge in the form of a coherent statement. Right now, for social and ideological reasons, this coincides with a position of mastery.

H: I don't know what you call "right now"; it has always been like that in our western societies. In our own history, the one we are still reacting to, that is what has happened and keeps on happening.

C: That's not entirely true. There is a history of mastery, for us among others, that runs through the history of national education, via the major schools of teacher instruction, via Jules Ferry, via the struggles for a state school, et cetera. And I really think that, from women's point of view, there have been some rays of light in that history and some moments when women had mastery. Not that they have had economic mastery, of course, but it has come about that they had symbolic management of an intellectual activity. An example would be the time of the trouvères and troubadours . . . at the same time, what's more, as a mythology of the "inspiring woman" opposing this mastery.

I believe that *cultural* oppression of women coincides with economic evolution and is accentuated by the development of capitalism. Think of the "précieuses," who are not at all well known or well liked. There have sometimes been women in possession of knowledge.

H: There has always been a split between those who are in possession of knowledge and culture and who occupy a position of mastery and the others. I don't rule out women's having been on that side, but even then they are not in the masters' position. I am not saying that knowledge is always associated with power, or that it must be: but that is its danger. And I am not saying women are never on the side of knowledge-power. But in the majority of cases in their history, one finds them aligned with no-knowledge or knowledge-without-power.

C: By *power* you don't mean political power, you mean that scrap, that reflection

---

Common public instruction for all citizens is to be created and organized and to be free with regard to those fields of instruction which are indispensable to all men. ([French] Constitution of 1791)

The institutions of instruction in their entirety were opened up to the people free of charge, and, at the same time they were cleared of any interference by the Church and the State. Thus, not only was instruction made accessible for everyone, but knowledge itself was set free of the chains which class prejudices and governmental power had laid on it. (Karl Marx, *On the Commune*)

of political power that the teacher exercises metaphorically and imaginarily. What exactly is the teacher's "power"?

H: Where is the division between "powers"? It's impossible to separate them. I believe teaching goes hand in hand with ideology.

C: I don't think so. If that was true, there would be no reason at all to struggle for a truly democratic transmission of knowledge – on the contrary! It is true that whole segments of knowledge are "trapped" in the dominant ideology, but still they are conveyed. There are, for example, Marxist historians; they teach history in a "history" program. It is not because they are in a position of mastery within the teaching structure as it is now that the *content* of their knowledge goes hand in hand with ideology. The division is more complex: it is between the subject's position in relation to knowledge and *the specific effects of the knowledge itself.* The transmission is effective in any kind of structure; even if it is attenuated by the instructional system, it is not *wiped out.*

H: It is almost wiped out. Thank god there is always a tremendous resistance – young people's flexibility, for instance. Take people when they get out of high school, private schools, no matter what school, and see what you get. Zero.

C: But they are receivers and under difficult conditions. . . .

The peoples whose women must work much more than is proper according to our ideas often have much more real consideration for women than our European populations. Civilization's "lady," who is surrounded by feigned respect and who has become a stranger to any real work, has a far lower social position than the woman who is a barbarian, who worked hard, who counted as a real lady (*dame, froxa, Frau: domina*) and who, moreover, was one because of her character. . . .

H: Receivers are what they have received. Certainly there are always tightly held lines, like a certain type of philosophical instruction. But that never has more than a limited and postponed effectiveness. Despite absolutely incredible setbacks, it does keep alive a certain kind of spirit of change. But that's not what has taken power. Power lies always in the same direction. It always has.

We are confronted with this new form of family in all its severity among the Greeks. As Marx noted the position of the goddesses in mythology represents an earlier period, when women still occupied a freer and more respected place, in the Heroic Age, we already find women degraded owing to the predominance of the man and the competition of female slaves. . . . The modern conjugal family is based on . . . admitted or masked domestic slavery of woman, and modern society is a mass made up exclusively of conjugal families, like so many molecules. In this day and age, man in the great majority of cases, must support and nourish the family, at least in the propertied classes; and this gives him a sovereign authority which does not need legal privilege to back it up. Within the family man is the bourgeois; woman plays the part of proletariat. But in the industrial sphere, the specific character of economic oppression that weighs on the proletariat is only manifested in all its severity after all the legal privileges of the capitalist class have been suppressed and complete legal equality of the two classes has been established; the democratic republic does not suppress the antagonism between the two classes, the contrary is true: that is what, first of all, provides the ground where the struggle is going to be resolved. (F. Engels, *The Origin of the Family, Private Property and the State*)

C: In the same direction because the bourgeoisie, the dominant class, is in power. But you can't say that on one side there is the dominant class with its power, its system of transmission and the content of that system—and that is ideology, and on the other side is everything else. I don't think that is an actual split.

H: That there could be a culture without culture or a world, a society without education is something I never thought.

C: At the moment, it seems to me, you are making mastery absolutely coincide with knowledge, except in a few exceptional cases.

H: Sure. But rather than mastery coinciding with knowledge, I would say that, with few exceptions, knowledge is constantly caught up in, is entrapped by a will for power. I know which people conveying knowledge don't seem to be dealing with the exercise of power. There are very few. In reality, most of the people I know make use of knowledge, consciously or unconsciously, and use it for something else or for themselves.

C: It is inevitable on a certain level that they make it serve themselves; nothing can ever be done about that. Satisfaction is essential to avoid falling into what I've called "oblativity." The desire to teach has to find some satisfaction!

The non-master must be imagined.

H: It's a question of quantity. I'm saying that people for whom the process of return is a normal process of revenue are rare. They get a certain satisfaction, of course, that's normal, but that satisfaction can take any form. You can be gratified by the feeling of drawing others to your high level or, on the contrary, of going down to their level, et cetera. The most usual satisfaction is not generous. "Masters," in general, try to really obtain an increase in value from mastery, a feeling of accrued superiority, an inflated narcissism. . . .

C: Partly that's true. But all the more so when the knowledge has less support. It is particularly true, therefore, of the literary person—for example, where a personal gloss has considerable importance just now, where the discourse has progressed so slightly into theory that it is upheld only by a huge amount of inspiration, whose coherence is literally neurotic and which has no other way to defend itself. It is not knowledge that is being conveyed there but something on the order of the poetic. Perhaps the misunderstanding is about the idea of knowledge. When it is a question of knowledge, I am talking about a body of coherent statements that is not a neurotic coherence, hence one that isn't held together by the *singular* phantasmic specialty of the one who does the conveying.

Cultural prohibition.

H: Mastery is at play in the Imaginary as well, where interpretation plays a part and is always cropping up. When one talks about mastery, it is a mastery that can very easily become permeated with something going beyond the object, something that is a mythical power, an Imaginary power that is held sacred and that adjoins a scene of a different sort from knowledge. Everything on the order of culture and cultural objects has a prohibition placed on it, which causes class positions in relation to culture. Likewise, woman is uneasy in relation to a certain sort of production—the production of signs. . . . We don't go straight for it. We even wonder if we *can* go there. We say to ourselves: that possession is not for me. All that has been internalized for ever so long. What would this kind of power, belonging to the mastery of knowledge and, moreover, concealed, be in a field that doesn't pass through discourse? If, instead, it went through concrete practices, like manual work or even in the business world where there are mechanisms you can really dominate, where things probably don't escape you. Always for us, working in humanities and literature, there is a part that is uncontrollable. Mastery goes through real concrete power, in that case, political power, money, all the possible forms of power that are the equivalents of the sacred power of the master's word.

C: What bothers me is this collusion between power/knowledge, invested with an effectiveness that I don't believe it has. The power to change—or to inhibit— knowledge comes through mediations that are too complex for us to judge what they might be. The power of power is first of all economic. What you describe is true on the level of a sort of huge, imaginary, mythical, ideological space. It is not true for things that are part of the real functioning of those structures.

What remains of me at the university, within the university?

II: For me ideology is a kind of vast membrance enveloping everything. We have to know that this skin exists even if it encloses us like a net or like closed eyelids. We have to know that, to change the world, we must constantly try to scratch and tear it. We can never rip the whole thing off, but we must never let it stick or stop being suspicious of it. It grows back and you start again.

C. Let's go back to the discourse of knowledge, the discourse of the university; as for myself I'm hanging on to it, I accept the dunce cap so readily put on the academic's head at the moment, but can I say that it is as a woman that I hold on to it, or not? I don't think the question is at all pertinent.

H: You're right that it has no pertinence in that instance. As a subject, I always suffered from being made inferior or was crushed by what comes through the surrounding knowledge, even if, to defend myself and out of curiosity, I said to myself: "I'm going to go see what it is." I didn't do as Kafka's peasant did; I went to see, but that comes from the fact that when I was in ignorance—which I was for a very long time—when I was "theoretically naive," as they say, I felt myself constantly under attack, aggressed, because it is very hard for people with a knowledge at their disposal not to be aggressive sometimes, even the best of masters. I'm thinking of B. . . . , who is a very intelligent woman with extraordinary talent. Recently I saw she was deeply troubled; a few people whom she had just seen had told her, "You know, women don't have to enter the Symbolic anyhow." It's ridiculous. For her it didn't mean anything, and for good reason—how could one expect her to know what "enter into the Symbolic" meant? The people she was talking to didn't even bother to say to themselves: she doesn't know what the Lacanian concept of the Symbolic is. It's not exactly your everyday word after all. From the moment one begins to *use* what can be called a concept, when it is mastered and enters your discourse and gets lost, it becomes an ordinary word; but that isn't true at all for everybody else. That is mastery's trap. Being so much a master that you forget you are one.

Give me the password.

C: What you said was "the best of masters," but then you described a mockery of a master. In other respects, however, I gladly invest a positive value in aggressivity, even that of the master, even that of the best of masters. Being aggressive is also allowing the other self-definition, it is *showing* oneself as a subject.

H: Being able to organize or give order to a discourse and being able to make progress are absolutely indispensable, but there are opposite, negative effects as well. For example—controlling and censoring imagination, free production, other forms, et cetera. As a writer, even though I don't know very much, I'm already saying to myself, "That's enough. I know almost too much about it. Let's not slow down."

C: With that, let's get back to writing, words, thought, feminine thought processes, whether there is coherence or not. You and I immediately agreed that when one made use of this discourse for transmitting, it didn't matter whether one was a man or a woman. Why did we agree so easily about that? Why is that so obvious?

H: Because, precisely, I think it is a discourse that annihilates sexual difference—where there is no question of it.

C: So—in other discourses it could be a question?

H: It is a discourse agreeing more with masculinity than with femininity.

C: We don't have any way to know that.

H: Yes, I have ideas about it. There is something in woman's libidinal organization that doesn't enjoy this kind of discourse. . . .

C: When you say that, you are moving in the direction of the women who say that feminine discourse can come only from splitting?

H: No. I was very exact. I said, "Woman doesn't enjoy herself in it." I never said she was incapable of it. And I am sure of it—femininity doesn't enjoy itself there. I keep coming back to this: we are all bisexual. The problem is, what have we done with our bisexuality? What is becoming of it?

The Untenable

Double history of seduction.
What woman is not Dora?
She who makes the others (desire).
The servant-girl's place. Does the hysteric change
the Real? Desire, the Imaginary, class struggle—
how do they relate? What are the yields?

H: I got into the sphere of hysteria because I was drawn—called. I knew absolutely nothing about it. I had read "The Dora Case," but didn't see myself in it. Once into it, though, I made great headway.

First, still rather naively, I produced a text on it. Later, I had a sort of "aftertaste," and I started working on the question. I arrived at a whole series of positions; some of these positions, perhaps, are contestable. It is impossible to have a single, rigid point of view about it. If it is only a metaphor—and it's not clear

---

"Her or me": if Dora felt for her father a more lively interest than that which one would have expected from a daughter, she felt and acted more like a jealous wife, as her mother would have been in the right to do, because it is the mother who has the right. But it is *the daughter* who has *the name*: if Dora said "her or me" when she made scenes for him, when she had no right to do so, that bad little girl, it was because she was her father's daughter. He was a very active man, with unusual talent, an important manufacturer, enjoying a fine material

147

that this is so, it functions well, it has its use. I started with Dora; I read that text in a sort of dizziness, exploding over the situation presented, where at heart I found myself siding frenetically with the different characters. I immediately worked out a reading that was probably not centered the way Freud had wanted it to be. I had to bring center stage obliterated characters, characters repressed in notes, at the bottom of the page, and who were for me in the absolute foreground. I read it like fiction. I didn't worry about an analytic investment at that moment, and besides, I couldn't have.

She identifies herself.

One never reads except by identification. But what kind? What is "identification"? When I say "identification," I do not say "loss of self." I become, I inhabit, I enter. Inhabiting someone, at that moment I can feel myself traversed by that person's initiatives and actions. (Actually, that has always disturbed me. When I was younger I was afraid because I realized I was capable of mimicry. Then I accused myself of thieving flight.) I turned round and round. I found myself caught up in those characters' same state, because they too were identify-

---

position . . . when his daughter was born he felt fulfilled, having already had a son who would succeed him. . . . He gave the baby the name Dora. All the other names in the story are without importance except for Dora's. During the first eight years of life, Dora was adored by her father. It was a love with no contract. From the age of eight, this little treasure suffered respiratory problems. She caused her father a great deal of worry. This kind man forced her to visit skillful doctors. What Mrs. K. was doing, couldn't Dora have done it?

| | not Mummy— | | put me to sleep— | some gold for Dora |
| DADDY— | | MUMMY— | | DORA— |

| Mr. K. | only for Mrs. K.— | only for Daddy— | not Mrs. K.— |
| MONSIEUR K.— | MADAME K.— | DADDY | MADAME K.— |

only for Dora— will have Daddy
    adore some gold for Daddy—
golden case— won't get—   not   my lady—

| DORA— | | DADDY— | | MADAME K.— |

           adore
    lie Daddy—   no gold to show—
only for Mummy—   not Dora—   will have my treasure—

| MUMMY— | DADDY— | DORA— | MY TREASURE— |

ing. . . . Almost all those involved in Dora's scene circulate through the others, which results in a sort of hideous merry-go-round, even more so because, through bourgeois pettiness, they are ambivalent. All consciously play a double game, plus the games of the unconscious. Each one acts out the little calculations of classic bourgeois comedy — a comedy of clear conscience on the one hand, a comedy of propriety on the other. First of all, "you don't divorce"; then you make a combination of structures with interchangeable elements to get the greatest possible pleasure from an adulterous situation. And that can hold only if there is a social pact that is observed. That pact is, "no one will say what he knows." Everybody knows, but everybody is silent, and everybody profits from it. Therefore, one is in a world that rests on a system of silent contracts, contracts of general hypocrisy. And it is a chain: "*I* won't tell what you are doing and *you* won't tell what I do." As I was reading, I heard voices sighing in the

mummydaddy—   adore
my goof   play Daddy—   not Dora— will have—
MY PEARL—   MY GEM—   DADDY—   DORA—

  get it?—   gold cage—
my (chatter)box.—play Mrs. K.—   I gold—   Mrs. F(reud)
MY GEMLET—   MADAME K.—JEOR—   MADAME F.—

                  bick . . .
  some gold for god—   my lady god—   will be—
DORA— GOD THE SECOND—MADAME GOD THE SECOND—MY BOX—

show—   . . . er, bicker—
my treasure—   but they have my marbles—
MY TREASURE—   MY HOUSE—   MY MARBLES—   MY DAUGHTER—

                  get it?
                (chatter)box   help!
notnot   play—   D's
DADDY—   MY GEMLET—   MY DICE—

Madame K. has rights
Mr. K. has rights
Daddy has rights
Mummy has rights
Only the gemlet has none
But she has the name. (Hélène Cixous, *Portrait du Soleil.*)

text—voices of people who, in the chain, were finally those on whom weighed heaviest the great weight of silence, those who were crushed, who obtained no satisfaction in the roundabout. In the front line was Dora, who fascinated me, because here was an eighteen-year-old girl caught in a world where you say to yourself, she is going to break—a captive, but with such strength! I could not keep from laughing from one end to the other, because, despite her powerlessness and with (thanks to) that powerlessness, here is a kid who successfully jams all the little adulterous wheels that are turning around her and, one after the other, they break down. She manages to say what she doesn't say, so intensely that the men drop like flies. We can very well see how—at what moment, in what scenes, by which meaning—she has cut through. Each time cutting through the marshmallow ribbon that the others are in the process of spieling. A hecatomb.

It is she who is the victim, but the others come out of it in shreds. The father, Mr. K., Freud—everybody passes through. They all drop. Doubtless a symbolic carnage because the men always regroup. Then, afterward, comes a reflux, and you have the party of men who come, reiterating the father, repeating the famous scene of Dora in bed, Dora lying down, Daddy standing and looking at Dora. In the end *she* makes *them* lie down; they fall: the most beautiful image is the one of Mr. K.'s accident. Before Dora's eyes, he was run over by a cart. All of this was linked with a criticism of society which touches me because I belonged to that lower middle class when I was little: the criticism passing through a secondary figure. In the same way that the woman is the man's repressed in the conjugal couple, there is this little character who is in the process of disappearing from society and on whom rested the family structure: the servant-girl.

Maid in the family.

C: She is everywhere, in all Freud's analyses. The servant-girl is a character who is just beginning to disappear from analyses. And she is always on the side of eroticism.

H: The seductress. She is the hole in the social cell; "it" goes through "that," it goes through her body. In "Dora" what was terrifying was that these archetypical servants were put by Freud himself in "the maid's room"—that is, in the notes. There are two who are identical. Both are called "the servant-girl," "the governess." One succeeds the other in Dora's life, with years in between, but they have exactly the same role. They have the same history: seduced by the boss and then eliminated for having been seduced by the boss. Woman's situation carried to the paroxysm of horror. So, the servant-girl is the repressed of the boss's wife.

C: The boss's wife is the lady: "madame." She spends her days in bed, or she buys smoked salmon. She is a strange, absent face. But certainly servant-girls are there only as fantasy objects, like animals. Grouscha, in the analysis of *The Wolfman*, is both the maid and a pear—the child says it straight out. He links it together out loud: pear striped with yellow, maid, butterfly, sex between a woman's legs. There are the servant-girls, stuck in between fruits and bugs. Elsewhere Freud speaks of a bottle of pineapple liqueur; it is spoiled, this liqueur; it smells bad. And Martha Freud, the slut, makes the most of it by saying: "It should be given to the servants."

And Freud says: "No, because it's spoiled we can throw it away." Good soul . . . unless, because it concerns one of Freud's own dreams, he made the most of it by blaming the sentence on his wife. . . .

H: That situation—why doesn't it appear in the cases that Freud recounts? Dora's case is archetypical, "the servant-girl is the boss's wife's repressed," but in Dora's case, Dora is in the place of the boss's wife: the mother is set aside. She is dead, she is nothing, and everybody has agreed to bury her. Including Freud. Not for a moment does he analyze the reports given him about the mother.

She is "in the hole." Which is exactly what permits Dora's rising to the fore and this sort of Oedipal idyll that is going to be played out between her and daddy. What does that mean? It means that, for Freud, the mother, once her role is fulfilled, is through. As the Germans say: "Der Mohr hat sein Pflicht getan, er kann gehen." The Moor has done his job, out with him. Now he can go. That is Othello in "The Moor of Venice." You can replace "the Moor" with the mother. She is done making kids, so she is made secondary in the story.

C: There is another reason, which is Freud's blindspot, not only about the Oedipal but also about class attitudes—a banality we must not forget to mention.

H: That is why I say that it is not significant that there is no boss's wife. It is significant that it is Freud who sets the stage, who puts covers on those things that are not important to him, who isn't in the play, and who puts the most important people in the best seats. It is certain that that corresponds socially to something quite real: the servant-girl, the prostitute. . . .

C: Eroticism happens through what is "clandestine," not through what is "official." Remember the text on sensual love and affectionate love in which Freud opposes them as almost incompatible. But Engels, after all, doesn't say anything different. That is all very coherent, and at the same time, there are sharp contradictions. What is coherent is the opposition of the legal wife and the prostitute and their complementarity in the family. The contradictions would be Freud's

---

In my opinion, it still had to be explained why Dora felt so offended by Mr. K.'s advances—the more so because I began to understand that, in this affair, for Mr. K. it was no frivolous attempt at seduction. I interpreted the fact that she informed her parents of this incident as an act which was already influenced by a morbid desire for revenge. . . .

We are back at the scene by the lake. . . . Mr. K. began rather seriously; but she did not let him finish. As soon as she understood what it was about, she

silences—the things he couldn't see in his own ideological misunderstanding. The family does not exist in isolation, rather it truly supports and reflects the class struggle running through it. The servant-girl, the prostitute, the mother, the boss's wife, the woman: that is all an ideological scene.

H: Freud didn't give the servant-girl enough recognition. Never do you see her in the body of the text—she is always in the kitchen, in her station: she appears in the notes. When Freud speaks of Dora's sexual initiation, entirely acquired from books, it is automatically attributed to the normal sources of this sort of pernicious education—it is probably the maid's doing, and indeed it is the servant-girl whom we find in a note.

Also, we always say that Freud failed to make the analysis of transferal—that he didn't see what was happening. The truth (which he saw only once when he was really put down) is that, in the system of exchange, me in your place, you in my place . . . Freud in relation to Dora was in the maid's place. It is Freud who was the servant-girl, and that is what is intolerable for Freud in the Dora case—that he was treated as one treats maids, having been fired the way you fire a servant-girl. There is no failure worse than that. The knot, the crux of the Dora case, is that Dora was afraid of being the maid, and, on the other hand, she was afraid of being nothing, like her mother. That "nothing" is stressed in the words the married men are saying. They are the words of comedy. At the same time,

---

slapped his face and ran off. I wanted to know what words he had said; she did not remember anything except this explanation: "You know that my wife is nothing to me."

. . . For she understood perfectly well what her father, who couldn't sleep without his cognac, needed. . . . Her father did not sleep, because relations with the beloved woman were lacking. . . . "My wife is nothing to me."

"I do not doubt," says the father, "that this incident is the cause of Dora's temperamental change. . . . She demands that I break off my relations with Mr. K. and especially with Mrs. K., whom she used to adore. But I cannot do that, because first I think Dora's story about Mr. K.'s dishonorable proposals is a fiction that has forced its way on her; besides, I am deeply attached to Mrs. K. by real friendship, and I would not like to hurt her. The poor woman is very unhappy with her husband. . . . We are two wretched people who . . . console each other with friendly sympathy. You know that my wife is nothing to me." (Freud, *Le cas Dora. Cinq Psychanalyses* [*The Dora Case. Five Psychoanalyses*].)

they pass on dramatic metaphors: Mr. K. says to Dora, and to the servant-girl whom he tried to seduce, "You know very well that my wife is nothing to me."

Freud as servant-girl.

No woman tolerates hearing (even if it is about the other woman), "My wife, a woman who is my woman, can be nothing." That is murder. So Dora, hearing it, knowing that the servant-girl had already heard it, sees woman, her mother, the maid die; she sees women massacred to make room for her. But she knows that she will have her turn at being massacred. Her terrific reaction is to slap Mr. K. This girl has understood, all her actions in the story Freud tells and is telling blindly show how she has seen each time the ignominy and the enactment

---

There had been at the house a person who, prematurely, had wished to open Dora's eyes about her father's relations with Mrs. K. . . . That was her last governess. . . . The teacher and pupil got along rather well for a while, then Dora suddenly became hostile to her and demanded her dismissal. As long as the governess had influence, she used it to stir Dora and her mother up against Mrs. K. . . . But her efforts were in vain. Dora remained devoted to Mrs. K. and wanted to know nothing of the reasons there might have been to think her father's relations with her shocking. Dora, on the other hand, understood very well the governess's motives. . . . She saw that the governess was in love with her father. When he was present, the governess seemed an entirely different person; then she was amusing and obliging. . . . But Dora even let that pass. She only became angry when she realized that the love which had been lavished on her was really meant for her father; . . . Then Dora broke off with her completely.

The poor governess had made Dora understand in an undesirable light part of her own behavior. Dora had acted with Mr. K.'s children . . . as . . . the governess had with her.

"Do you know, doctor, that today is the last time I shall be here?" . . . (Freud): "You know that you are always free to stop the treatment? When did you decide this?"

"Two weeks ago, I think."

"Those two weeks remind me of the notice a servant or governess gives of departure."

"There was also a governess who did that in the K.'s household."

. . . She was acting very strangely towards Mr. K. She didn't greet him, didn't answer him, she treated him as if he did not exist. . . . "She told me that Mr. K. . . . when Mrs. K. was absent for a few weeks, had wooed her and begged her to refuse him nothing. He told her that his wife was nothing to him, and so forth." (Freud, *Le cas Dora*)

of woman's murder. And to that must be added that in Dora there is a very beautiful feminine homosexuality, a love for woman that is astounding.

Dora seemed to me to be the one who resists the system, the one who cannot stand that the family and society are founded on the body of women, on bodies despised, rejected, bodies that are humiliating once they have been used. And this girl—like all hysterics, deprived of the possibility of saying directly what she perceived, of speaking face-to-face or on the telephone as father B. or father K. or Freud, et cetera do—still had the strength to make it known. It is the nuclear example of women's power to protest. It happened in 1899; it happens today wherever women have not been able to speak differently from Dora, but have spoken so effectively that it bursts the family into pieces.

Yes, the hysteric, with her way of questioning others (because if she succeeds in bringing down the men who surround her, it is by questioning them, by ceaselessly reflecting to them the image that truly castrates them, to the extent that the power they have wished to impose is an illegitimate power of rape and violence). —The hysteric is, to my eyes, the typical woman in all her force. It is a force that was turned back against Dora, but, if the scene changes and if woman begins to speak in other ways, it would be a force capable of demolishing those structures. There is something else in Dora's case that is great—everything in the nature of desire. A desire that is also, often, love—for love. The source of Dora's strength is, in spite of everything, her desire. The hysteric is not just someone who has her words cut off, someone for whom the body speaks. It all

---

She sat for *two hours* in contemplative and dreamy admiration before the *Sistine Madonna*. When I asked her what she liked in the picture, she replied in a confused way. Finally, she said: "The Madonna." (Freud, *Le cas Dora*)

starts with her anguish as it relates to desire and to the immensity of her desire—therefore, from her demanding quality. She doesn't let things get by. I see the hysteric saying: "I want everything." The world doesn't give her people who are "everythings"; they are always very little pieces. In what she projects as a demand for totality, for strength, for certainty, she makes demands of the others in a manner that is intolerable to them and that prevents their functioning as they function (without their restricted little economy). She destroys their calculations. The reckoning, for example, that consists of saying, "My wife is nothing, therefore, you can be everything"—because she knows that it isn't true, she knows what "everything" is, she knows what this false-nothing is, et cetera. I also thought the famous scene of the Madonna was terrific. It is the capacity for an adoration that is not empty—it is the belief in the possibility of such a thing.

The ones on the margins and social upheaval.

C: That is certainly why it is somehow also a containment. It is metaphoric, yes—a metaphor of the impossible, of the ideal and dreamed of totality, yes, but when you say "that bursts the family into pieces," no. It mimics, it metaphorizes destruction, but the family reconstitutes itself around it. As when you throw a stone in the water, the water ripples but becomes smooth again. The analysis I make of hysteria comes through my reflection on the place of deviants who are not hysterics but clowns, charlatans, crazies, all sorts of odd people. They all occupy challenging positions foreseen by the social bodies, challenging functions within the scope of all cultures. That doesn't change the structures, however. On the contrary, it makes them comfortable.

H: I am not sure that is where I would put hysterics.

C: But yes—it all comes together. Ethnologists, analysts, or anyone naively able to say this, at the same time recognize in them an exceptional capacity for language and an *exclusion correlative to it.* In that position, they are part of one of the deepest reenforcements of the superstructures, of the Symbolic. It keeps the net of the Imaginary in a tight grip, and the hysterics are inside it. If I am the network between witch and hysteric, passing one on through the other, through the same signifiers, it is certainly because the hysteric seems to me to inscribe herself within that line.

H: I think there are degrees. I imagine hysteria as distributing itself along a scale of the possible intensity of disturbance. Along with, beyond a certain threshold, something that makes a complete victim of the hysteric. She loses all effectiveness, then, because she herself is the place where everything is turned back against her; she is paralyzed by it, physically or otherwise, and thus loses her impact. There are structures characteristic of hysteria that are not neuroses, that work with very strong capacities of identification with the other, that are scouring, that make mirrors fly, that put disturbing images back into circulation; because only if you're not an Iago can you play your little game of hypocrisy, only if you don't say to yourself, "I — am a filthy creature." Because in general the system's functioning is based on blindness, on denial. There is also the fact that there is no place for the hysteric; she cannot be placed or take place. Hysteria is necessarily an element that disturbs arrangements; wherever it is, it shakes up all those who want to install themselves, who want to install something that is going to work, to repeat. It is very difficult to block out this type of person who doesn't leave you in peace, who wages permanent war against you.

C: Yes, it introduces dissension, but it doesn't explode anything at all; it doesn't disperse the bourgeois family, which also exists only through its dissension, which holds together only in the possibility or the reality of its own disturbance, always reclosable, always reclosed. It is when there is a crossing over to the symbolic act that it doesn't shut up again. At the back of my mind, I was thinking of Flaubert while you were talking to me. Flaubert the hysteric, Flaubert in the family circle . . . second son of the family. The father a very traditionalist doctor, a specialist in dissection at the charity hospital, one whose work is death. But also of the mother: they make a first son who is the true son, the heir. From that moment on, Mme. Flaubert wants and expects a girl. She has male children who die. Gustave is the third, he survives; but there you have it, in his mother's desire, he should be a girl. Therefore, insofar as he is a boy, he must die. He stays alive but as the "family idiot," not knowing how to read, stupid, considered abnormal. He is in a situation of exclusion, putting him obligatorily in a feminine position, both because he should be a girl and because the others are dead. Flaubert has no other solution than to go into writing, very precociously, and that is what Sartre demonstrates in his astonishing book. The first tales he writes are fantastic tales in which he is in the subjective position of the monsters. One of his first texts tells the story, in the first person, of a creature born of the encounter of a woman and a monkey. Later, to get on to other texts, he has to pass through crises whose immediate result is that his father mothers him. It is an absolutely pure schema. Yes, hysteria does upset and disturb the Flaubert family but very little in relation to his writing, which is the passage to the act, the political act, the passage to inscription in the Symbolic. But otherwise it doesn't, and Dora doesn't. For me the fact of being passed on to posterity through Freud's account and even Freud's failure is not a symbolic act. That is already more true of Freud and Breuer's hysteric who became the first welfare worker and who made something her hysteria. The distinction between them, between those who nicely fulfill their function of challenging with all possible violence (but who can enclose themselves afterward) and those who will arrive at symbolic inscription, no matter what act they use to get there, seems essential to me. Raising hell, throwing fits, disturbing family relations can be shut back up.

H: It is that force that works to dismantle structures. There are some who are not effective, and others who are; it is a question of circumstances, of degrees. Dora broke something.

C: I don't think so.

H: The houses that "resided" on her, whose stability was ensured by her. . . .

C: What she broke was strictly individual and limited.

H: Because at that time it was impossible to go any further.

C: Listen, you love Dora, but to me she never seemed a revolutionary character.

H: I don't give a damn about Dora; I don't fetishize her. She is the name of a certain force, which makes the little circus not work anymore.

C: Let's take that metaphorically: that is true of hysteria, agreed, but why limit that to the hysteric and hence to the feminine? From a certain point of view, the obsessive person does an equally destructive job, in the sense of passing limits in the direction of law, constraint, and conformity, which he transforms into caricature. In adding more to the rigidity of structures, and in adding more to ritual, he works destructively.

H: I'm not sure. When Freud says that what is obsessive, on a cultural level, yields the religious and that what is hysterical yields art, it seems right to me. The religious is something that consolidates, that will reenclose, that will seal and fasten everything that is rigid in the social realm. There is a difference between what makes things move and what stops them; it is what moves things that changes them.

C: Do you know the games like "taquin"? They are games where you move a piece in a system in which you can move only a limited number of pieces to explore the possibilities of permutation without the "taquin's" moving. One shifts an element within a perfectly rigid structure, which is all the better for it. Language only moves one square to the place of another—that's all; the real distribution of elements, the real change cannot happen on that level.

Can one put desire to sleep?

H: I don't think that the revolution is going to happen through language either. But there is no revolution without a conscious grasp—without there being people who get up and begin to yell. I think that is where I make a connection with Bataille's analyses. I think that what cannot be oppressed, even in the class struggle, is the libido—desire; it is in taking off from desire that you will revive the need for things to really change.

This land is not mine, nor this land, nor this land nor this land nor this sex nor this sex. I revolve around the Revolution as if around the sun with an unmoving, eternal desire like hell around heaven. . . . A race of exhausted men take my place, they die easily: they tumble down the slopes beneath my eyes, these diminished men are merry. . . . I imagine their burial. . . . They imagine

Desire never dies, but it can be stifled for a long time. For example, in peoples who are denied speech and who are on their last gasp. One ceases to move the moment one no longer communicates.

C: Except in taking what you say poetically, I have to admit that these sentences have no reality for me. Take an example. What *is* a people that doesn't communicate?

H: One can very easily smother desire. Let's take France, in fact. From the moment that you no longer circulate discourse, when you circulate only a dead, stereotypical discourse. . . .

C: But who is "one"? Who circulates? Who are the subjects? Where are they?

H: A certain power. The class that holds power has exercised it for a long time, but it has gotten worse, it is getting worse and worse, it systematically crushes all the places where the imagination is inscribed: the mass media, publishing— everywhere the word and its inventive forms can get through. This deals a heavy blow to political consciousness.

C: Obviously what you are describing is censorship. . . .

H: Yes, and when one censors, one lowers the rate of desire and it takes forever for it to revive. It doesn't communicate. It doesn't know where to go. It is tired; it is going to sleep. That's how it feels. It is not going to budge. That doesn't mean it is dead but that censorship and prohibition are really very effective historic brakes.

C: That is a level of description where I do not recognize anything of what I think in political terms. Not that it is "false," certainly. But it is described in terms that seem to me on the order of myth, of poetry. It describes a sort of collective subject, fictitious, desiring—a huge entity by turns free and revolutionary or subjugated, by turns sleeping or awake. . . . In reality these aren't subjects. Let's even admit into the political register the term desire, which in my sense and for the moment isn't pertinent: if you are thinking at the same time "desire" and "class struggle" (but they are heterogenous levels of language), the smothering of what you call "desire" is impossible; the putting to sleep, unthinkable; the

---

my burial but they think better of it: this land is not mine. And this belly and this History and this Sex?

They take their tommyguns and fire. Now that History is over, it is the unknown *outside*, banished but *where*, expropriated, but by what right? Emptied, in my own bosom where I have no place, I am witness to the violent debates of race and sex. I, my substitute. They ask me about Femininity. I keep down but standing. Substituting, can I affirm myself as substitute? And what is Mr. Freud's position?

They are keeping me in a harness: men, and the men's women, and the women-men, and the two of them. (Hélène Cixous, *Portrait du Soleil*)

class struggle never ceases to become harsher and harsher, more and more stirred up through its contradictions. What you are feeling as censorship and the putting to sleep of imagination precisely corresponds to a period of struggle such as there has not been in France for a long time; it is a reality that power is trying to erase. The stifling of it (which isn't the stifling of "desire") happens through abusive use of all means of information. Not astonishing that one can feel that, but is it necessary to be taken in by it? The idea of putting to sleep, therefore, is incompatible with the very notion of struggle contained in class struggle. Class struggle does not stop. There is imagination, desire, creation, production of writing (you see I am trying to find different names for the same experiences), and then somewhere else, on another level of reality, there is class struggle, and within it, women's struggle. There are missing links in all that, which we should try to think in order to succeed in joining our two languages. Sometimes desire and artistic production anticipate class struggle in its unfolding but also, dialectically, they are fallout from it, a more or less unconscious effect, with all its mediations, unthought at the present time. A conflict so fundamental for intellectuals that it informs the totality of consciousnesses, wherever they are situated, caught in impossible contradictions, whether consciously or not, whether they lean more toward guilty conscience or toward blindness. One is always situated there, in the struggle, in a precise position.

H: Class struggle is this sort of huge machine whose system is described by Marx and, therefore, is now functioning. But its rhythm is not always the same; it is a rhythm that is sometimes very attenuated.

C: It can *seem* very attenuated, especially if you are bludgeoned into thinking so. But there is a considerable shift between the reality of class struggle and the way in which it is lived mythically, especially by intellectuals who have difficulty being able to size up the reality of the struggles directly, because they are in a position where work on language and work on the Imaginary have fundamental importance and can put blinders on them.

II. Right now, I am pessimistic. There is, in a very generalized manner, a loss of voice in the world of writing, of literature, of creation. It is symptomatic and it will have effects; it isn't by chance that reading is on the retreat in almost all countries of the West. So that means that all the governments united, whether right or reformist, are saying: "You, if you still have eyes, shut them, and intellectuals of all countries, your mouths, and don't start making analyses, and besides, it isn't worth the trouble." One sees the development of an international

---

When a political man exercises pressure for the art of his time to express a given cultural world, it consists of political activity, not of artistic criticism: if the cultural world for which one struggles is a living and necessary fact, its expansiveness will be irresistible, and it will find its artists. (Antonio Gramsci)

intrigue that is leading toward capitalist imbecilization in its most inhuman, most automatic, most formidable form. The selling out of all the countries, their handing themselves over the way France has done with the United States, is also done on condition of a complicitous silence. And to achieve it, they will not only silence the bulk of the production of writing—of literature in general, whatever it may be—but they will also silence poetry, even though poetry isn't going to talk about international relations. But somehow, they fear it, and they gag it.

C: And yet, in the same period, in the same movement whose capitalist reverse side you are describing, imperialism is coming apart, is defeated: in Indochina—what an event! in Europe. And that is fundamental. Pessimism should be only a limited look, only one point of view, only one perspective. I believe that the need for *dialectic* (which is how I always see it in depth) is making itself very real and that we will not succeed in thinking the struggle for women's liberation without this means of analysis and of comprehension, which is not natural for us, which is difficult, but which is the only true method.

H: History is always in several places at once, there are always several histories underway; this is a high point in the history of women.

Glossary

Glossary

In a few important instances, the vocabulary of *La Jeune Née* reflects the cultural milieu of Paris, 1975. Ten years later, this vocabulary has entered our culture in certain academic settings; however, *La Jeune Née* was written to reach a wide audience. In the U.S., such a wide audience is far less likely to have been nourished on a mixture of structuralism, Marxism, deconstruction, and psychoanalysis with a Lacanian bent. In particular, Jacques Lacan's interpretations of the work of Freud have supplied some of the key words in this text. The work of Clément and Cixous stresses the importance of mistrusting the "discourse of mastery" in which these words normally function; nonetheless, they insist on the necessity of woman, as an adequate subject, taking for herself whatever tools of analysis will give her access to history. For a reader, vocabulary would certainly be one of these tools.

Although the "definitions" proposed here should be useful in revealing some of the assumptions underlying *The Newly Born Woman*, I have tried not to give too much background or to stray from the idiosyncratic definitions emerging from the book itself—which should be available to anyone who reads closely.

There are difficult words in this book; words that are too-full of sense (direction, meaning, feeling; common, uncommon) to be rendered by any one English word. One may hear, for instance: in *coupable*, both "culpable" and "cuttable"; in *voler*, both "to fly" and "to steal"; in *dépenser*, both "to spend" and "to unthink"; in *encore*, both "in body" and "still more." Rather than breaking the rhythm of the text, I have tried to follow a process of accretion, not choosing a single meaning and indulging in wordplay where the disruption could bear the

163

same relation to written English as the "original" did to written French. But this wordplay is not fully translatable, and it is an important technique for changing the focus of discourse, hence making and finding new discourses, letting the repressed come into language. It is a practice used by Clément and Cixous to subvert the univocal, patriarchal meanings that have constituted the authority of language. Cixous would have us be "moles" (*taupes*/topoi/ground mines) undermining a Symbolic structure that systematically excludes women. Two other words, *jouissance* and *propre*, have such significant political undertones that I have included them in the Glossary, along with the title *La Jeune Née*, in which one must hear more than *The Newly Born Woman*.

Imaginary/Symbolic/Real

Capitalized, these words are used in a Lacanian sense and must be distinguished from their everyday and their more technical, "structuralist" meanings. Lacan's Imaginary, the order of perception and hallucination, is fantasy-full but never fanciful. The Symbolic, the order of discursive and symbolic action, demystifies the symbol, which can no longer pretend to represent an adequate "truth." And the Real is not simply "reality" but the designation of what is absolutely unrepresentable.

There is no pure instance of any of the three. Predispositions toward the Symbolic arise in the earliest alienation of the Imaginary "mirror stage"; Imaginary constructs survive after entry into the Symbolic by the acquisition of language; and neither the Imaginary nor the Real can even be considered except by means of the Symbolic.

Lacan's prolific production over many years is notoriously full of ambiguities, and his concepts are far from static. Catherine Clément and Hélène Cixous take the "commonplaces" of Lacanian theory for their own purposes. Cixous, in particular, revalues the Imaginary, which Lacan consistently devalues in favor of the Symbolic.

imaginary

When spelled with a lowercase "i," imaginary is used (commonsensically) to describe a conception that is a conscious mental image.

Imaginary

The Imaginary is both a chronological stage in individual maturation that is dominated by the perceptual and the later survival of sense-making patterns marked by these preverbal, pre-Oedipal forms of understanding. In its central event, the "mirror stage," the young human identifies its own image, forms an idealized human image (*Imago*), and internalizes this identification as the beginnings of its ego (*moi*). This takes place on the ground of nonindividuation in relation to the body of the mother that characterizes primary narcissism. The illusion of the possibility of oneness and the binary spatial relationships of inside/outside will persist as Imaginary constructs, the latter particularly in positional judgments (good/evil, self/other, etc.). Many women writers in France emphasize and affirm the relationship with the body of the mother in this pre-Oedipal period, whose interchangeable relationships of love and aggression take on different meanings at Lacan's alienating "mirror stage." In the life of *la jeune née*, as in the life of the young child, the Imaginary comes first, and it persists.

jouissance

The reincarnation of this word in the English language has been accompanied by a certain amount of dictionary rattling. Apparently it did indeed exist in the eighteenth century with some of the fullness of current French usage. Total sexual ecstasy is its most common connotation, but in contemporary French philosophical, psychoanalytic, and political usage, it does not stop there, and to equate it with orgasm would be an oversimplification. It would also, as Lacan pointed out (when faced with the Madison Avenue commandment "Enjoy Coca-Cola"), be inadequate to translate it as enjoyment. This word, however, does maintain some of the sense of access and participation in connection with rights and property. Constitutions guarantee the "enjoyment of rights"; courts rule on who is to enjoy which right and what property. It is, therefore, a word with *simultaneously* sexual, political, and economic overtones. Total access, total participation, as well as total ecstasy are implied. At the simplest level of meaning—metaphorical—woman's capacity for multiple orgasm indicates that she has the potential to attain something more than Total, something extra—abundance and waste (a cultural throwaway), Real and unrepresentable.

On the phonic level, one can hear: *jouissance*: *j'ouis sens*: I hear meaning. "Meaning," for contemporary French thought, (see *writing* is about as elusive (illusory) as the desired "fusion and community" (p. 29) of *jouissance*, but the search and desire for it goes on. So, yet another level of activity is implied here, one in which the word is all-important. In *La Jeune Née*, the disturbance leading to hysteria (Clément's and Cixous's accounts of Freud's account) is often something heard but not yet understood (p. 46); and the reign of the Symbolic begins in myth when "insistent death penetrates the Great Woman through her ears" (p. 106). For the latter, it is the fiction of paternity that destroys her power as the Great Mother—"just" words, mere fiction, mind over matter. In the case of the hysteric, "what is heard" provides the clue for these driven women that all is not as it seems, all is not well. Even though they repress the knowledge and cannot speak it, their bodies must tell what they know. The Great Mother heard her death; the hysteric heard an unacceptable sense.

La Jeune Née

Hear here: *La Genêt*: a feminine writing outlaw. (The reference is to Jean Genêt, French writer, homosexual, and convicted criminal, who wrote of outlaws, outcasts, sexual masks, and social roles.)

Là je n'est: There I, a subject, is not.

Là je une nais: There I, a subject (a feminine one), am born.

Clément and Cixous seek what has been set aside as not-the-subject. By taking what is not-the-subject for their subject, they write themselves into history. To do this, they do not hesitate to steal, in their capacity as outlaw (*la* Genêt), past Freud's blind spots to take his instruments to do their work.

mirror stage

In Lacanian theory, this is a stage in the chronological development of the child, between six and eighteen months, in which the child emerges as an individual differentiated from the mother. The fragmented body images of early infancy begin to coalesce and produce an identity organized around what the infant sees of other identities, which, in turn, identify the infant. This first identification is the basis of all other identifications. Alienation is implicit in this stage; there is no self-present Self, because the Self thus identified represents an irreconcilable separation, not only between the young child and his or her mother but between all the child's perceptual awareness and this Self, this ego, that the child will call himself or herself. The alienation is most often referred to by Clément and Cixous as a "gap" (see *object a*). This "gap" also appears, in a positive sense, as a "space between," where difference is experienced as pleasure, and in "writing's" infinite deferral of meaning.

object a

Another Lacanian reference, "a" refers to *autre* (other) if it is not capitalized. In chronological, developmental terms, *object a* would be the earliest perceived instance of differentiation and lack (gap) that the child experiences. The child's perception that it lacks the mother's breast prefigures but is not identical with the child's later construction of an ego through reflections of the Other.

Other/other

In Lacanian theory, the ego is formed out of the internalization of the other (see *Mirror Stage*). On another scale, whole cultures locate themselves in relation to things that they are not—their Other. Spelled with a lowercase "o," other is generally specifically experiential; with a capital "O," it is more hypothetical. Depending on one's situation, in its later manifestations, the Other can be what is repressed or the Law repressing it.

Propre

I have translated this as Selfsame: ownself. It has overtones of property and appropriation. It also means "proper," "appropriate," and "clean." Clément repeatedly employs the euphemism *en voila du propre* (whose English equivalent is "what a fine mess!"), using the antiphrasis at points where what is "appropriate" is radically called into question. Since woman must care for bodily needs and instill the cultural values of cleanliness and propriety, she is deeply involved in what is *propre*, yet she is always somehow suspect, never quite *propre* herself.

Real

"The Real is full and 'lacks' nothing." (Jacques Lacan, *Ecrits*, Paris: Editions du Seuil, 1966, pp. 851, 852.) It is available to us only through the mediation of the Imaginary and Symbolic orders. It is what is, what has been, and what will become, and, though itself, it is nonnarrative and nonrepresentational, like history, it can be thought only when it is textualized. One must participate in this unthinkable Real because it cannot lack our participation. Also, like history, it can be experienced as the site of resistance to individual desire. For Clément and Cixous, when the Imaginary, the Symbolic, and the Real intersect in the subject, it is possible for one to "know," taking charge of the Real by means of the Symbolic, "what she," the Imaginary She, "becomes" (p. 57) that is Real.

symbolic

Spelled with a lowercase "s," and used with words such as "systems" or "structure," this word, though related, is not the same as Lacan's Symbolic. To establish her use of the word, Clément provides the following statement by Lévi-Strauss:

Every culture can be considered as a complex of symbolic systems, in which language, the rules of matrimony, economic relations, art, science and religion rank foremost. All these systems aim at expressing certain aspects of both physical reality and social reality, as well as, and more importantly, the relations which these two types of reality maintain between them and that the symbolic systems themselves maintain with one another. (p. 6)

Symbolic

The Symbolic, the order of language, is privileged by Lacan because it structures and represents the Imaginary and the Real. One enters the Symbolic order when one is introduced to language, in which abstract, shifting relationships free one from the immediacy of the Imaginary and make its mastery possible. The name (*nom*) and the prohibition (*non*) of the father are the abstractions that will allow the child to take his or her place in the cultural system. There, learning to speak the language, he or she is limited and alienated, "spoken by it." The Law is the name of this arbitrary order of abstraction whose power derives from the threat of castration as signified by the phallus. Despite its overwhelming patriarchal content, because the Law of paternal authority is (like any signifying system) necessarily *arbitrary*, *abstract*, and *fictional*, Clément and Cixous see women's active entry into language, into "writing," as the possible and necessary access to their formation and participation as subjects, rather than objects, in the Real.

writing

The act of writing is an act of production whose result, writing, continues to produce, independent of its "author." Through unlimited readings and rewritings, it defers meaning. In this infinite deferral of meaning, it undermines notions of representation and truth which hold that there is some original presence, some source of truth that can be restored to the text. These notions are the props of western metaphysics, fixing woman in a series of binary relationships and always in the subordinate position. Cixous is very specific that, although women have a privileged relation to writing (because their Oedipal structure does not require them to leave the Imaginary so decisively), *écriture feminine* can be written by men as well (men who are able to let some feminine through). Clément is more insistent on the use of writing as a means of entering the Symbolic, as a means of achieving an adequacy of subject. Both of them urge women to begin "writing"; they believe this act will undo cultural repression and replace censorship of difference with a free and powerful inhabiting of this difference.

Hélène Cixous, born in Algeria in 1937, is head of the Center of Research in Feminine Studies in Paris, which is the only center of its kind in France. Since the publication of *La jeune née* in France in 1975, Cixous has become one of the major writers and theoreticians to come out of the French feminist intellectual movement. Many of her books have been translated into Danish, German, and English. She has also written several plays; her latest, about Cambodia, was performed by the Théâtre du Soleil.

Catherine Clément is diplomat in charge of cultural exchanges at the French Ministry of External Relations. Formerly editor of cultural science for the Parisian newspaper *Le Matin*, she is the author of books on structuralism, psychoanalysis, and Marxism, and has written several novels.

Betsy Wing earned her B.A. degree in the history of art from Bryn Mawr College in 1958; she also attended Columbia and Miami universities. Her translations of some of Hélène Cixous's other essays have appeared in *boundary 2*, and she is translator of Denis Hollier's *The College of Sociology*, forthcoming from Minnesota.

Sandra M. Gilbert is professor of English at Princeton University; her book *The Madwoman in the Attic* (co-authored with Susan Gubar) was runner-up for the Pulitzer Prize in Non-Fiction in 1980. She is co-editor, with Stanley Aronowitz and Jackson Lears, of the University of Minnesota American Culture Series.